FINDING

MISS

FONG

he Life Of Lee Lye Hoe

James A. Wolter

The Life Of
Lee Lye Hoe

James A. Wolter

FINDING

MISS

FONG

JAMES A. WOLTER

atmosphere press

Note: The names of Peace Corps personnel and others in this book have been changed to preserve their privacy. This story tells about a naïve twenty-two-year-old guy from the northwest side of Chicago trying to find his way in an unfamiliar world back in 1961. As a biologist from a working-class background thrust into post-Colonial Malaya to teach biology, I found myself caught up in unexpected adventures while struggling with disillusionment in work and juggling entanglements in love.

PROLOGUE

It was the first time we spent the night sleeping together, in Moke Chee's bedroom, the room she grew up in, the room where she assembled all her little treasures and the room where, on previous nights, we sat on the floor talking until midnight. But tonight, September 11, 1963, in Georgetown, the capital of Penang, Malaya, I held Moke Chee in my arms, our bodies melding one into the other and breathing together as one. She breathing out, I in, synchronized, I in, her out. We were one. She nuzzled her face against my neck just under my chin, and we talked in whispers. Whispered dreams for the future, our future, filled the air until we fell asleep and lingered until morning when we awoke, still holding each other, still breathing as one, living our dream. We went downstairs and then out back to take our bucket baths. This time together. I shaved with the little aluminum bowl of hot water that my new mother-in-law set out for me. Moke Chee helped set the breakfast table. We had breakfast together as husband and wife. It was, it seemed, as it should be, the perfect but ironic ending to a Peace Corps odyssey that started two years and one month ago in Illinois. But it wasn't.

The next morning, I boarded my flight to Chicago, not knowing when we would see each other again. The uncertainty made departing all the more disconcerting.

CHAPTER 1

In August 1961, I accepted the Peace Corps' invitation to train as a biology teacher for the Peace Corps Malaya project. I was a twenty-two-year-old Catholic kid from the northwest side of Chicago, trying to find my way after graduating college and attending medical school in Chicago. Why did I decide to join the Peace Corps? I hated being asked that question back in 1961 and still do to this day. But I hated my answer even more: "I want to serve humanity and be of service to my country. I want the personal challenge of working under difficult circumstances to help people in a developing country." But I felt like a hypocrite. As noble as those reasons were for joining the Peace Corps, they were not the full answer. It would have appeared too shallow of me to admit that joining the Peace Corps was also a way to gracefully avoid getting married. It's not that I had anything against marriage. And it's not that Lolly, the college coed who I was dating, would not have been an excellent catch for me. It's just that neither she nor I were ready for marriage. We were being steamrolled into it by our mothers.

Lolly and I had been dating each other for a semester. She was still an undergraduate student at my alma mater, Northern Illinois University, attempting to boost her credentials for admission to her mother's alma mater, Bryn Mawr College. I had just been granted provisional admission to medical school in Chicago with assurances of full admission the next academic year as long as I successfully completed one full year working as a research technician at the med school under the mentorship of Dr. John Nickerson and successfully bolstered my anemic academic transcript with courses in organic chemistry and advanced calculus. To my surprise and her mother's disappointment, Lolly transferred to Roosevelt University in Chicago rather than Bryn Mawr College in Pennsylvania, so we could continue seeing each other.

One evening, while driving Lolly home after seeing "The Flower Drum Song" on stage at the Shubert Theater, we discussed the merits of arranged marriages as opposed to love marriages. It was a purely academic discussion, not at all pertaining to us personally.

Lolly's mother, Irma, took joy in Lolly recounting her dates with me. On this evening, Lolly told her mother about our conversation about marriage. That was all Irma needed to telephone my mother to share the good news and invite her to lunch to start planning for our nuptials. They met the following Sunday, unbeknownst to me.

My father, learning of this, took me aside and said: "You're young. Why would you want to get married? Don't do it. Have some fun. Live before you get married. And don't tell your mother I told you this."

He said this all in one breath and then just walked away. I was stunned. I thought he might be drunk, but he didn't exhibit any of his usual telltale signs of a blotchy red face, a wide toothy grin, and watery, bloodshot eyes. His clear-eyed, expressionless face was dead serious, and he spoke in a hushed monotone voice as if passing a secret for my ears only. I had never seen him more stone-cold sober and serious. And while understanding his words, my twenty-two-year-old self didn't have a clue what he was talking about.

At their Sunday luncheon, the would-be mothers-in-law concluded that if Lolly and I were in love and would eventually get married, then the sooner, the better. As executor of

Lolly's trust, which was left to her by her grandfather, Irma established a no-interest loan from the trust to pay my tuition, Lolly's tuition, and an allowance to cover our living expenses. The catch was that I would start paying off the loan after joining the family's medical practice.

To push the impending wedding along, Irma supplied us with tickets to the theater, opera, and ballet. She brought us to dinners and cocktail parties, where we were introduced to local Chicago celebrities, entertainers, city officials, and artists. It was all very heady.

I knew I was being groomed by Irma to provide Lolly with the lifestyle she desired for her only child, and I initially welcomed being transformed from a "goose to a swan." But there was a rumbling inside me. Irma had my future all laid out. All I had to do was follow her script. I felt trapped.

Visiting Lolly on nights not arranged by her mother, I wanted to stay in and listen to music or watch a movie on television. Lolly wanted, like her girlfriends, to go to concerts and join friends clubbing on Rush Street. She accused me of not caring for her and being distant. I admitted to being distant. I cared for her, but instead of telling her, I accused her of being immature and selfish. On those nights, my drive home was filled with self-recrimination, and after arriving home, I immediately telephoned Lolly to apologize for my behavior. Most of the time, she answered, sobbing on the other end, and forgave me. Other times, she just let the phone ring.

Still, Lolly convinced herself that I was everything she wished for in a husband. Her mother and father were now on civil terms but had divorced when Lolly was a child old enough to remember terrific battles with vulgar words and objects thrown. By comparison, our differences were minor. It was intoxicating for me to be Lolly's chosen one. I felt the envy of other men. Lolly's lavender eyes lit up each time she greeted me, and her flirty smile melted my heart. It was almost perfect, but I was exhausted.

When I needed surgery to remove a pesky abscessed cyst, Lolly smiled as my mother lavished praise and appreciation on her for visiting me in the hospital for two days and then caring for me the remainder of the week at my parents' house while I recovered. Lolly loved the role of the attentive and devoted sweetheart. She just turned nineteen years old and was in love with the romantic notion of being in love. Lolly relished the excitement and the attention showered on the soon-to-be betrothed. She told me she loved that I accepted the social engagements her mother planned for us and was proud I passed the family's scrutiny. She was particularly proud that her girlfriends envied the catch she landed. Our mothers had all the pieces in place—but one.

Irma had given Lolly a list of possible venues to hold the formal engagement announcement. When Lolly didn't give her an answer after two weeks, Irma went ahead and selected one. Lolly continued to procrastinate, and there were a few arguments between them. But what troubled Irma the most was that Lolly kept skipping her appointments with the dressmaker to be fitted for her engagement dress. Also, Lolly and I skipped an appointment with the family jeweler to select a design for the engagement and wedding rings. Irma called me. It sounded like she was sobbing.

"Will you do me a favor?"

"Of course, Irma. What is it?"

"I'm at wit's end. She won't listen to me. Will you talk to her?"

"I'll try."

I didn't tell Irma that Lolly and I were having issues. We were trying to talk them out. As promised, I did talk to Lolly. I started by confessing that I couldn't keep up with the social schedule Irma had us on—on top of my work and classes. I was surprised that Lolly felt as overwhelmed as I did with the whirlwind we were caught in. She, too, needed some space and time. We enjoyed being with each other, but neither of us was ready to get married. And neither of us felt strong enough to stand up to the united front of our mothers. Help came via a power outage and a telegram.

In early August of 1961, Dr. Nickerson's lab experienced a power outage, so I had the rest of the day off. I knew Lolly didn't have classes, but instead of driving to her house to see her, I drove home to have time alone to think. As I drove up the driveway to my house, I noticed a yellow paper flapping in the breezeway door jamb. It turned out to be a telegram from the Peace Corps. The breezeway door was a door we seldom used, and there must have been a half-dozen telegrams stuffed between the storm and entry doors. All were from the Peace Corps, inviting me to participate in training programs for Ghana, the Philippines, and Malaya. This one was for Malaya and said something to the effect that my name would be removed from the potential candidate list if I did not respond to this invitation since I hadn't responded to the earlier ones. I called Lolly immediately.

"I need to see you right away."

"What's wrong? Are you alright?"

"Yes. I need to see you in person. Can I come over?"

"Of course. You're sure you're alright?"

"See you in half an hour."

Lolly was waiting at the front door when I arrived. I handed her the telegram and said, "Take a look at this."

"Have you been drafted? They can't draft you. You're a med student. You're invited to join the Peace Corps and go to Malaya? Where's that? What are you going to do?"

"It depends on what you want to do. Do you want to get married to me?"

"That doesn't sound like much of a proposal to me. You can do better."

I hadn't realized until that moment that I never actually asked Lolly to marry me.

"Our mothers pretty much took care of that for us," I said. "Well, do you?"

"If you want me to marry you, I will."

"I wish I felt ready for marriage, but I don't. Not right now," I replied.

"I thought so. Neither do I."

"In two years, if we're meant to be together, things may be different."

"I'm not going to sit at home waiting for you. I want to be free to date other guys."

"Understood. Anyone in particular?"

"Zoie's brother, Martin. He joined a dental practice near campus. He joins us for lunch when he can. He asked me out."

"Oh."

"You're not hurt, are you? I don't want to hurt you." Lolly started crying.

"No. It's OK. I'll give my folks the news tonight. You'll let your mom know?"

That was the last time I saw Lolly, standing at her front door crying, watching me drive off. Irma called me after that to congratulate me on joining the Peace Corps. That call turned out to be a ruse to talk me out of it.

CHAPTER 2

Peace Corps training was supposed to start in August at Cornell University but was delayed until October, and training was moved to Northern Illinois University in DeKalb, Illinois. I was excited to get on with saving the world, but having to now train at my alma mater, NIU, was a bummer. I had just graduated a year ago, and returning there didn't feel like I was moving forward.

I continued living with my parents and fulfilling my proviso by taking classes and working for Dr. Nickerson as a lab technician at Chicago Medical School until it was time to report for training. Finally, October arrived, and the directive from the Peace Corps said to be at the passenger-pickup island C at Chicago's O'Hare airport at 10 a.m.

My father and mother dropped me off about 9:30 a.m. Two other men were already at island C when I arrived, standing about twelve feet apart from each other. I slid out of the back seat, pulling my suitcase behind me. It was a quick goodbye. I was grateful my parents weren't into displays of affection.

I went up to the guy standing nearest to me and asked, "Is this the Peace Corps pick-up place?"

"I hope so." Looking at the watch on his right wrist, he smiled and said, "I've been waiting about forty minutes. My name's Hosae Johnstone."

I smiled back, stuck out my hand, and said, "Hosea?"

He shook my hand and said, "It's biblical. Old Testament, but I go by John. It's equally biblical and New Testament."

His grip was firm and assertive, but not overly so. John had an easy manner with a broad toothy smile that was warm and welcoming. His blue eyes, alert and intelligent, sized me up.

I said, "Jim Wolter. I'm from Chicago, St. Celestine Parish.

"Why did you join?" John asked.

"Didn't have anything better to do. How about you?" I didn't want to go into details and was thankful John took the lead in talking about himself.

John offered, "For me, it was either enter the Naval Officer Training Program or the Peace Corps. I didn't see a lifelong career as a Naval Officer. Too few career options. But the Peace Corps can lead to a sundry of career opportunities."

John shared that he was the younger of two boys from central Illinois, the son of a Protestant pastor. His mother was a full-time pastor's wife whose main responsibility was to make the pastor and his family look good in the eyes of the congregation. John said, "Hence, the biblical name," and added, "That's what I'm looking for in a wife. The kind of wife who will help me get ahead in my career. A helpmate like my mother."

Pretty shitty life for her, I thought to myself. Too calculating, too boring. He should meet Irma.

John described attending a small, private liberal arts college on a scholarship set up by his father's parishioners. It seemed that he carried a burden of expectations like I did. They weren't as overt as the expectations Irma placed on me, but nonetheless, a burden. John didn't complain. Instead, he described a charmed undergraduate life in a fraternity, participating in school musicals, taking pre-med courses, belonging to the photography club, and studying overseas. His intellect, grades, and social skills earned him admission to medical school. He said that he hated the first-year drudgery of memorizing body parts in the anatomy lab. When grades came out at the end of his first year and he had to retake anatomy, he decided to drop out. He was not going to be the country doctor his family and community desired.

In response to my disappointment in going to DeKalb, he said it was an advantage because I would be the "go-to guy" for getting around town. I admired his ability to rationally take a long view and the bright side of our current situation.

While John and I were talking, island C filled up with more people, and shortly after 10 a.m., a van with the NIU logo on its side pulled up along the curb. The driver got out and directed us to take a seat in the van.

On the way to DeKalb, the driver told us that the Rice Hotel would be our residence during the training. The Rice was built in 1927 and had seen better days, but in its day, the two-story, seventy-room Spanish Revival was considered a gem and the best hotel west of Chicago to the Mississippi River. It hosted such notable guests as Amelia Earhart, Eleanor Roosevelt, Ronald Reagan, and then-Senator John F. Kennedy in 1958, who stayed in the VIP suite. The Peace Corps' Trainee rooms were less luxurious. The Rice, still the best hotel in DeKalb in 1961, lost its luster of yesteryear with fading paint and stale air, as well as an ambient musky odor of dusty carpeting, talcum-powdered old people, and mothballs. It now served as a residence for retirees living on Social Security, travelers passing through town, and visiting college athletic teams.

All thirty-eight male and female Trainees were housed on the same floor of the hotel. We were assigned two to a room, with one Trainee sleeping on a standard single bed and the other on a fold-up cot. John was down the hall from me. My roommate, Mike Frazer from Berkeley, California, had already arrived and announced that he claimed the only bed in the room, leaving me with the less comfortable cot.

Coed dorms were not the norm at the time, but here we were—young men and women living on the same floor of the hotel and sharing bathrooms down the hall, which resulted in a morning parade of Trainees in pajamas strolling the hallways.

There were gender-specific bathrooms, but the Trainees pretty much ignored the gender designations and used whichever was available in time of need. And yes, Trainees did couple up.

A Date with the Boss' Wife

I didn't think of it as a date, but she did and called it a date in the letter she wrote to her husband that night. Sheridan Baxter was in her late twenties, but seemed more mature and worldly than I was at twenty-two. And she was the wife of my future boss—Luke Baxter, the in-country Deputy Director of Peace Corps Malaya who was in his mid-thirties. Sheridan joined our training program toward the end of our first week of training. It was an opportunity for her to meet the Trainees and—in her words—"get away from being the perfect wife and mother for a couple weeks." She spent two weeks with us while Luke was in Malaya setting up the program, and their two children were staying with Luke's mother.

John was right when he said that I would become the "go-to guy" in DeKalb. As the Trainee with ties to NIU, I felt obligated to assist other Trainees and to ensure Sheridan's stay in DeKalb was full of positive moments. Each morning on the way to campus for our daily lectures, we walked past my old undergraduate Sigma Pi fraternity house. To impress nurse Trainee April Jennings, I offered my fellow Trainees a tour of the frat house. It was the first time Sheridan and most of the nurses had been inside one. Paul Schultz, the fraternity president, invited us to an upcoming house party.

Sheridan asked me: "Do you think I'm too old for a fraternity party?"

I replied, "Not at all."

"What happens? I've never been."

I explained: "There will be soft drinks and Housemother

Mrs. Myers' canapés. The guys will mingle with the girls and make sure that each lady doesn't sit out more than two dances in a row."

"Will you be my escort?" she asked.

"It'd be my pleasure, but let me ask you." I bowed toward her, swinging my right arm out in a slow, exaggerated motion imitating actors playing Southern gentlemen in late-night movies on TV, and said: "Sheridan, would you grant me the pleasure of your company to the Sigma Pi dance this Saturday?"

Sheridan said, "You're being silly. But it's sweet. I hope you're not making fun of an old married woman with two kids trying to reclaim a bit of her youth."

I started to say, "I'd never ..."

Sheridan didn't let me finish. "Of course, you'd never. All I packed was my little black party dress. Will that do?"

"Perfect. I'm just wearing khakis, a sports jacket, and a tie. Things usually get started at about seven. OK if I drop by about a quarter to?"

Unsettling Evening

When I knocked on her door Saturday evening, Sheridan was just about ready. "I couldn't get the zipper all the way up," she declared. "Luke usually has to do me up. Can you lend a hand, please?"

I had never zipped up a woman before and worried about being all thumbs poking her back. Thank God I was able to zip Sheridan up without brushing my knuckles up against her bare back.

"While you're at it, hook that little hook at the top, and will you please hook up my chain?" It was a thin, gold chain necklace with a tiny plain gold cross. Sheridan lifted her light sun-streaked brown hair from her neck with both hands and tilted

14

her head slightly forward, giving me clear exposure to her neck. The skin on the back of her neck, lighter than her hands or arms or face, was a lustrous white. On TV, I saw actors kiss the back of their wife's neck while hooking up their necklace. I fantasized about doing that with my wife, but Sheridan was Luke's wife. The clasp on the chain was tiny and tricky, but I managed, thankfully, without knuckling Sheridan's neck.

Sheridan faced the mirror, tugged at the sides of her dress, and wiggled her body to adjust its fit. She ran her fingers through her hair and gave her head a shake, fluffing her hair out and making it fall perfectly over her shoulders. Turning to me, she handed me a black cardigan and then turned her back to me again. I slipped the cardigan over her bare shoulders. Facing me once more, she seemed to be fishing for a compliment.

"Presentable?"

I responded, "Adorable."

That word surprised me. It wasn't in my functional vocabulary. Compliments were to be sincere and, ideally, spontaneous. Mine was spontaneous, alright. But Sheridan wasn't a real date. She was Luke's wife, and Luke was going to be my boss. I knew I had to compliment her, make her feel good. It had to be sincere, but I couldn't make it personal. Could I?

"One more thing." Sheridan handed me a small bag. "My heels. I can't walk all that way in heels. Can I change when we get there? Will the other girls be wearing heels?"

Sheridan was thinking of herself as one of the "other girls." I liked that. I felt like a big brother escorting his little sister to her first dance.

When we arrived at the Sigma Pi house, I offered Sheridan my arm. We climbed the four stairs. Greeting us was an attending pledge who escorted us to Paul Schultz.

Sheridan had shared her favorite songs and artists with me earlier in the week. I made a list and passed it to Paul. He had the DJ add Sheridan's favorites to the playlist for the night. Sheridan and I found a place to sit where she could change into her high heels. When the music started with one of Sheridan's favorites, I stood up and asked, "May I have this dance?"

Sheridan held out her hand. I took it and led her to the dance floor. I made sure to hold her at a respectable distance. She said, "I just love this song."

The next song was a swing tune and then a cha-cha. We danced nonstop, or at least Sheridan did. Paul and then Glen Engelhard cut in during both numbers. The DJ put on a waltz. This time, Richard Vanjoulski cut in. He was tall with wavy black hair and was the best dancer in the fraternity. I was going to cut back in as I had with Paul and Glen, but the smile on Sheridan's face and the swaying of her body exuded pure delight. Richard escorted Sheridan back to where I was waiting.

Sheridan said, "Would you mind if we sat the next couple out?"

"Not at all."

"I know you put them up to it."

"Put who up to what?"

"Don't play dumb. Cutting in. I was the only girl they cut in on."

"That's only because they have exquisite taste, and you are the ..."

"Enough small talk. I have a serious problem, and I need your help."

I thought to myself: She must be desperate if she needs my help. I'll do what I can, but constructing a memorable evening was one thing—helping a married woman with a serious problem was a different matter. And she wasn't just any married woman. She was my future boss' wife and had two kids. No way. This night is over. The sooner I get Sheridan back to the Rice, the better.

Sheridan spoke to me almost in a whisper. "I need a favor. I hate to ask you, but you're the only one I feel I can trust."

I felt like saying: What makes you think that, sister?

But I kept my mouth shut.

"I need you to save me from Penn."

"Save you from Penn?" Dr. J. Pendergrass (Penn) Winter was our Peace Corps Training Director at Northern Illinois University.

"I don't know what it is about me that attracts men like Penn. I must come off as the 'safe type' to men like him. Luke has a few clients and friends like that. Middle-aged men who saddle up to me, monopolize my whole evening, and force me to pretend to be interested in what they're saying. I always get stuck while the other women have a grand time. Tomorrow night at the Peace Corps party, when you see Penn monopolizing me, will you cut in and rescue me?"

"Consider it done." This will be easy, maybe even fun. I couldn't wait.

I caught the opening bar of the next song and knew it was the most favorite of Sheridan's favorites, a slow "golden oldie." I said, "May I have this dance?"

Again, I held Sheridan at a respectable distance. She said, "Are you going to hold me like a prune-eating old spinster all night?"

I said, "Huh?" She nodded her head to each side. "Have a look at the other couples."

I pulled Sheridan closer, but not so close that our bodies would touch. I held her right hand to my chest like the other guys. Her left hand moved higher on my right shoulder to the nape of my neck, and her forehead brushed against my cheek like the other girls. She seemed more at ease, and that made me feel more at ease. Another of Sheridan's favorites followed. "A little birdie tells me someone had something to do with the music selection," she said.

I pulled back enough to look Sheridan in the eyes. "What? You don't believe in coincidence?"

"I believe in coincidences. And I like them. Especially when my date is a man who, by coincidence, lassos the moon to create a special evening just for me," Sheridan then said: "Eight thirty-eight already. I feel like Cinderella at midnight. We should go."

I gave Sheridan my arm to navigate the stairs and was surprised she continued holding it as we made our way back to the Rice. "Where do you take a date when not attending a fraternity dance?"

"The Hillside Café for hot chocolate on a chilly night like tonight. It's on the way back. Are you game for a hot chocolate?"

"Definitely."

We went to Hillside, and our hot chocolates arrived with their traditional peppermint candy cane stirrers. Sheridan swirled the cane in the chocolate. "Is this another of your special extra arrangements?"

"It's tradition."

"Speaking of which. You gave me all the extra I needed. By getting involved with Luke, I missed so much of college life—dating, partying. In one night, you gave me four years of experiencing life as a young, starry-eyed coed."

Sheridan confided in me that hanging out with the Trainees, a fraternity party, and the Hillside Café made her feel young again. "I can't believe ten years have passed so fast. I was just a seventeen-year-old country girl starting college when I met Luke. He was a twenty-five-year-old city guy who was in his last year of law school. My girlfriends drooled over my tall, handsome Naval Officer. My mother insisted he was too good a catch to let pass. I was so young, early out of high school, with a world of living to do, but of course, my mother and my friends were right. How often could a girl expect a Luke Baxter to come into her life? We were engaged early on in our relationship, married shortly after graduation, and then came the children. Luke was moving up the professional ladder, and I was his helpmate living the American dream. But my American dream was like Swiss cheese full of holes. Tonight, even though it was just one night, those holes were filled."

I thought I detected Sheridan blush, maybe realizing how

much she was confiding in me. She said, "This must be very boring to you, me talking only about me. So, tell me, who is she?"

"Who, who is?"

"The one you're stewing over."

"Oh, Lolly."

"Yes, oh, Lolly."

"Didn't know I was so obvious."

"My dear Jimmy Wolter, you are so transparent. Noella is throwing herself at you. You're passively going along with Noella's advances while eyeing April Jennings but letting John out-hustle you for April uncontested."

Sheridan paused as if expecting a denial or confirmation. I remained silent.

"April's not all that taken with him," she said. "You have a real shot at her. All you have to do is make your move. But I don't have to tell you that. Do I?"

"Not really."

"You're a good guy, Jimmy Wolter. Don't settle for just anyone. You deserve the best." Sheridan paused as if choosing her next words, "Speaking of which, I have a younger sister finishing up college. I'm trying to talk her into joining the Peace Corps. If I gave you her address, would you drop her a note about it and about yourself? She'd make a great pen pal. Would you like her address?"

"Not really."

"If you change your mind, just let me know. I've already put in a good word about you to her." Sheridan looked at her wristwatch. "It'll be the kids' bedtime soon, and my mother-in-law will be waiting for my call. We'd better get back."

We headed back to the Rice. Sheridan didn't take my arm this time. We didn't speak on the way back either.

Reaching Sheridan's door, she said, "I brought a bottle of vintage chardonnay from my favorite vineyard. I have a glass each night while I write Luke. Would you like a glass before calling it a night?"

I didn't. The evening had been a success, and I wanted it to stay that way. How could I say no?

Sheridan was staying in the hotel's VIP room. She disappeared into the bathroom and reemerged with two bathroom glasses. We drank vintage chardonnay out of the hotel bathroom glasses, with her sitting on the bed and me on the only chair in the room.

It was approaching ten o'clock. Sheridan looked at her watch again. I stood up.

"Before you go, I have just one more favor, please. I need to be unhooked."

I was pleased that this time I didn't take forever with the necklace clasp.

I was extremely anxious to leave. I turned for the door. Sheridan escorted me to the door and thanked me for a memorable evening. I said, "The pleasure was all mine."

Then Sheridan said, "I really mean it, Jim. I can't begin to tell you what this night has done for me. After I telephone my mother-in-law and the kids, I'm going to pour myself another glass of wine and write Luke a letter all about tonight and then bury my face in my pillow and cry myself to sleep."

I didn't know how to respond and simply said, "Sleep well."

The next night at the party in the Rice party room, Penn sat next to Sheridan just as she predicted. I asked Sheridan to dance; nurse Trainee Eva Gentile got Penn up to dance. The Peace Corps ladies kept Penn entertained all evening, and likewise, the guys—mostly lanky Bob Reed—kept Sheridan dancing the night away. Sheridan was leaving for California the next day, and that evening would be the last we saw her until we reached Malaya. At the end of the evening, Sheridan thanked me for protecting her and making sure she had another wonderful evening and added: "Nothing could top being a Sigma Pi princess last night. I wrote Luke all about it and told him to assign you to a school in Malacca."

I was glad we were dancing at the time, and she couldn't

see my eyes because I was feeling some trepidation over what she included in the letter. Luke was going to be my boss, after all. What would he think when he received a letter extolling my virtues and the attention I afforded his wife at a dance? I knew some men, like my father, could be crazy jealous when it came to their wives. From Sheridan's description, Luke sounded like the kind of guy that wasn't jealous.

I didn't get to see Sheridan off. She departed for the airport while I was at a lecture, but she left a note for me at the front desk that read: "I'll tell Luke to find a teaching assignment for you in Malacca." Over hot chocolate at the Hillside Café, she had asked where I would like to be assigned in Malaya. I had told her I was fascinated by the history of the city of Malacca, and if I could pick an assignment, I would select Malacca. Sheridan also left her sister's name and address. I didn't keep it.

CHAPTER 3

The most common refrain heard during Peace Corps training was "be flexible." The need to be flexible was obvious before training even started. The Peace Corps originally gave instructions to report to Cornell in August for twelve weeks of training that would also include Outward Bound training in Puerto Rico. I wanted to train at Cornell University, an Ivy League school, and I wanted to experience the physical, mental, and emotional challenges of Outward Bound. Training couldn't start soon enough.

But then training was postponed from August to September and then from September to October, and then it was transferred to my alma mater NIU in DeKalb, Illinois. That was a personal disappointment to me.

The formal training of Peace Corps Malaya I finally kicked off in the Swen Parson Auditorium at Northern Illinois University in October 1961. The training had a formal planned aspect, probably more than ninety percent by scheduled clock hours, that took place mostly in the Swen Parson Library Auditorium. Penn introduced himself as the Peace Corps Malaya Training Director and then introduced Dr. J. Norbert (Norb) Patton, Chairman of the NIU History Department, who was the designated in-country Director of Peace Corps Malaya.

Norb started by providing a general overview of the geographic significance, history, and culture of Malaya. He informed us of what to anticipate in regard to living conditions and environment. He emphasized the importance of keeping a journal to document the highlights of each day, or minimally each week, so when writing a formal academic paper at some future date—or just wanting to recall a very special time in our lives—having notes to read will jog our memories.

I took his advice to heart and stopped by the NIU bookstore during lunch break and bought five of my favorite lab notebooks. I started keeping extensive notes, paragraphs long, until we were told about the postcard incident in Nigeria.

The Postcard Incident

We gathered in the auditorium for our usual lecture schedule on October 16, but instead of Penn handing out the weekly schedule, he handed each of us a photocopy of a postcard written by Marjorie Michelmore when she was a Peace Corps Volunteer stationed in Nigeria and asked us to read it. The postcard was packed with so many words covering every part of the card that I could barely read it.

After a few minutes, Penn asked what we thought. We concluded that Marjorie's words painted a picture of a pretty desperate and poverty-stricken place lacking basic sanitary standards. It may have been dramatically written to impress a boyfriend, but it probably was pretty accurate. We didn't see anything wrong with it. Penn then told us that the postcard became public, which resulted in public protests, a students' strike, and calls for terminating the Peace Corps in Nigeria.

Penn asked, "Does that put a different light on things?" We concluded that, while what Marjorie wrote was probably accurate, it was not prudent to write it on a postcard that could become public.

The postcard and its newsworthiness resulted in bringing

unwanted attention to me. A swarm of reporters from Chicago descended on DeKalb to interview Peace Corps Trainees. Specifically, they were seeking Jim Wolter because he was an NIU graduate and Trainee from Chicago. I ran whenever I saw a reporter. In one instance, while standing with a group of Trainees, a cameraman and reporter approached me. The reporter asked: "We were told Jim Wolter is here. Which one of you is Jim?"

I didn't want to be interviewed, so I said: "He was here. You just missed him. He went that way. You can still catch him if you hurry." I scurried off in the other direction.

The postcard incident caused me to alter my journaling. I had taken the advice of Norb and other authorities and kept a journal. I had been writing in sentences and paragraphs up to that point but altered my writing to a personal form of symbolic shorthand that I developed in case my journal would fall prey to prying eyes.

Insecurities

The hours spent in the Swen Parson Library Auditorium were intellectually captivating and entertaining. Yet the most vivid memories were of the times not accounted for on Penn's agenda—the downtime spent with other Volunteers from around the U.S. who spoke English in various accents. My thick northwest-side Chicago accent was difficult for some to follow. My roommate Mike had a perfect California Bay accent and could easily have been a radio broadcaster, but Tammy Printer, a nurse from Brooklyn, had an accent so strong that I missed chunks of her conversation and had to ask her to repeat to the verge of annoyance. And then there were the words spoken by April Jennings. To my ear, her lyrical Boston accent deserved orchestration.

Getting to know each other through shared experiences and conversations woven together in a rainbow of regional accents and dialects opened a world unknown to me. I realized my life experience and worldview were narrow and parochial. Meeting, living with, and getting to know the other Trainees opened my eyes to horizons I didn't know existed. It was magical.

Let's face it. Growing up in an all-white neighborhood, going to an all-white city school, and attending a rural college with mostly a white student population from northern Illinois gave me limited exposure to the world. As the naïve twenty-two-year-old that I was and the relationships I fell into, I could appear to be a ladies' man and a cad, but I really was an emotionally insecure, socially unsophisticated guy. I worried that I would not become a Peace Corps Volunteer, which was what I was training for while trying to be accepted by my peers.

In 1961, something like the United States Peace Corps had never been done before. We were reminded that as the first group, we would determine whether the program as President John F. Kennedy's first initiative as President would succeed or fail. We also were reminded that just because we were in training didn't guarantee we would become Volunteers. We could be told to go home. We weren't told what the criteria were to be selected. So, for me, the most comforting aspect of training was my relationships.

During our training, we had daily physical fitness drills, which included demonstrating water survival skills, and we had lessons on maintaining our personal health. Wash our hands with soap and water frequently, don't touch our faces, drink boiled water, don't eat street food, avoid STDs, and don't do anything you wouldn't want your mother to witness. We also received technical training in our specialized areas. Nurses learned about the Malayan health system, teachers learned about the Malayan education system, and so on. I was designated to be a high school biology teacher.

Flirtations

Flirtations, romance, and heartbreak weren't the immediate images that came to mind when I received an invitation to participate in the training. But thirty-eight mostly young single men and women sharing close living quarters in the same hotel and spending sixteen hours a day, seven days a week together preparing to go on an exotic assignment—flirtations, romance, and heartbreak were sure to follow. It did for me.

Mike had an ingenious solution for the quest for privacy. He was clever in that kind of way. I had to hand it to him. There was a wall-mounted hall lamp outside our room that had a little lampshade that matched the wallpaper. If either of us had company, we simply tipped the lampshade toward the door as a warning not to barge in without knocking. Then we would give a quick double rap and wait for a response.

In our small group of commingling men and women living together in confined quarters, gossip was rampant, secrets not closely held, and practical jokes the norm. It didn't take more than a few days before the guys were straightening out the lampshade—or at least that was Mike's story—and Mike would come bounding in without knocking and say, "Oh, don't mind me. You forgot to adjust the shade."

This is a good place to talk about entering a relationship with Noella. After all, I joined the Peace Corps in part to end a relationship that was barreling toward marriage. While I wasn't ready for marriage, neither was I ready to become a Trappist monk, and there were many women in our group who weren't ready to become cloistered nuns. To me, April Jennings, a nurse from Boston, stood out. I loved her accent and could listen to it all day. A natural smile graced her full freckled apple-cheek face, and she had the loveliest bluest smiling eyes this side of heaven and a low-key easy-going personality. She struck me as someone whom I would never tire of spending quiet time with.

But as one of the Peace Corps trainers said, "You're not here to meet your future spouse." That sounded like very sound advice, but still, young women and men did what young women and men do.

I was open to and welcomed casual relationships with multiple women that were more platonic in nature than romantic. That was an aspect of April I found alluring, and I think she found that attractive in me. We felt safe and comfortable not having to work at impressing each other or controlling one another. It was refreshing.

One day while waiting in line to purchase lab books at the NIU bookstore, I recognized Mia Galletti at the front of the line. She was short in stature, but her red hair and blue eyes stood out. We dated casually in college before I got involved with Lolly. There was no pretense with Mia. She said what came to her mind without coyness or filter. I liked that. She paid the cashier but lingered until I checked out.

Mia greeted me with, "I never expected to see you here."

We headed out of the store together and started walking across campus. "I'm with the Peace Corps," I responded.

"Last I heard, you were in med school."

"That didn't work out."

While walking, she asked, "If you have nothing better to do, how about joining me at the Autumn Fest party on Saturday?"

"I'll be there. What time?"

"Seven." We parted ways, and I continued walking.

Seven. I repeated it in my mind as the cool crisp breeze pushed along the blacktop path to the library. I was reminiscing about my unencumbered undergraduate days when I heard, "Penny for your thoughts."

I looked up. It was Noella walking alone toward the bookstore. The sun, hovering in the sky, struck her strawberry hair, making it glow like a halo. A simple "hi" would have sufficed, but I was caught by surprise, and the words that tumbled through my mind and out of my mouth were: "Your hair. It's glowing like a halo." I think Noella took it as an invitation to flirt.

She raised her shoulder nearest to me and tilted her head toward me while scanning me out of the corner of her laughing, flirtatious blue eyes. I felt naked. I could feel my cheeks grow hot. She flashed a wide, luscious, ripe, red-lipped smile. Her loose-fitting white long-sleeved blouse fluttering in the breeze was in contrast to her form-fitting slacks. Her slacks were as ripe red as her lips—hugging her long sensuous curving legs and outlining her round ripe red zaftig cheeks. I was doing to her what she was doing to me, but she wasn't blushing.

She said, "It came out of a bottle."

I said, "What?"

She said, "I have some left. You can have it. Then you'll have a halo, too."

She was flirting with me. I was sure of it. She just gave me an open invitation to flirt back. I didn't. I said, "Oh."

I knew it was a lame response. I didn't know what else to say, so I smiled and moved on.

If only that were the end of it. But it wasn't. On Friday, the group gathered at Friendly's bar across from the Rice Hotel before journeying to the university natatorium. This was the night we were to be tested on water survival techniques. I arrived at Friendly's late, and it was packed. I saw Noella waving me over, pointing to an empty place next to her in a booth shared with John, Mike, and a couple others.

After just one beer, I said, "I wish we didn't have to go back to the pool."

Noella said, "You look bushed, poor baby." She put her arm around my shoulder and pulled my head down to rest in her lap. I was tired, and her lap was dreamingly comfortable. My cheek rested against her lower tummy—the pelvic region. The rhythm of her breathing and the movement of her tummy were hypnotic. I closed my eyes and so wanted to sleep—lost in the lap of a woman where nothing else existed, nothing else mattered.

Noella's fingers stroked my eyebrows, then stroked my eyelids. Soon her lips were nibbling at my eyelashes. She began kissing my eyelids and then my mouth. Right there, in public. I felt cheap and shallow, letting myself be used, letting myself be seduced. Still, I reciprocated.

The gang was getting up to go to the pool when I realized that I left my swimsuit at the hotel. I quickly bolted for the Rice. After getting my swim trunks, I hustled the one-and-a-half-mile trek back to the swimming pool. John was the only one still in the men's locker room when I arrived. As I got ready for the nightly pool plunge, he said: "You sure looked like one very content fellow lying there in Noella's lap, sucking it all in."

"I was drunk." An excuse I heard my father use to explain away any number of transgressions. "Didn't know what I was doing."

"Don't kid yourself. You were lapping it up."

"I have no idea why Noella picked me. This is going too fast. What is she looking for?"

"Guy, you're over-analyzing. You don't have to understand to enjoy it. Just go with the flow and enjoy the ride while it lasts. You can always get off anytime you want."

No, I can't. I told myself. The image of Lolly standing at her front door sobbing as I drove away after we broke up still haunted me. I felt awful and wanted no part of that again. On the other hand, I valued John's counsel. He was more experienced than I was. I convinced myself that John was right. The Friendly's episode likely wouldn't go any further. It didn't have to develop into a full-blown relationship. Did it? I liked April but unexpectedly got waylaid by Noella.

John and I made our way to the pool just as the whistle sounded for the first forty-five-minute Heads-Above-Water test. Our instructions were to remain afloat until the sound of the next whistle. Noella passed easily along with maybe two-thirds of the group, including John and Bob Reed. I was hanging on the side of the pool between Art Swanson and Ben Lake. Noella swam over to me. "Stop fighting it. Relax. I'll get you through this. I've taught hundreds at the Y. Trust me."

I did. I needed to pass.

"Purse your lips and take a deep breath," explained Noella. "Now let the air out slowly through your nose. That's it. Relax. Again. Now this time, close your eyes. Breathe in. Now out slowly. Now lean back. Relax. I'm holding you. Don't panic if water washes over your face. Think of it as washing away all your fears. Keep your eyes closed, breathing in, out. Imagine the most peaceful, most beautiful place you have ever been. And now, think of the most trusted person you know. Now that person joins you. The two of you are in the most peaceful, most beautiful place, safe in each other's company."

The next thing I heard was a sharp whistle and Noella shouting to me: "I told you that you could do it!"

We climbed out of the pool. I gave my name to the graduate assistant. Noella identified herself as Nelda Koser. She cunningly had taken and passed the test for her friend. She and Nelda did not resemble each other in any way. Now if that weren't enough, Nelda wasn't even suited up. Also, Bob Reed stood in for Art Swanson and John for Ben Lake. Later, celebrating back at Friendly's, I said. "Are you guys crazy? If you got caught, you could have gotten kicked out of training."

Reed was the ringleader. "Not a chance. We were just names the grad assistant was charged with checking off a list. The sooner we passed, the better it was for him." I loved being part of this group. And Noella—there was much more substance to her than her form-fitting red slacks.

Noella and I Become an Item

Saturday morning Noella sat with John and me at breakfast and then lunch and dinner. She wanted to know what she and

I could do after dinner and suggested seeing a movie at The Egyptian, which was one block from the Rice Hotel. I told her I was attending an Autumn Fest party at a house on campus. She assumed it was at the Sigma Pi house and asked what she should wear. Bold, I thought, and presumptuous. That irritated me. I told Noella: "Mia, a friend from my undergraduate days, invited me to her house party. We have a friendly platonic relationship. I'm like a big brother to her."

Noella stood up, stiffened her body, and walked out in a huff. She muttered something, but I didn't catch it. Well, that's the end of that, I thought.

I didn't like the way it was ending—whatever "it" was—but I was happy it was over. I was glad tomorrow was Sunday. We could avoid seeing each other until Monday, when once more, we would be swept up in lectures and forget anything happened. It had been only twenty-four hours, and I already longed to go back to being just Jim. I had no desire to be one-half of Noella and Jim.

Mia's house party was a costume party. Mia was dressed as Raggedy Ann. Gosh, she was cute. I didn't have a costume and felt out of place at an undergraduate costume party. Mia and I spent the evening sitting on the front porch swing, reminiscing about "old times" and talking about what we wanted in the future. Mia was more certain: "First, graduate in June, become a fourth-grade teacher, have a Catholic marriage with a good man, have a large family, and live in a comfortable home." I told Mia, "Except for being a fourth-grade teacher and marrying a Catholic man, I wanted about the same thing."

She punched my shoulder and said, "Don't tease me."

We both laughed, and she added, "Why don't you skip the Peace Corps and become a science teacher? The school I'm student-teaching at needs a science teacher. I'll talk to my principal."

"The Peace Corps is for me right now. We'll see what happens after that. Do you know what time it is?" I walked Mia the few steps to the porch door. She said, "Who thought sitting and talking the night away could be so much fun. Can we do this again?"

"I wish we could. I haven't had such a good time since I don't know when. But I have to remain with the Peace Corps group. I will call you over Thanksgiving or Christmas break if we get one."

"Promise?" She asked.

I shook my head yes.

Mia replied, "I would like that." She reached up on tiptoes, planting a quick kiss on my cheek, then disappeared like a wisp beyond the door, leaving me puzzled. I heard her say from the other side of the door: "Remember, you promised."

That was unexpected but nice, I thought. Our relationship was platonic. We have never kissed before. Just a spontaneous expression of gratitude, I told myself, but an awfully nice way to cap a memorable evening. I walked back to the Rice feeling light as a feather. I was ready to climb into my lumpy cot for a night of blissful slumber. Entering the Rice lobby, a frigid pall hit me. Noella was sitting cross-legged in a chair next to the fireplace facing the entryway with her arms folded across her chest. She had fire in her eyes.

"Well?" she said in a cold voice.

"Well, what?"

"Don't well what me. Do you know what time it is?"

"Yeah." I nodded toward the wall clock. "The big hand is pointing to two, and the little hand is pointing to eleven."

Noella said, "Don't wise mouth me." Then Noella said in a sing-song voice, rolling her head side to side, mocking me, "Mia and I have a platonic relationship. I'm like a big brother to her."

She snapped, "You liar."

I snapped back, "We do. But what's that to you? You don't own me."

"Platonic my foot. Is that lipstick on your cheek platonic?"

With that, Noella got up and stormed away. That's the end of that, I thought with relief.

It was a crazy forty-eight hours with Noella. A flirtation, a seduction at Friendly's, a helpful survival lesson in the natatorium, and two explosive "walk-outs." This wasn't normal. I wanted off this roller coaster. Noella and I managed to avoid each other on Sunday, but come Monday morning, she sat in the seat next to me in the auditorium during lectures. She joined me at lunch in the cafeteria as if nothing happened. I knew I was being a fool but went along with her.

A Promise Kept

Penn arranged for those Trainees who weren't going home for Thanksgiving to stay at the Drake Hotel in downtown Chicago. With each Trainee having a room to themselves, Noella told me she was looking forward to spending a romantic weekend with me. I told Noella that I wanted to spend this last Thanksgiving with my parents and family. I also thought Noella and I needed a break from each other but didn't tell her that.

Noella sat next to me on the charter bus from DeKalb to Chicago but ignored my attempts at small conversation. I felt foolish. I wanted to change my seat, but we were seated at the front of the bus, so if I changed my seat, all the other Trainees would see. I felt stuck. The bus stopped at the front entrance of the Drake Hotel, and we all got off. I was about to walk to the subway to catch a train home when Noella finally spoke, "Are you sure you won't change your mind?"

"Sorry. I can't." The illuminated hand on the walk sign of the Michigan Avenue traffic light turned from red to white. I grabbed my bag. "Gotta run." I was worried Noella would throw a scene, so I rushed across the street, dodging a taxi.

I did keep my promise and called Mia when I got home.

She told me, "I'm too busy preparing lesson plans to go out on the weekend. The principal is going to observe me teaching on Monday."

Before I could figure out a polite way of ending the conversation, Mia added, "But you can join me at my family's Thanksgiving tradition. We serve Thanksgiving Dinner to residents of the Misericordia Home. I think you'll enjoy it. Would you like to go?" I accepted.

When our group returned to DeKalb, Noella got angry with me once again on our last night of training. Earlier that day, we gathered as usual in the auditorium. The selection ended. I was in, and all but two Trainees made it: Naome, who was from Alaska and allergic to the sun, deselected herself on medical grounds; and Tex, who was an architect and was to teach architecture in Malaya but had no work experience other than building a few garages for family.

It was Thursday and the last night as a Trainee. In the morning, we would head to Swen Parson to be sworn in as Peace Corps Volunteers and receive our clothing allowance and travel vouchers. I should have been swept up in the joy and sense of accomplishment. I wasn't. I was at odds with the party atmosphere. There was a sense of relief, but training would continue for four more weeks in Malaya. And our travel plans changed.

Initially, we were to leave the day after Christmas by ship from California to the Philippines and receive Malay language instruction during the trip. But a previous group of Peace Corps Volunteers going to the Philippines was so rowdy aboard their ship that this plan was canceled. Instead, our language instruction would happen at the University of Malaya in Petaling Jaya. Be flexible. I was disappointed to not travel by ship and to not receive Malay language instruction before arriving.

I was drained and wanted to turn in early. Noella followed me to my room. "I'll give you a back rub to help you relax and plan for the break." Earlier, Noella had brought up spending

Christmas at her family's ski cabin before leaving for Malaya, but I put her off by saying we didn't know whether we would both go to Malaya.

Now that Noella and I were both selected, my excuse for not spending the break with her no longer held. Noella sang while giving me a back rub. What she did next stunned me.

Noella climbed on top of me in my cot. Yes, we spent time alone in my bedroom before, but never in bed. She kissed my ear and whispered, "Now, we can plan for the future. How about spending the break at my family's ski cabin?"

"I don't have skis."

"No problem. You can use my brother's."

"I don't know how to ski. Never been."

"No problem. I'll teach you. We'll have plenty of other things to do besides ski."

I said, "I want to spend time with my family."

Noella snuggled closer to me and nuzzled my ear. "No problem, silly. Your parents can drive up with mine. There's a nice lodge they can stay at in town. And there's a nice little chapel in town, too. I know the pastor, and I'm sure he'll marry us on short notice. We can have a skiing honeymoon with an extended Malayan honeymoon."

I said, "I don't think getting married at the same time as entering the Peace Corps is a good idea. Who knows what we'll face when we get there?"

"Whatever it is, we'll face it together. What better way to begin a marriage."

I said, "We hardly know each other."

"What do you mean? We spent every day, all day, together for eight weeks. I know you well enough."

I said, "Then you know I'm not ready for marriage. I wish I were, but I'm not."

Before I could tell Noella that I was sorry, she shot out of bed, gave me the most hateful look, and slammed the door.

The next morning, Noella buzzed around the auditorium

hugging each female and kissing each male, saying, "Goodbye. Until we meet again."

Noella kissed all the men, including John, who was standing next to me, but made an exaggerated U-turn as she came to me. John laughed and said, "What's with Noella and the theatrical snub. What did you do to engineer such a colossal fall from grace?"

I said, "I don't know. Guess she thought it's time to dump me." I wasn't about to talk about rejecting Noella's marriage proposal.

"So, did you get any? All that time alone in your room."

"No. We just sat on the floor and played cards, gin rummy mostly. She got a kick out of beating me. Luckily, we weren't playing for money." That was the truth.

"Just look at that body. Don't you wish you had?"

"I tried. Believe me, I tried." This time I lied, and John bought it. I was glad.

This Is It

Finally, after eight seemingly never-ending weeks, Friday, December 1, 1961, arrived. The day we—the Peace Corps Malaya I Trainees—would be sworn in as official Volunteers. Penn stood at his usual place on the front left corner of the auditorium stage. He called the Trainees to order.

Guests were present for the occasion. Penn gave instructions for checking out of the hotel by noon and other travel arrangements. And then the swearing-in ceremony. I took pleasure in looking around the auditorium and listening to my fellow Peace Corps Volunteers take our oath of office. Each Volunteer stood erect, right hand in the air, a serious look on their faces and a seriousness in their voices as we recited together our oath to defend the U.S. Constitution against all enemies. I had goosebumps.

There were a few more government-employee tasks. Clothing allowance checks were distributed along with advice to purchase wash-and-wear summer clothing in the U.S. because it was not possible to purchase clothing off the rack in Malaya, and Malaya did not have laundromats. As our travel vouchers were being distributed, we were told that rather than departing two days after Christmas, we would leave after New Year's Day. And instead of three weeks of training at the University of Malaya, we would have four.

That bit of information was a bit of a bummer. I was ready to leave for Malaya as soon as I was sworn in. I didn't want any more waiting. I was ready to go. Instead, I was returning to my parents' house to wait.

I was in limbo.

The time between completing training in DeKalb and departing for Malaya was an uneasy time. The underlying unease of whether I would be selected was replaced with a discomforting feeling of limbo. I had to wait four weeks before departing to Malaya to teach biology. I was living at home with my parents under an uncomfortable truce. I was anxious to leave but knew my mother didn't want me to go. I could see the disappointment in her eyes. She wasn't one to keep her feelings, especially disappointment and anger, to herself, and I expected her to let me have it any day, but she didn't. I didn't know this person—defeated and sympathetic, masquerading as my mother. I didn't like it. As the time for my departure drew near, I hoped she would snap out of it. I longed for just one more tongue-lashing, a classic bouquet of curse words, arranged and rearranged, entwined in all my wrongdoings and all her years of sacrifices until she exorcised the demons plaguing her. It never came.

Finally, on January 2, 1962, all thirty-six newly minted Volunteers for Peace Corps Malaya I gathered at O'Hare airport in Chicago. Penn was taking charge once more, but this time as our travel escort. We were excited to begin our journey to

Malaya. Not so quick. A snowstorm hit, and we had to spend the night at O'Hare. Morning greeted us with clear, beautiful, baby-blue skies. We finally boarded our flight. We first flew to Anchorage, Alaska, changed planes, and then flew to Hong Kong. After a three-day layover in Hong Kong, we flew to our ultimate destination of Kuala Lumpur, Malaya.

CHAPTER 4

We landed on the tarmac in Malaya and used a staircase to exit the plane. The hot, humid air walloped me in the chest. I grabbed the handrail and saw our boss Luke standing at the bottom of the staircase. After meeting Sheridan in DeKalb, I was looking forward to meeting her husband. Luke was handsome, tall, and tan with a slender, muscular, Naval Officer build, just as I had pictured.

He greeted each Volunteer by name and with a large smile as he directed each of us to various transport vehicles. When I reached the bottom of the stairs, his smile disappeared, and he said, "Jim Wolter—wait here. You're riding with me."

Wow, I thought. Sheridan must have put in a really good word for me. I have it made. The boss asked me to ride with him.

Luke said, "I've been anxious to meet you. I wanted to size up my competition."

I thought he was jesting. I was going to respond in kind but held my tongue. He eyed me with an intense competitive squint and asked questions about my education. "You went to Wright Junior College, did you?"

"Yes."

"I went to the Great Lakes Naval Station for officer training school, but I learned to tie knots at Wright. Not much of a place back then, more like a junior high school building good for learning to tie knots. Is it still that way?"

"I only attended one semester."

"Ah yes, then you went to Northern Illinois University. If I'm not mistaken, it's not a ranked college."

I didn't know what he was talking about, but I was sure it was part of an ongoing putdown. "It was a good school for me."

I added, "I had a fellowship offer from Chapel Hill for a Ph.D. in genetics and was accepted by the Chicago Medical School." I thought to myself: Put that in your pipe and smoke it, buster.

"What's the ranking of the Chicago Medical School?"

I knew what he was after. The Chicago Medical School wasn't considered a prestigious school, but it turned out very competent physicians who built very successful practices. "Last I checked, it ranked first in the percentages of students passing the National Boards on their first attempt."

"So why would you give all that up to join the Peace Corps?"

I didn't want to answer that question, so I simply said: "I gave everything up to join the Peace Corps for the same reason as you." That would have been enough, but I had to add, "Except I didn't have a wife and kids to bring along." I smiled. I was pleased with myself for not adding that your wife and kids had to give everything up to follow you.

Luke drove to the University of Malaya, pointing out various landmarks. He was giving me a private tour, and I unexpectedly felt privileged, even after his interrogating questions. Maybe I misjudged him. Maybe that's how men of the world talk.

Meeting My Roommates

Luke dropped me off at the University of Malaya's men's dormitory. I carried my luggage to a reception area. A college-aged man scanned my name on a list, handed me a key, and said,

"Room one-twelve." My three Malay roommates were waiting in the room when I arrived. They seemed shy. I introduced myself. Each of them had Mohamed as part of their name, but only one was actually called Mohamed. I was confused. "Just call each of us Mohamed," one said. My new roommates and I shared a stark but comfortable room.

The room had four narrow beds lining the walls. Between each bed was a combination desk-dresser. Each of the four dressers had three drawers. It was a plain, utilitarian room. I placed my suitcase on top of the only empty desk and said, "Mine?" They said yes in unison. For appearing to be initially shy, they changed when I opened my suitcase. They drew near me as I unpacked, eyeing each item that I pulled out of my bag. My clothes filled the dresser drawers, and what didn't fit remained in the suitcase, which I slid under the only unoccupied bed and again said, "Mine?" They remained quiet until I placed my five NIU bookstore bargain lab notebooks on the desktop, along with a box of pencils. They spoke in Malay among themselves. I didn't have time to ask what they were saying because I had to go to my first Malay language class.

I grabbed my notebook and a pencil. As an afterthought, I placed the four other notebooks and the remaining pencils in the desk drawer before heading out.

I smiled and waved goodbye. I then left and joined the other Volunteers to walk to the lecture hall.

We gathered in a large hall for our language training. I was looking forward to an interactive language learning experience where we would learn useful conversation that we would immediately apply. What I found was boring. We were taught "proper Malay" that would be understood throughout Malaya but not necessarily spoken. The readers reminded me of the old *Dick and Jane* books I read in primary grades. They contained dialogue that I was unlikely to use. I didn't progress in Malay as much as I desired.

When I returned to the dorm after class the first day, I

found only one notebook left on my desk and only one pencil in the pencil box. I asked my roommates, "Do you know what happened to my notebooks and pencils?"

Mohamed Talib, who became the trio's spokesperson, said, "You had five. We had none." I said: "You took them?"

"Yes."

"I'm going to need them."

"You can get more. We cannot."

I was pissed but tried not to show it. I shared the incident with Jack May. Jack was third in command at the Peace Corps office in Kuala Lumpur. He told me it was customary to exchange gifts. My roommates may initially have thought I was going to give them the notebooks. Beyond that, since the notebooks were left out in the open, in their mind, they felt free to help themselves.

Jack explained that my roommates and I were operating on two different value systems. He said, "You're joining them, they're not joining you, so you have to adapt to—not necessarily adopt—their value system."

After one evening out on the town, I came back to my room and was ready to write in my notebook a few notes about my day, as was my customary routine. But the notebook wasn't on my desk. I looked around and found it on Syed Mohamed's desk. The pencil that I habitually placed inside my notebook as a bookmark was now sitting on top of the notebook. It was obvious that he and probably all three roommates had read my journal.

I didn't say anything. Initially, I had thought about locking my notebook in my suitcase but thought it would indicate to my roommates that I didn't trust them. My notes, even those in my form of shorthand since the Marjorie postcard incident, were innocuous. Still, I resented my roommates going through my things. I told myself not to take it personally, but I didn't leave my notebook or mail from home on my desk after that.

As Peace Corps Volunteers, we were magnets to Malaysian

and international students and faculty. We would gather together in the dining hall, and that's where Jennifer, an Australian graduate student in her mid-twenties, picked up John and me. She invited us, really John, to her apartment for a party that evening. John told me he had dibs on Jennifer. I expected John to leave with me at the end of the party, but he stayed with Jennifer. I didn't see my Peace Corps buddy John much after that except in class.

I missed hanging around with John during non-class time. But soon, while sitting alone in the dining hall, I was adopted by a group of six Chinese students and two Indian students—all male and all studying economics. I called them The Posse. They decided I needed to know my way around Kuala Lumpur, and we spent weekend afternoons walking the streets. They introduced me to The Oasis Creamery, which was indeed an oasis. It was an air-conditioned paradise within walking distance of the Peace Corps office. Entering it was just like walking into an ice cream parlor in Anywhere, USA.

Be Flexible

It was finally the big day. Norb would give us our assignments, and we would depart in all directions blanketing Malaya by plane, train, and taxi. Earlier in the week, we had been asked which towns and states we desired to be posted to. I had only one. It remained Malacca because of its historical significance and cultural history. Sheridan said she'd put in a word for me, and recently she and Norb assured me I would be assigned there. The motto "Be Flexible" in my case again was "Be prepared for disappointment."

Assignments were handed out in alphabetic order. When it came to my name, Norb said, "Jim, we have to talk."

While the other Volunteers were hugging, laughing, and

generally celebrating, Norb pulled me aside, "I need you to go to Kuala Trengganu. The General Hospital has changed their request from one to three nurses. I was sending Eva Gentile up there and Jenny Evers to the secondary school. But I had to send nurses Cindy Mann and Noella to join Eva. Four women in one town, the most isolated of all assignments, my team thought that was a recipe for failure. We thought you, with your sense of humor, could help Eva keep a lid on things if any interpersonal disputes arose. I'm counting on you, Jim. We all are."

"Why did you ask our preferences if you were going to ignore them?" I asked.

"I assure you we didn't, but this time we had to think of the good for the whole program."

"But why did you assure me I was going to Malacca?"

"You were at that time, but circumstances changed. You have to look at it from our perspective and take in the big picture."

Didn't these fools have eyes? Didn't they see Noella go out of her way to snub me in public and try to humiliate me? Didn't they see Cindy castrate any man within arm's length? Eva, fine, I love Eva. I would do anything for her, but going to Kuala Trengganu to help keep Cindy and Noella from causing problems is not something I joined the Peace Corps for. It was unfair. If the Peace Corps thought Noella and Cindy were potential problems, they should be sent home.

Volunteers were asked how they wanted to travel to their assignments. I wanted to fly out that afternoon, but the three nurses wanted to go by train to see the countryside. Norb told me, "Jim, I don't want the nurses traveling alone. You'll have to escort them." That made me angrier.

CHAPTER 5

This is what I was waiting for. I had wanted to be assigned to Malacca, but my disappointment was short-lived. If I had made a second choice, it would have been Kuala Trengganu. Eva, Cindy, and Noella were delighted by the prestige of being assigned to what the Peace Corps considered the most remote assignment.

Kuala Trengganu was a small fishing village located at the mouth of where the Trengganu River emptied its tea-colored water into the South China Sea. It became a center for trade and was the capital of the State of Trengganu. John, my main Peace Corps buddy, and I made our final farewell. We had experienced adventures and secrets together. Now I was headed to the east coast while John was staying on the west coast. I felt, for the first time, a distance between John and me.

Someone, I don't know who, maybe Norb, referred to the three nurses and me as "Jim and his harem" in Kuala Trengganu. I'm not sure who resented that more, the nurses or me. I desired to establish my own identity—apart from the nurses and even, as odd as it might seem, apart from the Peace Corps. I simply wanted to be known as Jim, the biology teacher who was friendly, competent, and hardworking.

Since Eva, Cindy, Noella, and I were not scheduled to catch the train to Kuala Trengganu until the next morning at Gemas, we waited and watched the other Volunteers head to the airport and board taxis. We saw all the other Volunteers off until it was our turn to pile into the Peace Corps van for the three-hour journey to the Gemas Government Resthouse. The Gemas train station was the station where the train started and headed toward Kuala Trengganu, and the nurses wanted to see as much of the countryside as possible. In the morning, it was a short walk to the station. The six o'clock train arrived a little more than half past the hour at the blush of dawn.

We had the cabin to ourselves. Rows of wood benches, similar to church pews, provided ample seating. There were perhaps twenty rows, but the three nurses sat together on one bench seat, and I sat by myself on another. It didn't take long before we were underway.

The nurses chatted among themselves. During our twelve weeks of training, Eva, Cindy, and Noella didn't hang out together. Now they will live together for two years. They needed to get to know each other, and I was a distraction. I would have to amuse myself on the day-long journey.

As they huddled together in intense conversation, I left them for a tour of the kitchen car. When I returned a short time later, I found Eva, Cindy, and Noella each on their own bench, fast asleep. I only hoped it was by mutual agreement that they needed the rest and not the result of a squabble. They were so sound asleep that they didn't wake when the train stopped and more passengers boarded. The nurses had lobbied to take the train to see the countryside but remained sound asleep. I thought about waking them but figured sleep was good for them and even better for me.

When the sun was low in the sky. The nurses began to stir. "Where are we? What time is it? I'm hungry."

I answered, "We're nearing where we get off."

"Why didn't you wake us? We missed the entire trip," said Noella. She was snarky, but at least she was speaking to me.

Finally, We Arrive

It was twilight by the time we arrived at our destination. My school Headmaster, Bankim Daarun, was pacing the station platform smoking a cigarette. He had a light brown complexion, was slender, about as tall as me, with a long narrow nose and thin lips. He was dressed in dark trousers and a long-sleeved white shirt rolled up to his elbows and wore leather open-toe sandals.

After introducing himself, he said, "Jim, you're late. Why didn't you fly or take a taxi?"

I figured he was making a statement rather than seeking answers, so I just extended my hand and said, "Pleased to meet you, too."

"May I introduce you to Mr. Lim Teh Eng? He has graciously agreed to share his accommodations with you. Of course, you'll share expenses."

Teh Eng and I barely shook hands before Bankim said, "And may I have the pleasure of being introduced to your lovely traveling companions?"

Bankim chatted with the nurses while we waited for the Matron to pick them up. Teh Eng and I got to know each other. He was a few inches shorter than I was, with a slender build. He had a handsome face with well-proportioned features. He was seven years older than I was, just like my older brother Ed. He was married and had two sons living back in Penang. He attended the Penang Free School and had taught geography there since graduating from Singapore University. He longed to be back in Penang but had to accept a two-year teaching assignment on the east coast to be considered for a promotion in the Ministry of Education. "This is my Peace Corps assignment." Teh Eng rolled back his head in laughter at his own joke.

The Matron arrived, and the nurses left.

"Teh Eng, how about you and I take Jim out for a drink?" asked Bankim.

"I'm afraid not tonight. I have assignments to correct and lessons to prepare for tomorrow."

"Jim, what do you say?"

"I'd like to settle in and look over my class schedule and the biology syllabus."

"There will be plenty of time for that tomorrow."

"But I'm already three weeks late. I want to be prepared."

"You can't get those things until tomorrow."

"Will I observe the substitute teacher to learn what the students are working on?"

"Your classes were covered by multiple teachers. They've been anxiously waiting for you to relieve them, so don't count on them covering your classes any longer."

"But I'm not prepared."

"Just spend the first day introducing yourself to your students. You'll be the first American they meet, and they will have plenty of questions. You can ask them what they've been studying."

I remained silent and thought: I still don't know what I'll be doing, but I'm here, and I hope I don't fail. We drove in silence.

We finally swung into the school compound and up on the front lawn of Teh Eng's house, soon to be my home for the next two years. It was a two-story stucco duplex with metal shuttered windows and an attached one-car garage.

Teh Eng unlocked the front door and handed me a key.

I followed Teh Eng through the front door of his house, and he gave me a quick tour of the ground floor. Immediately ahead was a stairway. Four steel shutters covered the front windows while wall-to-wall, floor-to-ceiling accordion wood doors opened and blanketed the opposite wall if we wished to bring the outdoors in. On the other side of the staircase was a dining area. An electric kettle, a tea caddy, and a thermos sat on the buffet, and on the table sat two stacks of student papers waiting to be corrected.

Teh Eng said, "I work at this end of the table. You can work at the other end if you like. I keep hot water in the thermos and tea in the tea caddy. Help yourself. No need to clean up. The House Boy will take care of cleaning in the morning."

I poked my head in the kitchen. There was a two-burner electric stove with an oven and a deep porcelain sink. Quickly I followed Teh Eng who was about to show me my room.

We walked up the stairs to a corridor that led to three bedrooms and a bath with a Western-style toilet and shower. Teh Eng's room was the end room with a window facing the front and one facing the back. I selected the bedroom that had three windows—one facing the front, one facing the back, and, best of all, one facing the sea.

I popped my suitcase onto the bare bed frame. "I'll need to get a mattress and bedding."

"We'll go to Bong's tomorrow and get bedding and a mosquito net for you," said Teh Eng. "I'll let you settle in while I finish correcting papers."

"Thanks; I'll be down after I shower."

After my shower, I returned to the dining room. Teh Eng said: "I have something for you. The previous biology teacher left this behind." He handed me a book that looked something like *The Old Farmer's Almanac*. I asked, "What's this?"

"A compilation of five years of biology questions that were asked on the Cambridge Examination a decade ago. The questions tend to repeat. This will give you an idea of what your students will be expected to know. You'd be well advised to study the questions and plan your lessons accordingly."

"Thank you." While Teh Eng finished marking his papers, I studied the questions. It was a start.

CHAPTER 6

Who hasn't experienced the elation of the first day of school or a new job? I was excited about the new experiences and challenges awaiting me at Sultan Sulaiman Secondary School in Kuala Trengganu. And I wondered and worried about how I would fit into the established order. I walked into the faculty room with Teh Eng. In the faculty room, I noticed the women teachers' desks were nearest the door, and the men teachers' desks were in the rear of the room. Teh Eng introduced me to the assembled faculty. Mrs. Ang said, "Here's an empty desk, next to mine; you may have it, if you like."

As it happened, Mrs. Ang lived in the other half of the duplex occupied by Teh Eng and me. That vacant desk, now mine, was the dividing line between the women's desks and the men's desks. The desk on the other side of mine belonged to Low Tim Fook, Assistant Headmaster. He also was a graduate of the University of Singapore in chemistry. And next to his desk was Teh Eng's desk. Mrs. Ang, Mr. Low, and Teh Eng were all senior faculty with teaching experience.

The Malayan education system followed the British system, which was structured to identify talented students and cull weaker students at a young age—determining their education and future. For example, at the end of the American equivalent of sixth grade, students would take their first and possibly last exam—the standardized National Examination—to determine if they could proceed to secondary school or not. Another exam would be in three years, after Form III (the American equivalent of ninth grade or the freshman year of high school). Successfully passing the Form III exam earned the students the Lower Certificate of Education (LCE) and again determined whether students could continue their education through Form V. After Form V, students sat for the Cambridge Examination, which determined who would go to the next level of Form VI. Form VI lasted two years and culminated in taking the Higher School Certificate (HSC) exam and eventual admission to a university.

I felt anxious and intimidated. I questioned whether I was skilled enough. If I weren't, then my inadequacies would result in my students failing and ending their education, their career prospects, and their future standard of living.

My teaching assignment was Form V biology, Form IV chemistry, and Form V mathematics. My extra assignments were Assistant House Master of Red House and Assistant Scout Master. I was to report to the House Master of Red House and to the Scout Master for Saturday morning and after-school assignments.

Low asked, "Do you have any further questions?"

I looked over my class schedule. It was heavy, with two lab sciences and three math classes. I said, "I have a question. I'm a biology teacher. Why am I assigned to teach only one biology class?"

"Take that up with the Headmaster."

"What about syllabi for my classes?"

"I have one for chemistry, but the others, you will have to take up with the Headmaster."

My Classes

My first-period class was biology. Surveying the biology lab, it had the same lab setup I was familiar with: a chalkboard; a long, raised demonstration lab table at the front of the room; and rows of student lab tables. There were no microscopes, projectors, dissecting instruments, nothing, not even chalk for use on the chalkboard.

My students arrived, smiling and giggling. When they saw me, they quickly quieted down and filed into their seats over the watchful eye of the class Head Boy. When settled in, the Head Boy said, "Class stand." The students stood waiting in silence. I noticed every seat was taken, all forty-two of them.

I smiled and said, "Good morning, class." I received a re-sounding "Good morning, Sir" in reply. The students remained standing until I said, "Please sit." I introduced myself. I had intended to write my name on the chalkboard before my students arrived, but I couldn't find chalk, so I verbally spelled out my name. I told my students where I was from and a bit about my family and my education. I asked what they had previously been studying. I was surprised when my students responded: "Nothing, Sir." In my mind, I thought: the Cambridge Examination is in November, and they have missed three weeks of instruction. I'll have to start from the beginning.

I called on the Head Boy. "Did you go on field trips to study the seaside or the paddy fields across the road?"

"Sir, no. Never, Sir."

I asked him to be seated and outlined what we would study. The location of the Sultan Sulaiman, with the sea on one side of the school's compound and paddy fields across the road, was a gift to a biologist. I had noticed that an ecology question appeared on every past Cambridge exam. "We will start with studying the ecology of the seaside and a freshwater wetland. We will take field trips to our beach and the paddy fields."

I went to the chalkboard and started opening desk drawers in search of a piece of chalk.

The Head Boy stood. "Excuse me, Sir, there is no chalk. Sir must bring his own chalk to class."

"Thank you. Next time I'll bring chalk."

The chemistry lab had the same setup as the biology lab, except the lab tables' faucets weren't connected to a water source. Also, there were no test tubes, beakers, or chemicals. How was chemistry taught without chemicals? I had a minimal amount of chemistry in college and by no means was qualified to be teaching chemistry.

Each of my mathematics classes was studying plane geometry but a different topic. Again, I was not qualified to teach mathematics and, in particular, plane geometry. I specifically told Norb during training that I could get by teaching math from arithmetic to calculus, but I could not teach plane geometry. All I knew about plane geometry was what I learned doing my older sister's geometry homework when I was in seventh grade.

By the end of the school day, the excitement of teaching had abandoned me. I was stunned by what I got into. Biology would be difficult but not hopeless. There were workarounds for the lack of equipment, but teaching chemistry without chemicals was insane. But most ludicrous was me, a person who never had so much as one day of formal instruction in plane geometry, teaching three classes of plane geometry to students whose future depended on passing the Cambridge Examination in nine months.

I was pissed at the Peace Corps staff. I figured Bankim wouldn't be of any help either, but I still went to see him.

I said, "Thank you for finding the biology syllabus for me. It's going to be a big help."

"I'm sure that's not what you wanted to see me about."

"It's my class assignments. I'm a biology teacher. I don't know enough chemistry to teach it, and the math classes are studying geometry. There's no way I can teach students geometry."

"There is no one else to teach those classes. You're the American Peace Corps. Find a way. Is that all?"

"One more thing. We have no microscopes."

"There's no money for a microscope. If your microscope is so important, why didn't your government furnish one when they built the new science building?"

"That I don't know. But, if your answer is no, just say so." I got up to leave. I was pissed at Bankim. I noticed when he picked me up at the train station the night before that he had a way of maintaining a placid face without revealing the emotions behind his stinging words. He didn't smile, either. He exhibited a dull, flat, lifeless affect.

"Fine. No," Bankim replied with a hint of anger in his voice. I said, "Thank you." And left.

Call for Help

As I headed back to my house. I was frustrated. To make matters worse, the students would be sitting for exams that would determine whether they continued their education and, in turn, the future course of their lives. Norb had assured the Volunteers several times that he had personally made sure that each of us had an appropriate and meaningful job. How could he be so wrong? I needed to call him, but I didn't want to use the phone in the school office.

Teh Eng was already at the dining table with a cup of tea and a stack of papers to correct. He said: "My students came from your class and said you assigned them a question they couldn't answer and asked me, 'What is life?' "

"What did you tell them?" And then I sang, "Life is but a bowl of cherries." Teh Eng then sang a couple of bars, rolling in laughter. "Let's get you to town and get you a mattress, mosquito net, and bedding. We can't have you sleeping on the floor."

I added: "I also have to call the Peace Corps office but don't want to use the school phone."

"No problem," he said.

I climbed on the back of Teh Eng's Lambretta motor scooter, and he drove us to Bong's Import Export shop, which carried school supplies and a host of other things as diverse as bolts of beautiful Thai silk to American magazines and British electronics. He said he would have the goods I required delivered in an hour.

Teh Eng then said to Bong: "Jim has to make a telephone call to the Peace Corps Office in Kuala Lumpur and doesn't want to use the school phone."

Bong turned to me and asked, "Do you have the number?"

"Yes."

"Let me make the call."

Bong lifted the phone's receiver and asked the operator to connect him to the Peace Corps Office in Malaya. He then said: "Bong here in Trengganu. Can I speak to your manager?" There was a pause, and he said, "Never mind, let me speak to him." He handed the phone to me and said, "You can speak freely."

It was Luke on the other end. Norb wasn't in. I described my teaching situation to him and told him it was nothing like Norb described, and neither the Assistant Headmaster nor the Headmaster was willing to assign me to classes that I was qualified to teach. There must have been a terrible misunderstanding, and I wanted my teaching assignment at Sultan Sulaiman changed or transferred to another school that needed a biology teacher. Luke acknowledged that I had said that I couldn't teach plane geometry, but the Peace Corps Office could not interfere with the internal functioning of a school and could not arrange a transfer for me. I would have to "tough it out."

I asked, "Will the Peace Corps pay for a geometry tutor to teach me geometry if I can find one?"

Luke replied, "No, that would appear the Peace Corps was sending out teachers not qualified to teach."

"Luke, that's exactly what the Peace Corps has done."

"I'll arrange for Bob Reed to tutor you over the school break.

That's the most we can offer."

"In three months. That's the best you can do?"

"I did make arrangements for you to pick up a new Raleigh bicycle at Khoo's Bicycle Shop."

I hung up without saying goodbye and handed the phone back to Bong, "Thank you."

"Anytime." Bong smiled at me. He had a round face with soft features and an easy-going manner that made me comfortable.

Teh Eng said, "Things always look better on a full stomach. We'll have something to eat, then we'll go back and figure things out."

We went to Ah Soon's coffee shop, which we referred to as "The Green Door Restaurant" because of its green doors, and had his wonton soup for dinner.

On the way home, we stopped at Khoo's Bicycle Shop to pick up my bicycle. It was the tallest bike I ever saw. It was too tall for me. I didn't want to take it, but Khoo insisted that the Peace Corps boss had ordered this specific bike for me. I cycled home a bit uncomfortable, but as time passed, I became one with the bike and enjoyed sitting up high.

Teh Eng was right. Getting back to our house and after a bowl of wonton soup, things did not seem as desperate as they did earlier. His advice for geometry was to start with chapter one in the textbook, work on a few problems, and move on, chapter by chapter, until I caught up with the class. In the meantime, have the students take turns at the chalkboard and explain how they worked out the homework assignments. Teh Eng's advice worked.

Whenever Bong received a shipment of new magazines or records from America, he would wave me over if he saw me cycling in town. We read magazines and listened to music in the back room of his shop while drinking tea and talking about anything that popped into our heads. A few days later, Bong had me look over the newly arrived electronic equipment imported from England. One box contained a new model, portable, plug-in Philips radio-cassette tape player. We listened to BBC World News and a Mario Lanza tape.

Bong asked, "What do you think? Do you like it?"

"It's beautiful. Great sound. It will sell."

Bong said, "Then you take it."

"Sorry, I can't afford it."

"It's my gift to you."

"I don't think the Peace Corps will allow me to accept such an expensive gift."

"Then pay me what you want. Anything. Five ringgits a month, and I will buy it back when you go home."

I brought the tape player home. Teh Eng said, "I enjoy listening to the BBC to improve my English accent. Don't you think I sound very British?" Teh Eng tossed back his head in laughter.

Dying on the Beach

On Saturday, Bankim, the nurses, Teh Eng, and I joined Howard Brooke from the British Voluntary Service Overseas group at Dugong Beach. It was a beautiful day with a clear sunny sky even though it was monsoon season. The water was warm, with waves about two to three feet high. Howard and I were talking while walking in the surf about knee-high when suddenly I felt I had stepped off a cliff. As I slipped underwater, it felt like somebody grabbed my ankles and pulled me further under and further out to sea. I thought I was going to drown.

Just as suddenly as I was pulled underwater, I bobbed up, but I was far from shore. I saw Howard about two hundred yards away and swam against the current to him. When I finally reached him, he said, "I'm not touching bottom."

It was about another two hundred yards to the beach, and I was spent just reaching Howard. I said, "I don't think I can make it back on my own. Can you help?

He said, "Roll over on your back, and I'll try to pull you."

I did, and he started pulling me toward shore. Shortly after, maybe five yards later, he said, "I don't think I can make it, either, if I continue pulling you. I have to leave you."

I said, "Go ahead." and I continued to float on my back, remembering what Noella taught me back in the NIU swimming pool during Peace Corps training. I regained my strength. I was no longer swimming against the current and swam back to shore. I crawled up the beach exhausted and spitting out saltwater.

I looked up and saw Bankim. I expected him to say something. He obviously saw Howard and me pulled out to sea, but he said nothing. Eva and Cindy came over and asked if Howard and I were OK. Noella went over to Howard, but not me. When I stood up, I went first to Howard and thanked him for saving my life. Then I walked over to Noella to thank her and tell her the floating technique she taught me saved my life. Noella watched me approach, and as I was about to speak, she turned her back to me and marched away. Bankim, his affectless face now sporting an evil-looking grin that looked more like a smirk than a smile, said: "Jim, tell me, what is this comedy of errors between you and Noella?"

I thought that was an odd question, given that I almost drowned on an outing organized by him. I answered, "Noella and I were an item during Peace Corps training. She decided to call it off. That's all."

"Ah, so say you, but something tells me that's not all. A scorned and vengeful woman, methinks, lurks about seeking her due. It will be delightful to observe how this plays out."

An Unannounced Visit

As a biologist, senior Peace Corps staff in Kuala Lumpur reminded me of mushrooms. They just popped up unannounced and unexpectedly. It was in mid to late March when who should show up at the door to the faculty room but Norb Patton. He said that the Peace Corps Malaya II—the second group of sworn-in Volunteers—would arrive soon, and he was checking with Bankim on the possibility of a chemistry teacher joining me at the school. He added there would be two new nurses assigned to the hospital.

Norb said, "Jim, I know we can count on you to look after the new Volunteers and help the new teacher settle in."

"Yes, of course," I said.

Norb also mentioned that Bankim said I was doing a good job, but there was one area I had to work on: I had been pushing my biology students too hard and fast. I explained that I had pestered Bankim to see the biology syllabus before I started teaching. Not knowing the specifics of Malayan education, I thought the syllabus was for the first term when it was for the full year. I had worked my poor students unmercifully,

Norb also told me with a chuckle in his voice, "Your trousers look pretty baggy."

I said, "I know. I spent all of my clothing allowance buying wash-and-wear trousers before leaving for Malaya and then lost sixty pounds when I got sick during training in Kuala Lumpur. I'm waiting to have duty-free trousers made in Penang over the school holiday."

Norb said, "I'm afraid waiting isn't a luxury available to you. Bankim told me you have the nickname 'Baggy Pants' because your trousers are so loose. We can't have that. It's not the image you want to project."

That was a stinging personal criticism.

I said, "I got some bad advice in training and spent all my clothing allowance before coming to Malaya." I held back from telling Norb that the bad advice I received came from his wife.

Norb said, "I'm sure you'll find a way." He was smiling now as if he were relieved that he got my "performance review" out of the way and could move on to a new topic.

"Jim, I want you to fly to Kuala Lumpur this weekend to welcome the Malaya II Volunteers." I was still pissed at Norb but thought it would be fun to catch up with fellow Volunteers.

Making Holiday Plans

The following Friday, the Peace Corps Malaya II Volunteers had a weekend orientation to Malaya at the University of Malaya. During a party with the two groups of Volunteers and staff, April Jennings approached me and said: "If you have nothing planned for the school holidays in May, how about visiting Ayer Lanas. It's beautiful. A biologist's paradise. Mila and I can put you up."

I thought: April invited me to visit her. I had better accept it before she changes her mind.

"I'll be there. How about Thursday or Friday, the second week of May? The first week my neighbor invited me to join him in Malacca to eradicate an invasive species from rubber estates and fruit orchards. Then I'm going to duty-free Penang to get some trousers that fit."

April replied, "The ones you're wearing are perfectly adorable. They're so you. But I look forward to checking you out in your duty-free trousers."

My buddy John was talking to Regina Meale, who was described by the Peace Corps staff as "a woman who will be a definite asset to her husband's career." I didn't have a chance to visit with John, so I horned in on their conversation. For some reason, whether to make John jealous or because she wanted me to visit her, she said to me, "If you have nothing planned for the school holiday, how about visiting me in Alor Star."

I accepted, saying, "I'll be in Malacca hunting wild boar and flying foxes the first week and in Penang the second week to buy clothes that fit. How about I stop by on my way back to Kuala Trengganu?"

I could tell by the way Regina's eyes lit up that she was impressed with the image of me as a big game hunter and said, "I look forward to hearing all about your exploits."

I figured I'd take a taxi from Malacca to Kuala Lumpur and another taxi to Penang and shop for a day or two and then take a taxi to Alor Star for a day before flying to Kota Bharu to visit April in Ayer Lanas for four or maybe even five days. It would be a hectic and exhausting week of travel, but I was looking forward to spending time with April relaxing without others around. Yes, nurse Volunteer Mila Iverson would be there, but she was friends with me and knew how to disappear. April and I would have nearly a whole week together alone. Glory be.

Before we left, Norb said: "Jim, I know I can count on you to take Victoria under your wing and introduce her to the culture of Kuala Trengganu and make sure she has a successful acceptance and adjustment to Sultan Sulaiman. You'll also have two new nurses to look after."

A few days later, Victoria, the new Peace Corps chemistry teacher, arrived. Bankim directed me to let Victoria shadow me for a few days so she could become accustomed to the school. At the start of her third day of school, Low told me to take my lesson-plan book and all my personal belongings from my desk and report to the Headmaster. I wondered what that was about and headed for Bankim's office with all my things.

Reaching Bankim's office, I noticed a Peace Corps car outside. I entered his office and found Norb sitting there. I thought that was odd. It was too early to have driven in that morning. Norb must have stayed at the Resthouse overnight. Norb lumbered to his feet, smiled, shook my hand, and said, "I don't know how to tell you this, Jim, but you've been transferred to a new school."

Bankim said, "The Ministry has transferred you to Tengku Bariah Secondary School. You know Ang Boon Hooi. He's the Headmaster. You are to report to him immediately."

"Why?"

Norb said, "It's a new school, and they need a teacher."

I said, "If the new school needs a teacher, then send the new teacher to the new school and let me continue here."

Bankim said, "That is not going to happen."

I said, "Look, it took a lot of effort to get settled in here and to get my classes organized. Now you want to transfer me? Why can't the new teacher go to the new school? Why do I have to start all over again?"

Bankim said, "The Ministry determined you are no longer needed here. That's the way it is. But you can be thankful. I persuaded the Peace Corps to provide you with a motorbike because it is too far a distance to cycle."

I turned to Norb and said, "If I'm not needed here, then transfer me to Malacca. That's where you said I would be posted in the first place."

Norb didn't answer, but Bankim responded, "When you signed up for the Peace Corps, I'm sure it was to teach anywhere you were posted, and now you're being posted to Tengku Bariah."

Norb said, "You know he's right. Besides, now that there are four women here, we need you even more in Kuala Trengganu."

I said, "You could have, at the very least, given me an opportunity to say goodbye to my students."

Bankim said, "They're no longer your students. Ang Boon Hooi is expecting you. Do you need directions?"

I felt like I was being kicked out of my school. I walked out of Bankim's office, not bothering to shake hands or look at Norb or Bankim. "I'll find my own way."

CHAPTER 7

I descended the stairs from Bankim's office and passed Norb's parked Peace Corps car, feeling dejected. I wondered when Norb knew I was being transferred. Did he know a few weeks back when he popped in unannounced? It was then that he asked me if a new Volunteer could shadow me for a few days. Of course, ever-eager me agreed without realizing that was the prelude to my termination.

I was determined to find my own way. The Peace Corps posted me at Sultan Sulaiman in the first place, not so much to teach biology but to smooth out any problems three nurses might encounter or cause. Now, I was kept at Tengku Bariah Secondary School to babysit and bodyguard three nurses and a teacher in Kuala Trengganu. That was unfair.

I felt empty and numb walking across the school compound to Teh Eng's house.

I wanted to quit the Peace Corps right then and there and go home, but I might need a letter of recommendation from them. What would the Peace Corps letter say? *Jim was transferred to another school. He didn't like it. So, he quit.*

I decided not to quit immediately. I would remain in the Peace Corps until the end of the second term in August. This afternoon, I would write to my parents to let them know I was returning in August, and I would write to Dr. Nickerson, my medical school mentor, to inform him that I was returning a year early and ask him what I needed to do to get reinstated at the medical school. Later, I would tell the Peace Corps that I decided to leave early to return to medical school. I would find my own way and make the best of the remainder of my tour. I determined it was best to depart while leaving no burned bridges.

I got on my bicycle, feeling better, not great, but better. I had a plan. The end of my Peace Corps tour was in sight. I would make the best of it. I didn't need the Peace Corps. I would find my own way. Boon, the Headmaster of Tengku Bariah, was waiting for me.

Another Screw-Up

I pushed my bicycle hard. It took me about forty minutes to get to Tengku Bariah Secondary School. I parked my bicycle. I noticed the entire school compound was ringed by a cyclone fence. It gave the school compound the look of a prison yard. I was happy to find Boon at his desk. Boon was my neighbor, and he was my friend. He sponsored my admission to the tennis club and invited me to travel with him to his father's house in Malacca, where we would join his father's hunting party during the upcoming school holiday.

When he saw me, Boon got up from his desk, walked over to the door of his office, extended his hand, and said, "Welcome, Jim." He then took on a more professional demeanor. He said, "Jim, just before you arrived, I received a call from the Chief Education Officer's (CEO) office telling me to expect you and to find a job for you. I told the CEO that all of my teaching assignments for the term were set, and all I had for you were the Form III Ugama classes."

"What is Ugama?"

"It's Islamic studies."

I thought there must be some mistake. Norb would never have agreed to this assignment. I asked Boon, "Did Norb Patton meet with you to check out my teaching assignment?"

Boon replied, "I never met the gentleman. I just now learned you were assigned to Tengku Bariah."

Once again, I was placed in an assignment I couldn't possibly do.

I said, "Boon, I can't possibly teach Islamic studies. I don't know anything about Islam."

"Jim, I don't expect you to teach Ugama. All I expect you to do is take attendance and provide a supervised study period until the Ministry sends us an Ustaz."

Boon must have seen my angst and began speaking again. "I'm sorry, Jim. That's all I have for you. I have no choice in the matter either." I didn't see it Boon's way, and I felt I was stuck in an untenable situation.

"Boon, there has been a colossal foul-up here. There's no way the Peace Corps would assign a non-Muslim Peace Corps teacher to supervise Islamic studies classes. I need to call the Peace Corps office to clear this up. May I use the school phone?"

"Yes, of course." Boon pushed the phone toward me.

I knew Norb wouldn't be in the office and was glad because I was even more pissed at him. The Peace Corps secretary answered the telephone and transferred me to Luke. I skipped the usual exchange of pleasantries and asked straightaway, "Luke, are you aware of my transfer today?"

"I knew something to that effect was in the works but was not involved in the details. What's up?"

"I've been assigned to a new school where I'm to supervise Ugama classes."

"What's Ugama?"

"Exactly. My Headmaster is sitting here with me, and he says he doesn't actually expect me to teach Ugama but to provide the students with a supervised study hall until an Ustaz is sent to the school by the Ministry."

"When will that be?"

I turned to Boon and said, "He wants to know when an Ustaz will be here."

Boon replied, "I have no idea."

"Luke, he has no idea. Look, I joined the Peace Corps to teach biology to students that needed a biology teacher. I didn't leave my family, my friends, and medical school to travel halfway around the world to be a placeholder until the Ministry gets around to assigning an Ustaz to this school."

"I'll share your situation with Norb first thing when he gets back, and I'm sure he, or I, or someone, will be back to you. All I can say is if something like this had to happen to a Volunteer, it is comforting to know it was you because I have full confidence you will figure something out."

"I do have something figured out. Assign me to a school where I can teach biology or release me and I'll go back home."

"Jim, I understand. Don't do anything rash. As soon as Norb gets back, we'll get things straightened out. Hold tight, and we'll be in touch."

Luke listened to me, but he was second in command and had no authority to fix my situation. I was stuck. I made Luke the butt of my anger and didn't bother saying goodbye. I hung up the receiver and pushed the phone back toward Boon. I resented being used as a placeholder by the Ministry and felt like a political pawn abandoned by the Peace Corps. I didn't give a shit about the Peace Corps or holding up its image, but I appreciated Boon's candor and felt obliged to help him out.

I said to Boon, "I'll do my best."

He said, "I'm sure you will. I have one more question before introducing you to the staff. Do you have any boxing experience?"

"I boxed in college. I had two matches." I wanted to say more about quitting boxing because I thought it a barbaric activity, but Boon interrupted.

Boon stood up and said, "Good. Let's go for a walk."

The first thing that jumped out at me as I followed Boon was a boxing ring taking up the center third of the Tuck Shop "Mr. Ratnam, I want to introduce you to Mr. Jim Wolter, a Peace Corps teacher who has just been assigned to our school. Jim, I want you to meet Mr. Ratnam. He is our Senior Assistant and our Athletic Director."

Ratnam got up, offered me his hand, and said, "Pleased to meet you, Mr. Jim."

Boon said, "We have our Boxing Master. Jim here boxed in college."

This was my chance to get out of boxing. I said, "Just two fights. I quit. I'm the wrong person for Boxing Master." Boon turned to Ratnam and said, "I'll leave Jim with you. I'd like him to get the Boxing Club started by the end of the week."

Ratnam said, "You heard the Headmaster's directive. Now, you will have a class in a few minutes, so follow me to the faculty room for introductions."

As we approached the faculty room, I could hear talking and laughter coming from the room. Ratnam's authoritative voice called out: "Staff, listen up. This is Mr. Jim. You probably know him as the Peace Corps teacher at Sultan Sulaiman. He has been transferred here, and you will be relieved to know that he is taking over the Ugama classes, effective immediately. Introduce yourselves and point out an empty desk for him to use."

A cheer went up from the faculty. I knew three of the men— Koo Jin Leng, Leslie Foo, and Tan Tiong Kooi— because they lived in the bachelors' quarters across from Teh Eng's quarters.

Jin Leng jumped up on a desk, stomped his feet, and shouted, "Take this one!"

Ratnam handed me a lesson-plan book and class schedule. The passing bell rang. I walked to my assigned building and stayed there for the day. I found a desk at the end of the corridor on the ground floor. I thought it was an odd place for a desk, but it was in a quiet, peaceful place away from all the other teachers. I didn't want to be at Tengku Bariah. I wanted to be alone. I thought I had the perfect hiding place.

I was sitting quietly with my elbows on the desk and my face buried in my hands, trying to soothe myself, when I heard a high-pitched irritating man's voice that I recognized as Jin Leng's.

"Here you are. I've been searching for you." I kept my face covered, hoping he'd go away. "I'm here to collect your $17.80M."

"For what?"

"The NUT picnic to Pulau Perhentian over Easter recess."

"What's NUT?"

"The National Union of Teachers. Pulau Perhentian is a beautiful coral island off the Besut coast. We leave Thursday after school and return Saturday."

"I'm not a union member."

"The picnic is a chance for union members and nonmembers to mix so nonmembers can learn the advantages of membership."

"I'm in the Peace Corps. I can't join a union."

"We're not asking you to join the union. We're just asking you to join us on the picnic. Teh Eng and Victoria have already agreed to join us. You are the only one who hasn't paid up. We are counting on you. If you don't go, I'll have to recalculate the cost to everyone else."

The bell rang for the next class. I got up to go to class, said, "Sorry, I'm not going," and walked off to class, savoring the idea of being alone over Easter break.

Ugama Classes

I was officially assigned to teach Ugama. The routine for Ugama classes was to take class attendance and then dismiss the non-Muslim students who went to the Tuck Shop for an unsupervised study period. It didn't make sense to me to send the non-Muslims out of class when the Muslim students weren't studying Ugama. I kept all my students in class.

At the end of the day, I filled in the lesson-plan book. If there was a more stupid activity, I didn't know what it was. Writing "supervised study hall" five times every day was documenting the depths to which my service as a Peace Corps Volunteer had fallen.

When I arrived home, I immediately went to my room and wrote to my parents, telling them I'd been transferred to another school, didn't think my services were required in Malaya, and that I intended to end my service early. I didn't go into detail. I also wrote to Dr. Nickerson and confessed that he was correct in advising me not to join the Peace Corps. I told him my intention was to return home in August 1962 rather than as planned in August 1963 and asked if I could be reinstated at the medical school a year early.

That night, I was lying in bed waiting to hear Teh Eng turn in. When he did, I slipped out of the house quietly. It was not unusual for me to go for walks up the beach after dark, away from all the people. This time I wore my swimming trunks. The moon glowed on placid waters, creating what looked like a silver road leading west to the shores of the United States. I so badly wanted to be there where I was loved. I wanted to be as far away from Kuala Trengganu as soon as possible. I wanted to end my misery. I wanted to end it all. I swam out, hopeful that I would become exhausted and just sink. But it didn't happen.

I rolled over on my back and looked up into the night sky's sweeping, breathtaking majesty. I decided, regardless of the response I received from Dr. Nickerson about returning to medical school in August, that I would exit the Peace Corps at that time. Until then, I would forget about the Peace Corps and make my own way, serving as I saw fit. I felt a rush of energy. I swam back to shore.

The following day, Teh Eng approached me and said, "Jim, we have to talk. Do you remember when you told me that if you did something that was offensive, I should tell you?"

"Yes,"

"Well, that time has come. The Tengku Bariah staff think you are being one of those standoffish Europeans by taking a desk away from the faculty room and not going on the picnic. You have to use a desk in the faculty room, and you have to go on the picnic."

"The faculty room is too rowdy, and I look forward to being alone over Easter break."

"That's all fine and good, but you have to go on the picnic. Think of it as going with me, not NUT. Do you need the $17.80M?"

"No. I'll pay Jin Leng tomorrow."

"And you'll spend some time in the faculty room."

"I will."

CHAPTER 8

A decrepit orange school bus idled, belching fumes from its diesel engine that clattered like two sledgehammers pounding away angrily on a cast-iron boiler. Teh Eng shouted up the stairs, "Jim, hurry, the bus is here. I'll save a seat for you."

I was hiding out in my room, hoping Teh Eng would forget about me. I didn't want to go on the NUT picnic. I had given Jin Leng, the picnic organizer, my money for the picnic. That's all he was concerned about. I was counting on him leaving me behind if I were late getting on the bus. I wanted to be left behind, all alone, in Kuala Trengganu. Camping out for a night on an uninhabited isolated island in the South China Sea with two dozen or so teachers was the last thing in the world I wanted to do.

When I was forced by the Peace Corps to transfer to Tengku Bariah against my will and then forced by Boon to babysit the Ugama classes and forced again by Boon to coach boxing, I promised myself that I would serve my remaining five months in Malaya on my terms only. I was adamant. I would bend to the will of others no more. But here I was once again being coerced into doing something I didn't want to do. But, how could I say no to Teh Eng, especially when he took me in to share his quarters? In reality, he opened his life to me and mentored me when I needed mentoring and consoled me when I needed consoling. He said that he was looking out for my best interests. I trusted him. I couldn't refuse.

The orange road hazard on four wheels with "School Bus" painted in large black letters was parked on the side of the roadway between my quarters and the bachelors' quarters. Teh Eng was seated in the aisle seat across from the bus driver. When I got on the bus, Teh Eng swung his knees into the aisle and said, "I saved a window seat for you."

If I had to ride on a bus with a herd of teachers, Teh Eng ensured I had the best seat. I could look out the window at the passing scenery, watch the road ahead and not have to interact with anyone but Teh Eng. He was protecting me again, and I loved him for that.

I don't know what it is about a school bus that makes passengers want to sing. But as our bus rolled onto the ferry taking us to the other side of the Trengganu River, the teachers began singing "Ninety-Nine Bottles of Beer on the Wall." Never did I expect to hear that hideous tune in Malaya. I don't know how many courses of the song it took to get to Besut, but I was thoroughly relieved when the bus finally pulled off the blacktop road onto the one-lane dirt road leading to our destination.

The Most Beautiful Woman in the World

As our bus rolled into the dusty and drab Besut School compound, there she was standing alone, alongside a green Mercedes with the word "TAXI" painted in white on the front door—a beautiful vision that I first glimpsed from behind. A lovely easy wave of long dark hair flowed over her supple bare shoulders, whereas other Malayan women wore their hair in an ear-length cut that was referred to as a "Buster Brown Cut." And it would be a cold day in Kuala Trengganu before a teacher would wear a dress exposing their shoulders. She was wearing a simple sundress with red and white vertical stripes, and she held a long cigarette holder with a lit cigarette in her right hand, which I thought looked like a silly affectation, but otherwise, she looked stunning. I pointed her out to Teh Eng, who had already seen her. I said, "Wow, who is that? I've never seen her around Kuala Trengganu."

"That's Fong Moke Chee. She teaches in Kelantan and is a special guest of the Trengganu NUT."

"Do you know her?"

"I haven't met her, but everybody knows Miss Fong. She's a St. George's girl and just got back from studying art at Brinsford Lodge in England."

The bus rolled further, and I could see her profile and then her full face. I couldn't believe my eyes. In this little isolated, nowhere place—standing by herself on a dusty path and cradling a long cigarette holder in her hand—was the most beautiful woman in the world. Her eyes were big and brown and full of life. She didn't, I suspected by her appearance and stance, suffer fools lightly. She had a perfectly formed petite nose turned slightly upward, and her lips were exquisite, puffy, and pillowy, making me wonder what they would be like to kiss. I wished I could find out.

I told Teh Eng, "I wish I met her before she got married."

He said, "She's not married."

"But look, she's wearing a wedding ring."

"She wears that to ward off men. But she's not married."

"But she's wearing a maternity dress. She must be married."

"That's not a maternity dress. She's an artist. That's her own design. She wears them all the time."

"Are you sure? That sure looks like a wedding ring to me."

"I'm sure. It's been reported that she is engaged to some chap studying engineering in Australia."

"I hope I get to talk to her."

"You and every other man here. That's why Miss Fong was

invited. The men hope to talk to her and to see her in a swim-suit."

I didn't know what to say. After a brief pause, as though Teh Eng was collecting his thoughts or selecting the right words or both, he continued, "You may be in luck. Being an artist, just back from England and not constrained by conven-tionality, she is the only woman here, besides Victoria, likely to talk to you. But you'll have to out-fox all the other wolves." Teh Eng chuckled at his play on words. I thought his play on words was clever, but I was thinking about his earlier statement.

I hadn't thought about seeing Miss Fong in a bathing suit. Seeing her in her loose-fitting red-and-white-striped dress was more than enough to please my eyes. The bus came to a stop, and Jin Leng hustled us to our quarters for the night. I was assigned a spot on a rattan mat covering the concrete floor in Joe Dixon's room. Joe was a Peace Corps Malaya II teacher. But before turning in for the night, we had a chicken curry with yellow rice dinner followed by after-dinner enter-tainment. This is where things got interesting.

Fate Was with Me

Baby Pong, a physical education teacher, and Jin Leng had us gathered into one large circle. They explained we would then form teams and play "What's That Tune?" They had us count off as one, two, three, and four to form the teams. The men tried to figure out Miss Fong's number and jockeyed so they would be in her group. Teh Eng and I kept getting moved fur-ther away from Miss Fong, but when the time came to split the circle in two, I ended up in her group. The two groups again counted off, and the same jockeying took place. One fellow from the other group even tried to slip into our group but was quickly expelled by the other men. As it turned out, I ended up in the same smaller group as Miss Fong. My number placed me next to her. Now, we were instructed to form girl-boy teams. Fate intervened, bringing together Miss Fong and me as teammates for the first round.

The game itself was simple. Baby Pong or Jin Leng placed a record on the phonograph and let it play until the correct name of the tune was called out. I had an unfair advantage because all the tunes were Western tunes. Additionally, Mr. Everett, my former trumpet teacher, prepared me to play in dance bands, where I would have to play a song requested by the audience, so he trained me to recognize a tune after hearing one or two bars hummed even if it were hummed off-key. Mr. Everett's training enabled me to recognize every tune before all the other teachers. Initially, I called out the tune, but after a few tunes, I felt like a showoff and whispered the titles to Miss Fong, who called them out. Winning with Miss Fong as a partner was exhilarating, and even more so after we decided to keep silent and let other teams win so as not to spoil the evening for them. Our moments of not competing gave us a chance to talk to one another.

Another aspect of the game was to switch partners. But no other woman was willing to break the unwritten taboo of mixing with a European socially. Miss Fong rescued me from the indignity of being discriminated against and remained my partner. I was grateful and impressed that such a beautiful woman had the character and kindness to keep a foreigner from being isolated and embarrassed.

Miss Fong and I talked about the usual things recent college graduates talk about. Miss Fong told me tales of studying in England and hitchhiking through Europe during school holidays, which fascinated me. It was something I would have loved to do. We talked about our families and her tales of growing up during the Japanese occupation—singing the Japanese anthem to a Japanese soldier to keep herself and her nanny from being arrested on the way home from the market. Then, there was the frightful and chilling account of her father being interred under suspicion of being a British spy and being interrogated and beaten to near death by occupying Japanese forces. She also told me pleasant and fascinating post-occupation stories of being an only child playing with dozens of cousins at a huge family home with a large compound filled with fruit trees and overseen by her dowager maternal grandmother. I was impressed with Miss Fong's openness and candor.

Miss Fong asked me about my life, family, schooling, and why I joined the Peace Corps. My life, compared to hers, was pretty boring. She was surprised that my mother was opposed to my going to college and had wanted me to get a job and get married instead. Yes, I told her, there was a girl, Lolly, back home. Her mother and my mother were pushing us to marry, but we weren't ready. We decided that I would join the Peace Corps for two years and see if we were ready for marriage after that.

As the night wore on, Miss Fong insisted I call her Moke Chee, and she called me Jim. She said: "I'm glad we had a chance to talk. Initially, I thought you looked ridiculous wearing that sweatshirt and smoking a pipe. I thought, 'Who is he trying to impress?' But I see you are not so bad, not as bad as you look—a pretentious phony stuck on yourself. There's some substance to you."

"I'm glad of that. The sweatshirt keeps me warm, but it's not hot. It's an old college sweatshirt; I didn't want to wear my good shirts to a picnic. You're right about the pipe. I smoke it because I think it makes me look like a mature man of the world, but I don't know how to keep it lit, and tobacco smells better than it tastes. Now, you're telling me it doesn't make me look like a man of the world."

"It makes you look ridiculous. You should get rid of it."

I was enjoying our conversation. Even if Moke Chee weren't the most beautiful woman in the world, which obviously she was, I would still be enjoying our conversation. It flowed so naturally, and I felt so comfortable sitting and talking with this remarkably unpretentious woman. She was more than a pretty face. She was refreshingly truthful. If something were on her mind, she said it, and I felt I could be the same way with her. I asked the question that had been burning in my mind from the first time I saw her from the school bus window.

"Your ring. Why are you called Miss Fong when you're wearing a ring on your wedding finger? Are you married?"

"It's to keep the wolves at bay. Are you a wolf, Mr. Wolter?"

"I hope not. At least if I am, I hope I'm a harmless one."

"There is a boy. We are longtime childhood friends. Our families assume we are going to marry when he completes his studies in Australia. It's nothing formal. It's just an understanding. I'll have to cross that bridge after he completes his studies. He will have a good job as an engineer and is a nice boy and comes from a good family. I would have a comfortable life and would be able to care for my elderly parents and nanny. But he's young, only two years older than me."

"How much older do you think a man should be than his wife?"

"I think, ideally, a man should be at least eight years older but no more than ten."

"How old are you now?" I asked her.

"I'm twenty-two. How old are you?"

"I'll turn thirty-one in December."

"Then you're thirty."

I intended to add "December 1969" to my age but detected a glint in Miss Fong's eyes when she realized I was exactly eight years older than her. That was a calculated fib on my part, but I've told bigger fibs, and we were enjoying each other's company. Now, if I said I was joking, she might not see my fib as a joke and then become uncomfortable for being so gullible and resent me for making her the butt of my joke. She may question what other fibs I told her, and of course, it would make me look like the shallow ass that I was—or just another wolf willing to say anything to gain her favor. I decided to swallow my fib and hoped she would forget it.

At some point, it was inevitable that we would get around to talking about the upcoming school holiday. It was only two weeks away, and all the teachers were talking about their holiday plans. Miss Fong was going back to Penang to care for her elderly parents and nanny. I liked that. No, I more than liked that; I loved it. I wanted to shout to the world: The most beautiful woman in the world was going home during the school holiday to care for her elderly parents and nanny. She could go anywhere she desired, but she was going home to care for her family. That was so unselfish. I didn't know any other woman, any other person, who was that unselfish and thoughtful. Her beauty was more than skin deep. She was more than a pretty face.

An Invitation to Die For

When Moke Chee asked what I would be doing during the holiday, I told her I was accompanying my Headmaster to Malacca for the first week and looked forward to sightseeing. I left the hunting wild boar part out of the trip. While the prospect of hunting wild boar impressed Regina, after Moke Chee told me to get rid of my ridiculous pipe, I feared she'd think I was trying to impress her again. I told her that after Malacca, I had to go to Penang to do some duty-free shopping. I explained how I lost so much weight that my clothes became baggy, and I was given the nickname "Baggy Pants" by the students and staff in Kuala Trengganu. She gave me a response that I couldn't have dreamed of in my wildest dream.

"If you shop on your own, they'll charge you cutthroat tourist prices. Before we leave, I'll give you my address. Look me up when you get to Penang. I'll take you shopping, and we'll go sightseeing while your clothes are being made."

"Will that be too much trouble? I don't want to impose."

"When I was in England, seniors from my college and local people showed me around and made my time much richer and far less expensive. I pledged to myself back then that I would extend the same hospitality to visitors in need of help when I returned home."

It seemed our conversation had just begun when the clanging of a bell snatched our words in mid-air. Jin Leng was ringing a handheld school bell and shouted, "Ladies and gentlemen, it's nine-thirty, and the electricity will be turned off at ten o'clock. Besides, we have an early departure, so it's time to call it a night. You have a half hour to get settled in before it's completely dark."

Jin Leng's announcement interrupted Miss Fong mid-sentence. I wanted to hear the rest of what she was saying, but instead, we had to retire for the night with our respective groups of teachers.

"The night is ending too soon. I enjoyed talking with you. Sleep well, Miss Fong." I liked the sound of Miss Fong, particularly the "Miss" part of Miss Fong.

"Good night, Jim. I enjoyed talking to you, too, and if you expect me to show you around Penang, you will have to call me Moke Chee."

"Good night, Moke Chee. See you in the morning."

We went to our separate quarters. The women stayed in the women's hostel on one side of the school's Tuck Shop, and the men stayed in the men's hostel on the opposite side. When Joe Dixon and I were in his room alone, he said, "You've got every man here hating your guts."

"Why? What did I do wrong?"

"What did you do wrong? You monopolized Moke Chee all night. You kept her all to yourself. That's what you did wrong."

"It's not my fault all the other women at the party refused to partner with me. She took pity on me and partnered with me. That's all."

"Ya, sure. That's all. What about Victoria? She was looking for you to break away and partner with her. You have her pissed at you, too."

"What for? She had plenty of men jockeying to be her partner."

"Not the one she wanted. She'll extract a price out of you for that."

The electricity was turned off at ten o'clock as promised. Sleeping on the rattan mat was reasonably comfortable—or, more accurately, not miserably uncomfortable—but the concrete floor sucked all of the heat away from my body, and I was freezing by early morning. The prospect of the warmth of the rising sun and seeing Moke Chee at breakfast danced pleasurably through my mind.

CHAPTER 9

Morning came. Jin Leng was clanging away on the handbell shouting, "Breakfast is served!" Breakfast of tea and toast with kaya was prepared by the Tuck Shop operator and was one of those free-for-all, every man (and I do mean man) for himself grabbing what he wanted and to hell with everybody else. Women didn't have a chance at the food until the men grabbed what they wanted. It was barbaric. I used my size and my long reach to grab two pieces of toast and brought them to Moke Chee. I said, "Hold these. I'll be right back with tea."

Moke Chee said, "Thank you, and good morning."

She was seated at a table and reserved the seat next to her for me.

I asked, "Is anyone sitting here?"

"Don't be silly. Have a seat. I'm hungry."

I felt grungy. I didn't shower or shave. I didn't think there was a reason to do otherwise, but now having breakfast with Moke Chee I wish I had brought my razor to Besut and jumped in the shower. I said, "I must look grungy. I didn't shave or shower this morning."

"There's no need to. At least you got rid of that silly pipe."

Our conversation continued that most wonderful morning in the same easy manner as the night before. After what Joe Dixon had said to me about being hated by the other men, I was aware of them staring at me. I avoided making eye contact with them but felt their menacing glares. Besides, I could look into Moke Chee's eyes, and why would I want to look anywhere else? Further, rather than grab toast to stuff their faces, they could have done as I did and retrieved something to eat for Moke Chee or another lady of their desire. I wasn't there to change their manners, but I wasn't going to abandon mine. For me, it was always ladies first. If I gained Moke Chee's favor, that was my good fortune.

Tough luck, guys.

Our Journey to the Island

Jin Leng and Baby Pong started herding us down the dusty dirt pathway to a wooded pier where two motor launches were waiting. Moke Chee and I continued our conversation. As I motioned to the bigger of the two boats waiting for us, I said to Moke Chee, "Let's get in this one."

Moke Chee replied, "I'm frightened. I don't know how to swim."

I was surprised. Malaya was surrounded by water, so I thought all Malayans knew how to swim, and I couldn't imagine Miss Fong being frightened of anything. I tried to reassure her. "Don't worry. We're in the bigger, newer boat, and if anything happens, I can swim. I'll take care of you. I promise." I hoped I didn't sound like I was boasting, even though I was. I felt like a hero.

Victoria and some of her housemates, along with Jin Leng, joined our boat called the *Bintang Pagi*. Teh Eng, who I hadn't seen since we were split up at the start of the "Name That Tune" game, was in the other boat, *Udang Besar*, and had paired up with his badminton buddy Lee Ma Chow. Victoria and her friends sat in the stern of the boat with their backs resting against the transom. I asked Moke Chee to join me in the bow, not to be away from Victoria, although Victoria may have taken it that way.

I said to Moke Chee, "Let's sit up front, away from the diesel fumes. Also, if we're lucky enough to come across a pod of dolphins, they will swim off our bow." The *Bintang Pagi* was tied to the dock but was rolling gently with the waves. Moke Chee was unsteady walking in the rolling boat, and I offered my hand to steady her. When she took my hand, I felt the other men staring daggers at me, but I was just innocently offering a lady a helping hand, and she took it. Lucky me.

And my luck continued. Dolphins did appear off our bow within the first hour of our journey.

Moke Chee spotted them first and grabbed my arm. "Look, you were right. There they are."

She got up from her seat and leaned out over the bow. I don't know where her caution went, but she looked ready to jump in after the dolphins. More passengers tried to come forward for a better view of the dolphins, and the captain cautioned them to remain in their seats to keep the boat from capsizing. So, for the remaining four hours, the dolphins entertained us.

We lost sight of mainland Malaya. It was our smaller sister boat, our dolphin escort, and us alone in the open sea. I was sniffing the air. Moke Chee said, "What are you doing?"

I said, "Do you smell that?"

Moke Chee sniffed the air. She was so cute. She said, "I smell nothing."

"That's it. The smell of nothing; nothing but fresh air."

Scanning the horizon over the bow, I saw a green speck that appeared to float above the water where the sea met the sky. It was Pulau Perhentian, a welcome sight, as were our friendly dolphins.

The high-pitched note of engines reviving at high speed dropped several octaves to a low hum as the engines slowed while approaching the island. The water was crystal clear, and it was possible to look over the bow thirty feet down and see a magnificent array of corals and fish in the most gorgeous colors imaginable. We glided over the coral reef, which gave way to the sandy beach extending into the sea. The captain engaged the engine in reverse when we were at a depth of perhaps ten feet. The *Bintang Pagi* slowed to a near stop. The captain dropped anchor off the bow at about three-feet deep.

I was wearing my swimming trunks under my trousers, so I slipped my trousers off and jumped off the bow. The water reached my ribcage. Spike Razallie and the other men followed. We went to the stern and swung it toward the beach. That lowered the depth of the water by about two feet so the women could jump in the water and wade ashore. Moke Chee was still in the bow of the boat, so I walked to the bow and carried her to shore. She wrapped her arms around my neck. I cradled her in my arms and held her tight against my chest the way I saw Superman rescuing Lois Lane in comic books. Moke Chee was so light that carrying her made me feel as strong as Superman. It hadn't registered with me until now how much I missed a woman's touch. Carrying Moke Chee with her arms around my neck was paradise.

As I held Moke Chee tight, I said, "Don't worry, I've got you. I'm not going to let you go."

She held on tight but didn't say anything. My only wish was that the shore was further away, as I relished each step I carried Moke Chee toward shore. My quiet joy, my encounter with paradise, was interrupted by a shrill sound.

I heard an irritating voice calling, "Jim, me too, me too, me too, Jim." I don't know how Victoria got to the bow of the boat, but I wasn't going to fall for her trick. Fortunately, Razallie carried her ashore, quieting her caterwauling. The other men followed suit and started carrying women ashore who were fearful of jumping off the stern and wading ashore themselves. After carrying Moke Chee, I helped carry provisions from the boat to shore.

Island Rules

Baby Pong and Jin Leng divided the beach into three sections by tying large red ribbons on two coconut trees and drawing a line in the sand from the water's edge, up the beach, and to the tree line. The section between the two marked trees was the co-communal area for women and men. The line to the north marked the women-only zone, and the line to the south marked the men-only zone. Beyond the two zones were huge rock outcroppings. Beyond the outcroppings were the respective open-air latrines.

Jin Leng gathered the men in the men's zone and went over the "island rules." First, absolutely no men in the women's zone and no women in the men's zone. Second, when nature called, we were to go behind the rocks, dig a hole in the sand, take care of business, cover the hole back up, and mark it with a twig so the next unsuspecting soul wouldn't find a surprise when he went to dig his hole. Third, Jin Leng assigned each of us to three-man teams to stand watch for two hours each from midnight to dawn. Before dismissing us, Jin Leng assigned us to gather firewood before swimming or partaking in any other activity.

Some of the ladies were wading in the sea, and others were scouring the beach for seashells, but most were huddled in the shade of casuarina trees by the time the men completed combing the beach for firewood. Moke Chee was in a group of four other women searching for seashells. I joined them. When I found a beautiful one that was fully intact, I held the shell out in my open right hand, offering it for the taking to any of the ladies. Only Moke Chee took the shells I offered. I coaxed Moke Chee to wade into the water.

Moke Chee said, "I love the water, but I can't swim." She was comfortable going only thigh-deep. I thought about who it was—Teh Eng or Dixon—who said that all of the men wanted to see Miss Fong in a bathing suit. Well, there she was in a bathing suit, still beautiful, but no more beautiful than in her sack dress. Malayan men had a way of looking at a woman, a way that looked like they were undressing the woman with their eyes. I wondered if they were doing that to Miss Fong now as she and I were playing in the water. I didn't look back at them to see if they were because, if they were, it would make me angry, and I would create a scene telling them to get their filthy eyes off her. The thought of them doing that to Baby Pong or Victoria or any of the other women didn't stir the same reaction in me.

Moke Chee had to help prepare the evening meal, so I went diving among the corals. I had seen movies about coral reefs as an undergraduate in biology class and on television, and the reefs were beyond beautiful, but the real thing was magnificently beautiful and breathtaking.

That evening, we had dinner around the campfire. Sitting around the campfire, women on one side and men on the other side, reminded me of middle school socials back in the States where the girls and boys would stay separate from each other. I was relieved. While I enjoyed Moke Chee's company, I didn't want to monopolize her time or prevent her from socializing with other teachers. I also didn't want to create the impression that we were becoming an item. As a group, we entertained ourselves by singing group songs. As the night grew darker and the sounds from the forest behind grew louder and nearer, it became time to tell ghost stories.

Teh Eng, Ma Chow, and I drew the 2 a.m. watch. Our job was to keep the bonfire lit with fresh wood and provide protection and assistance.

"I see you have met Miss Fong," said Teh Eng.

"Yes. It was by Fate initially when we became partners. When we had to switch partners, no other woman would partner with me. So that was that. She's very easy to talk to."

"So, you're no longer angry with me for pushing you to come on the picnic?"

"I was, but not now. You were right again."

"I know." Teh Eng laughed.

Time to Say Goodbye

Our final day seemed to come too soon. I felt the tone of the picnic change. The leisurely, relaxed, casual movement of teachers unwinding from the responsibility of educating their charges shifted to a swifter, purposeful, organized group effort of leaving the beach as we found it before we returned to the mainland. But there was enough time for me to tell Moke Chee that I saw several shells underwater, and I could fetch a few on my final morning dive. She said she would love to have more shells. I brought back two cowrie shells. "They are the loveliest shells I have. Thank you." And as she said thank you, she gave my arm a squeeze.

The boat came, and after helping Moke Chee get on board, I helped others. I was happy that Moke Chee saved me a place in the bow next to her. Moke Chee and I watched the dolphins weave their way up and over and under the waves. This time we watched in silence. We had talked almost nonstop since playing that silly game Thursday night. Now, we were silent. But it was a comfortable silence.

Neither Moke Chee nor I said anything about the May school holiday just two weeks away. I thought that maybe in the excitement of that first night, Moke Chee just gave me an off-hand invitation to visit her when I visited Penang, like when Americans say, "Let's get together," but have no intention of ever seeing each other again. But that would be so out of character for Moke Chee. She said she'd give me her address but hadn't. Maybe she forgot. Maybe I should ask her, but if she said no, I would feel awful. It's better to keep quiet. I had a melancholy feeling as this odd Alice in Wonderland picnic was coming to an end.

Moke Chee's taxi was already waiting to take her back to Pasir Puteh when we walked back to the school compound. I walked her to the taxi, and she thanked me for the shells and an enjoyable time. I told her the picnic would have been awful without her rescuing me and said, "I promise to get rid of that pipe. Leslie Foo has been admiring it, and I'm giving it to him."

"I didn't have a piece of paper to write my address," Moke Chee said. "It is 70c Irving Road. Can you remember that?"

"Yes, 70c Irving Road. I got it."

I opened the taxi door for Moke Chee and closed it behind her. She rolled down the window and said, "Remember, let me do the negotiating when you get to Penang."

The taxi pulled away. I waved and watched it disappear in a trail of dust.

Dixon overheard our exchange and asked me: "Did Moke Chee just give you her address?"

"She's going to keep me from being overcharged when I go to Penang to have new trousers made on my way to Alor Star. Regina invited me to visit her."

"Are you crazy? You have a chance to spend your holiday with Moke Chee, and you're thinking of visiting Regina."

"April Jennings also invited me to visit her."

"Don't be stupid. You've been invited to spend your school holiday with the most beautiful, if not the most interesting, woman in the world. Wouldn't you want to spend every day with her?"

"It's nothing like you think."

"I don't have to think about anything. I know every man here would kill to get an invitation from Moke Chee to visit her. Please do yourself a favor and skip Alor Star. It isn't worth it. I don't know April, but you won't find another woman like Moke Chee."

"She's got a boyfriend. They're practically engaged."

"I know about that. He's her boy friend, not her boyfriend."

The rattling old orange bone shaker was ready for boarding. This time Teh Eng was sitting with Ma Chow, and I sat with Leslie Foo. I gifted him my pipe, a pouch of tobacco, and a box of matches.

He held the pipe in his mouth, and I said, "The pipe makes you look like a sophisticated, wise man of the world."

Leslie was a jovial person and even more jovial with his new pipe. He shared with me that he, like Moke Chee, had just come back from college in England, but he attended Kirkby with Moke Chee's cousin, Peggy Fong. He laughed, "They're known as the beautiful Fong cousins of Penang. But they couldn't be more different. Peggy hides indoors to stay out of the sun. When she goes out, she carries a parasol and wears elbow-length gloves to maintain a fair complexion, and tries to act like an English lady, whereas Moke Chee is happy being Moke Chee."

CHAPTER 10

The much-anticipated May 1962 school holiday arrived. Most teachers cleared out of town immediately at the close of school on Friday afternoon. Boon had school work to complete, and he had to see his wife and young son off at the airfield on Sunday. Boon and I departed Kuala Trengganu for Malacca early Monday morning in Boon's white TR3.

It was a whirlwind holiday. I went on a wild boar hunt and a flying fox hunt with Boon's father. During the hunting trip, I managed to urinate on my Headmaster, Boon, while we were relieving ourselves in the jungle. I also visited the historical sites of Malacca. I had one more task to complete in Kuala Lumpur before meeting Miss Fong and shopping for new trousers in Penang—meeting Regina in Alor Star for a day of sightseeing and then spending the rest of the week with April.

I Want to Leave the Peace Corps

I returned to the Peace Corps office first thing Friday morning. I needed to see Norb to tell him I was terminating my assignment in August and to seek his help in securing a travel voucher for my return to Chicago.

Norb wasn't in the office. Neither was Luke. But Jack May

was in, and by the bored look on his face, I guessed he was not pleased being stuck in the office. Jack told me, "The third group of Volunteers—Peace Corps Malaya III—is on the way. Norb and Luke are visiting sites to check the specifics of each Volunteer's job assignment to ensure there is an actual job each Volunteer can fill."

"I wish they would have done that for me."

"I heard a little about that snafu." Jack proved to be a good listener. I filled his ears with my whole story. I told him how hurt and worthless that made me feel and how angry I was at Norb, Luke, and him for treating me like a political pawn and abandoning me instead of coming to help me.

Jack wanted to know all the details of how I was preparing my students without actually teaching religion content to my Ugama students. He said: "You understand, it's something we can't advertise. My advice to you is to keep it under your hat."

"It's a little late for that. This is Malaya," I replied. "My entire school and all of Kuala Trengganu knows. If the Peace Corps office knows, do you think the incompetents who manage the Ministry of Education don't know? I'm not advertising anything. I've had it with the Peace Corps."

"That shouldn't have happened to you," Jack admitted. "What brings you to Kuala Lumpur?"

"I want to find out how to get a travel voucher back to Chicago."

"Why leave now?"

"I made a mistake. This isn't for me. I want to go to medical school and get on with my life."

"You'll have to work out the details of obtaining a voucher with Norb. He's due here in a few minutes if you have time to wait."

Norb arrived. He was smiling as he entered the office, but the smile fell from his face when he saw me.

"Hello, Jim. I've been expecting you to drop by. Let's go to my office."

"I want to quit the Peace Corps early, and I need a travel voucher."

"I'd like you to stay, but if terminating early is what you want, that won't be a problem. And, of course, the Peace Corps will provide you with a voucher back to Chicago."

That was easy, I thought. There was no further reason to hang around, so I rose from my chair to leave and said, "Thanks, Norb. I appreciate it."

But Norb had more to say: "I appreciate you giving me advance notice of terminating early, and I'm grateful you're completing another school term. Jim, I feel it's important for you to know the first I learned of your transfer was when I received a telephone call in the Headmaster's office from the Trengganu CEO just before the Headmaster called you to his office. The CEO assured me that you were going to a brand-new school that needed a math and science teacher. Officially, as a matter of record, the Trengganu CEO has you listed as teaching science and math, and that's how we have you listed."

I wish Norb hadn't said that last sentence. Up to that point, I accepted that Norb was being open and honest with me. I lost my composure, "You know that's a crock of shit. The CEO knows, and you know. I'm willing to let the world know what I'm really teaching at Tengku Bariah. You're complicit in allowing the CEO to use me as a placeholder until a religious education teacher is assigned to Tengku Bariah. What's worse, when I called the office and asked Luke for help, the only help I got was, 'We'll get back to you.' But no one got back to me. Now you want to tell me I'm teaching math and science when I'm preparing two hundred kids to take the Ugama test. Give me a break."

Neither he, Luke, nor Jack got back to me when I called Luke and asked for help because they didn't know what to do. As long as they didn't "officially" know of a problem, they didn't have to deal with it.

I then expressed to Norb: "I've been wanting to unload on

you for weeks. Now I feel better."

He stood up from behind his desk. The broad smile that had been absent from his face returned as broad as ever. Thrusting his hand out, he said, "I feel better too. I'm glad you came by. It's been bothering me. If it had to happen, we were glad it was you because we were confident you'd handle it. And you did. Thank you, Jim."

I shook Norb's hand. It was getting close to noon, and I needed to get a taxi to Penang. At long last, I could look up Miss Fong.

Life was looking up.

CHAPTER 11

I walked the few blocks from the Peace Corps Office in Old Market Square to the taxi stand on Jalan Rahman Road. I was in luck. A taxi was waiting. I joined three other passengers who were bound for Penang and climbed in the front seat next to the driver.

After a few hours, the winding and twisting road came around a soft curve and turned into a flat, open area as far as my eye could see. The driver told us he didn't have a license to deliver us to our destinations in Penang, so he dropped us off at the Georgetown taxi stand. I decided to make the two-mile walk from the taxi stand to the Hotel Continental on Penang Road.

I checked in, took a shower, went back down to the lobby, and asked the desk clerk for directions to 70c Irving Road. I followed his directions by walking down Penang Road toward Macalister Road. I felt a sense of freedom walking along Penang Road because I wasn't the only European. I strolled past tailor shops, souvenir shops, and the Cold Storage ice cream parlor without attracting any undue attention.

After reaching Macalister Road, I turned right and walked a short distance to Lorong Susu and then turned left for an even shorter distance to Irving Road, where I turned right. Typical Chinese shophouses lined both sides of Irving Road. Miss Fong's house on this comparatively quiet residential street, where Europeans didn't venture, was just a short walk from Penang Road. I felt out of place on Irving Road with children following after me shouting, "Hey, where are you going?"

I found 70c easy enough. It was a little after seven o'clock in the evening, just turning dark, and the shutters to the windows on either side of the front door were closed. I figured Miss Fong's home was closed for the night and that it was probably too late to call on her, so I retraced my way back to the hotel.

Finding Miss Fong

The next morning, I woke up early, showered, and walked the now familiar route to Miss Fong's house. It wasn't even 8 a.m., so I stopped at a coffee shop and ordered what looked like a pancake folded over ground peanuts and crunchy brown sugar, along with a cup of hot, sweet, black Malayan coffee. I hung out there until a quarter after eight. I ordered another pancake to eat along the way, which earned me a big gold-toothed smile from the hawker.

It took less than another ten minutes to get to Miss Fong's house. The shutters on the front windows were open, so I thought it was not too early to call on her. As I climbed the three steps to the front stoop, I heard a loud, angry-sounding woman's voice coming from inside the house. I was hesitant to knock. It sounded like the woman was scolding someone. I didn't want to get in the middle of that. I waited for a while, hoping the scolding would subside, but it didn't. I debated turning around and returning later, but a group of children—about a half dozen ten-year-old boys and girls—had gathered on the street and stared at me standing on the stoop. They embarrassed me into knocking. I couldn't very well walk up the stoop, stand there, and then turn around and walk away, so I knocked on the front door. I didn't knock so hard as to sound aggressive, but I also didn't want to knock so soft as not to be heard.

An older woman with a squarish face looked out the window to the left of the front door. Her face was flushed, and it carried an angry look, as if she didn't want to be disturbed. This is not going to turn out well, I thought.

The old woman's face softened when she saw me standing at the door. She said, "You Mr. Jim?"

I said, "Yes, I'm Jim. Is Moke Chee in?"

The woman smiled and said, "You wait." And then I heard what sounded like the clang of two deadbolts opening and the sliding of two crossbars opening. The woman opened the door, smiling even more broadly, and said, "You come in."

I slipped off my shoes and entered a reception room with a Taoist altar the length of the wall facing the door and two huge mirrors facing each other on opposing walls, and a large round marble table and six round wooden stools in the center of the room. The old woman picked up my shoes from the stoop and placed them inside on the floor near the door. She said, "Moke Chee not here. She expect you. Up hill and be down. You write where you be at ten o'clock. She come for you."

The old woman shuffled to a back room and returned with a piece of paper and a pencil and said, "Sit. Write."

I sat on a stool at the large round marble table in the receiving room. Out of the corner of my eye, I saw that the group of street urchins who had embarrassed me into knocking on the door were now on the stoop themselves, peering through the front window bars, observing me. I printed: *I am at the Hotel Continental on Penang Road, Jim.*

The old woman disappeared again while I was writing. I sat at the table, waiting for her to return. She reappeared with a cup of tea and a plate of cookies. Still smiling, she said, "You eat? You want eat?"

I decided to practice the Mandarin that I learned during

the two weeks with my primary grade classmates at Chinese night school and, smiling, said, "Thank you," in Mandarin. She said the equivalent of "You are welcome" in Mandarin and then continued a conversation that I couldn't follow. I wished I hadn't tried to show off because now it would be obvious that I wasn't fluent. She hovered near me, watching me finish the tea and a cookie, all the while smiling. The smile never left her face. The smile was one of content admiration, the kind one might observe on a mother's face while she was looking at her sleeping child. Maybe because the old woman was hovering too close to me and her smile was so unwavering, it made me feel ill at ease. I wanted to leave but didn't want to be rude. I drank the tea and ate one cookie in a hurry. When I finished, she asked in Mandarin if I wanted more and then said in English, "More?"

I stood up and said in English, "That was delicious. Thank you. I have to go now." I walked to the front door, bowed, and said, "Thank you."

She unbolted the front door and slid the wooden crossbar to the side and slung the heavy wooden door open.

I said, "Thank you again and goodbye," but this time in Mandarin.

She replied in English, "Goodbye." She stood on the front stoop and watched me walk down Irving Road. I turned around once and waved. She was still smiling and nodded her head in acknowledgment.

Miss Fong Takes Me Shopping

I was in my room reading tourist brochures about Penang when the telephone rang. It rang in the distinctive British manner of two quick rings followed by silence and then two more quick rings again. The call was from the front desk clerk, who said,

"You have a guest waiting for you in the lobby, Sir."

I took the self-operated elevator to the ground floor. There I found a more beautiful Miss Fong than I remembered waiting with a smile. She wore no makeup on her face. Her hair was tied in a ponytail, and she was wearing a blue cheongsam and blue shoes.

She was with another woman. Miss Fong's companion was short and plump. She came up to the tip of Miss Fong's tiny nose, and she wasn't pretty like Miss Fong, but she was cute like a gnome with a bright smile that lifted her jowls and big dark smiling eyes framed by long dark eyelashes. She fluttered her eyelids to the rhythm of her speech as if communicating in Morse code.

"Miss Fong, I presume." That sounded like a stupid sophomoric thing to say, which I realized as soon as it came out of my mouth.

"Welcome to Penang, and call me Moke Chee. This is my friend Joo Ee. She's an art teacher in Kota Bharu and knows Jaron Knight."

Joo Ee extended her hand and said, "Welcome."

"Pleased to meet you. How's Jaron doing?"

Joo Ee's diminutive stature was counterpoised by her manner of speaking. With her eyelashes beating to the rhythm of each articulated syllable of every word, and with every word followed by a slight but definite pause, Joo Ee said, "Call me Joo Ee. Jaron is doing fine, living the life of a gentleman." Then she smiled.

That struck me as an odd comment, and I wondered what she meant by "living the life of a gentleman." And why did she smile? I wondered but thought it best not to ask.

Moke Chee said, "My mother told me you had a cup of tea and one cookie, and you looked hungry. Have you had any real food to eat yet?"

"Sort of. Before going to your house, I stopped at a coffee shop and had two pancakes with a cup of Malayan coffee."

"We'll get something to eat after we get you some trousers. How does that sound?"

"Great."

"We'll go to a couple of shops to look at fabric, get a price, and find out how much time it will take to complete your slacks. Remember, let me do the talking and negotiating."

Joo Ee said, "I'll leave you two at it. I have my own errands. Mokes, I'll catch up with you for lunch later." She added something in Hokkien that I didn't catch, but she was smiling and looking at me, so I figured it wasn't anything that I needed to worry about.

Then Joo Ee turned to me and said, "Remember, keep your big American mouth shut and let Moke Chee do the negotiating."

Joo Ee's directness and choice of vocabulary stunned me. All I could say was, "Yes, ma'am. It was a pleasure meeting you."

Moke Chee took me to the first shop. It was a shop where Moke Chee purchased fabric to make her own clothes. The proprietor knew her. We inspected fabrics and got a price and a delivery date. It was amazing to watch Moke Chee haggle with the proprietor over the price. Then she said to the proprietor, "We're going to get a price from your competitor."

"Why do you always do this to me? You know I give you the best product and the best price. Get another price, any price. I will beat it."

Moke Chee took me to a second shop—the first shop's primary competitor—and haggled with him. Then it was back to the first shop for more negotiating. I didn't know how the proprietor could deny Moke Chee's request. She was so cute when she lifted her chin to reject his offer and then immediately followed up with a counteroffer. Finally, the proprietor turned to me and said, "Your wife is asking me to sell you three pairs of slacks at cost. I can't stay in business like that. You look like a reasonable man. I have to make a little profit. I cannot reduce the price, but for twenty dollars more, I will make a very nice suit jacket for you."

The proprietor called Moke Chee my wife. Moke Chee was wearing the gold ring on her wedding finger. Of course, he would think I was her spouse. What would a married Chinese woman be doing with a European man if he weren't her husband? As if I could be so lucky. I wondered if she caught that. If she did, she paid no mind to it because she was not going to be deterred from getting me the best deal possible. Moke Chee countered his offer immediately: "Ten Malayan dollars, and you have a deal."

The proprietor said, "OK, OK. Make it eighteen but don't tell anybody. You're killing me. It will take a day longer."

Moke Chee asked, "How long, total?"

The proprietor responded as if he were exasperated, "Three days total."

Moke Chee countered, "Fifteen."

The proprietor sighed, "Fifteen."

Moke Chee turned to me and asked, "Is that acceptable to you?"

I figured three more days in Penang meant I would have to skip visiting Regina in Alor Star. Portraying myself as the "Great White Hunter" to Regina lost its luster, as did being used as John's competition for her affection. I'd rather stay three more days in Penang and then fly directly to Kota Bharu. That still gave me three days to visit April Jennings. I said, "Yes, of course."

The proprietor said, "Half now. The rest when it's finished."

Interspersed with shopping and haggling, Moke Chee asked me about my visit to Malacca with Boon. I told her about my feeling of being touched by history when I visited St. Francis' tomb, Stadthuys, the Dutch Clock Tower, and Christ Church because I had learned about the Dutch East India Company and the British East India Company as a schoolboy. I also told her how much I enjoyed visiting the Baba and Nyonya Museum and the Cheng Hoon Teng Chinese Temple and eating hawker food on Jonker Street.

Moke Chee said, "Good. I know where to take you." When we finished shopping, she said, "Are you up for a walk?"

"Sure."

"First, we have to take a detour to see Nanny. I told her I would stop by to see her today. Then we'll take a bus to Ayer Itam, and we'll visit the Kek Lok Si Temple."

CHAPTER 12

I thought we would walk back to her house, but we went to a different house near Irving Road but not on Irving Road. Moke Chee called something in Hokkien through an open window. An older woman came to the door. She was tiny and slender, maybe coming up to Moke Chee's eyes. Her pepper-gray hair was pulled back in a bun. She had a kind and handsome face with a clear, smooth, unblemished complexion and amazingly wrinkle-free skin. To say she smiled upon greeting Moke Chee would be an understatement. Her face and that of Moke Chee's exuded glee. In fact, both of them exuded glee as they clasped hands, and the warmth between them was palpable. Moke Chee introduced me to Nanny in Hokkien, and the only words I caught were "my friend," "America," and "Jim."

Nanny turned to me and nodded her head, smiled, and said, "Uh, America. Hello."

I was pleased she made an effort to speak to me in English and reciprocated by replying in Hokkien, "Have you taken rice?"

She seemed unimpressed with my mastery of Hokkien and simply nodded her head again and smiled at me long enough just to say, "Ah, ah, thank you." She turned her attention back to Moke Chee again, and they continued to talk for about ten more minutes. Before departing, the old woman said, "Goodbye," to me in English, and I responded, "Goodbye," also in English. As we were about to round a corner, Moke Chee turned back to wave to Nanny, as did I, and Nanny, still smiling, waved back. As things turned out, I followed Moke Chee to visit Nanny each day while I was in Penang.

We walked past some boys in their late teens who shouted comments at us—or, more accurately, at Moke Chee—in Hokkien. I picked up a few vulgar words. I turned toward the foul-mouthed louts, and Moke Chee grabbed my arm, "Pay them no attention. The best way to deal with street hooligans is to treat them with indifference."

We reached the bus stand without further incident. Moke Chee informed me of the history of Penang and all the wonderful food and good places to eat. There was a question that was on my mind, but I decided to wait until we were on the bus to ask.

The bus started rolling, and I said, "Nanny doesn't live at your house."

Moke Chee responded, "That's a long story. My mother couldn't get along with her, and now she's employed by another family, but I visit her every opportunity I can. Next school term will be better. I've been promised a reassignment to Penang to care for my elderly parents. Nanny can live with me and won't have to work."

I was in disbelief, in a good way, that someone my age—and a beautiful woman at that— could be so thoughtful and caring for her parents and Nanny. The concept was foreign to me. All my friends back home, including me, left our parents to strike out on our own as soon as we could; otherwise, what would I and all the other Peace Corps Volunteers be doing halfway around the world away from home.

It must have sounded stupid when I asked, "But don't you want to live a life of your own?"

Moke Chee said, "I do. I'm an only child. My life is to care for them. In the East, we call it filial piety. Some say it's respect for elders, but it's more than that. It brings me joy. It's who I am."

Her compassion and commitment to her parents and to

Nanny were something so foreign to me. Her sense of responsibility and her joy in meeting that responsibility vicariously filled me with joy. That joyous feeling was something that I had not experienced before, and it made me feel good about myself. I found Moke Chee so fascinating, so contradictory to what I expected, yet with a consistent value set so different from any woman I had ever met. She so easily discarded the superficial norm of Malayan women who refused to talk to a European man, yet she strongly adhered to the filial piety culture. The little I knew about the filial piety culture I admired, and Moke Chee saw it as part of her identity. I knew that I was very lucky to be invited by Moke Chee to visit her, but now I was overwhelmed by my good fortune and wished I could meet someone with her strong character and consistent principled values back home.

I was so engrossed in our conversation that I was disappointed when we arrived at Ayer Itam. We got off the bus, and Moke Chee said, "We'll eat first, at one of Penang's best and most famous hawker stalls. I'll order and let you know what you ate afterward."

Two bowls of a brown murky aromatic liquid with noodles and bits of indistinguishable things floating in it arrived at our table. It appeared to be some kind of soup. It didn't look particularly appetizing but smelled delicious. Moke Chee said, "Let's eat," and dug into her bowl with plastic chopsticks and a metal Chinese soup spoon. I followed her lead and dug in. It was surprisingly good.

She asked, "How do you like it?"

"It's delicious. What is it?"

"Penang's famous laksa asam. Fish soup."

"What about your friend?" I asked. "She said she would join us."

"In English, she said she was meeting us for lunch, but in Hokkien, she said she didn't want to be a third wheel and was going back up the hill. Also, she said she approves of you."

"That's odd."

"That she approves of you?"

"Maybe that too, but, you know, the English and Hokkien thing."

"Only if you know nothing about women."

We weren't for one moment at a loss for topics to talk about, and I don't know where the time went. The temple we visited next was built into the hillside with stairways leading to what seemed to be temples within temples. I clicked away with my camera, trying to capture the grandeur of the gold-leaf Buddha around each turn. I also focused my camera to capture images of Miss Fong in each frame I shot because I knew once my visit to Penang was over, I would need something tangible to remind me that Miss Fong really showed me around Penang and my visit wasn't just a dream. It seemed like we had been exploring the multiple-storied temple with multiple prayer rooms for minutes when it had been hours. There was still much more to explore, but it was hot and exhausting. Moke Chee said, "It's tea time. Let's go back to town."

We got back to the Macalister Road bus terminal, where there were several hawker stalls. We went to a hawker squishing eight-foot-long sugar cane stalks through rollers forcing the stalks to surrender their sweet chlorophyll-colored nectar. Moke Chee said, "This is my favorite. Fresh sugarcane water."

The hawker served up two glasses of freshly squeezed sugarcane water poured over chunks of ice. The cold, sweet yellow-green liquid with the aroma of freshly cut grass was heavenly and the perfect drink on a hot day.

We went to another stall. The hawker was an Indian man wearing a thin cotton towel around his head. He was frying some prawns and other ingredients in a saffron-colored batter.

Moke Chee said, "Pasembur, my father's favorite. We'll buy some for him."

Meeting Miss Fong's Parents

It was a short walk to Moke Chee's house. We ran across the same gaggle of street kids who followed me down Irving Road the day before. A couple shouted something in Hokkien while others called out in English, "Is he your boyfriend?" Moke Chee treated them with complete indifference. I did too.

We climbed the stairs to the front stoop of her house, and Moke Chee called through the open window. The old woman, who by now I knew was Moke Chee's mother, came to open the door. Moke Chee handed her mother the pasembur and then introduced me to her father. He invited me to sit down, which I did. Moke Chee's mother, who had disappeared to a back room, reappeared with a plate of cookies and a pot of tea.

Moke Chee said to her father, "I'm going to Grandmother's. I'll be right back." Then she said to me, "I won't be but a few minutes."

It seemed more than a tad awkward leaving me alone with her mother and father, whom I had just met, and really I hardly knew Moke Chee, but Moke Chee was so nonchalant about leaving me alone with her parents, and it happened so naturally. It wasn't like I was trying to make a favorable impression with a girlfriend's parents after meeting them for the first time, so it didn't feel too awkward. Moke Chee's father told her mother to bring out the pasembur. He said, "This is pasembur. You won't get it anywhere as delicious as in Penang. Try it."

I tried it. It was crunchy and savory. I liked it. But I only took one piece and nibbled on it because Moke Chee told me it was her father's favorite. I said, "I agree. This is delicious."

"There's plenty here. Don't stand on ceremony. Help yourself to more," Mr. Fong said.

I took another piece, but that was it. I liked Moke Chee's parents. Mr. Fong had a distinct British accent that sounded akin to the BBC announcers I listened to on the radio. He told me he learned English from the Lasallian Brothers as a schoolboy at St. Francis Xavier School on the land his father donated to the Lasallians for their church and school.

Mr. Fong was interested in the overall Peace Corps' mission and my specific assignment. He was curious about Chicago and wanted to know whether I had seen the great American bison and seemed disappointed when I told him I only saw one in a zoo. He told me his father built a miniature zoo for him on the family compound when he was a young boy. He pointed to antlers on a wall. Mr. Fong used his antlers as a hat rack and said, "Those antlers are from my pet Malayan antelope. I cared for it, but it wasn't able to survive in captivity. Some wild animals are able to survive in captivity, but most aren't."

Moke Chee was gone for several minutes. When she returned to the house, she was all smiles. She said, "It's all set. We're having dinner at The Green Parrot. I'll come to fetch you from your hotel at seven. You have had a full day. You best go back to your hotel for a rest and freshen up."

"I look forward to seeing you at seven." I was about to walk back to the Hotel Continental when Moke Chee hailed a trishaw. She said I'd done enough walking and then negotiated the price to take me back to the Hotel Continental. I enjoyed riding in Penang trishaws because the passengers sat in front of the driver and had a splendid view of the scenery, while in Kuala Lumpur, the passengers in trishaws sat behind the driver and had the driver's behind to look at.

CHAPTER 13

I didn't rest much when I got back to the Hotel Continental. I remembered seeing The Green Parrot written up in one of the tourist brochures populating my room but decided not to read the article. I was certain Moke Chee made a special effort to arrange dinner there. It was obviously something special, and I wanted to be surprised. I went down to the lobby to wait for Moke Chee at a little before seven.

It had been only about two hours since I saw Moke Chee, and she was transformed. She wore open-toe, high-heel purple shoes and a form-fitting purple cheongsam. Her hair was up in a French roll, held in place by a rose-colored comb that matched her lipstick. I preferred her hair down or in a ponytail because it showed the natural curl of her hair, but I guessed that she considered wearing her hair down too informal for an occasion that called for dressing up. Her face was made up with rose lipstick that made her lips even more appealing, if that were possible. But the dark eyeliner actuating and extending the lines of her eyelids detracted from the natural beauty of her beautiful, big fawn-like eyes. I figured she was making an artistic statement and should appreciate it. Still, Moke Chee was stunning.

Remembering my fraternity training to compliment a woman when greeting her for an evening out, I wanted to pay Moke Chee a compliment. Her being an artist, I wanted to be creative without sounding too forward, so without thinking, I blurted, "You look scrumptious." I don't know where those words came from. I had never said something like that before and regretted it as soon as the words left my mouth. It sounded so crude.

Moke Chee smiled and replied, "I don't know."

She paused, and I worried. She was still smiling and then said, "Should I say this?" She continued to look me in the eyes, but she was no longer smiling. I could tell she was turning something over in her mind. I worried that she would tell me to forget about tonight and walk out. Instead, she said, "I will."

Moke Chee gave a laugh, hooked her arm through mine, and said, "I'm not edible. Let's go; we have a car waiting."

I lucked out. Moke Chee turned my clumsy attempt at a compliment into a joke on me. I was so relieved at that moment that I didn't fully appreciate the physical joy of her taking my arm. I should have savored that gesture more, but I was thinking about being a kid back home when a joke went bad. We would say, "The yoke's on you" or "You have egg on your face." I certainly had egg on my face, but Moke Chee handled it all in good stride.

Moke Chee told me to get in the front passenger seat while I held the car door open for her to climb into the back seat. She introduced me to her two older cousins. Lim Sui Lay was driving. I reached my hand out, and he took it but didn't smile. Then Moke Chee introduced me to Lim Gim Lan, who was in the back with her. She didn't smile either when I greeted her. I gathered that these two dower-faced cousins were to be our chaperones for the evening.

Dancing at The Green Parrot

The Green Parrot was relatively near the Hotel Continental, and we arrived at the restaurant in short order. The Green

Parrot had a stunning setting on the edge of the Andaman Sea. It had an indoor venue and an outdoor venue and appeared to cater to a primarily European crowd, with a few Chinese couples added here and there. Moke Chee chose the outdoor venue, which had an open-air dance floor that jutted out into the sea. At the far end of the dance floor was a band shelter with sixteen music stands that read: "Guy Lombardo and His Royal Canadians."

I helped Moke Chee with her chair as we were seated at a table at the edge of the dance floor. The menu listed primarily European selections. Each of us ordered chicken chop. Moke Chee ordered a bubbly wine drink called Baby Champ, I had a local beer, and the cousins each had hot tea with cream and sugar.

The cousins didn't speak or smile during dinner. Moke Chee translated what I was saying into Hokkien, but they did not respond. The cousins' non-responsiveness made me feel uncomfortable. Thankfully, Moke Chee kept the flow of conversation going. The band started filing onto the bandstand. I naturally expected to see Canadian musicians, but the musicians were all Chinese dressed in tuxedos with red Canadian Mountie dinner jackets, except for the bandleader, who wore a glittering gold dinner jacket. The bandleader announced, "We just completed a two-month tour of Australia. We are here to entertain you with Guy Lombardo standards, and we welcome your requests. Now welcome from the land Down Under, our very own Australian nightingale, Miss Audrey Lane, who will sing 'I Love You Truly' for Elsa and Mike on their first wedding anniversary."

There was applause from the audience. The band started playing, the Australian nightingale started singing, and Elsa and Mike took the floor. The setting—moonlight dancing on the rippling waves, air freshened by a silky sea breeze, a star-studded inky blue sky, and live music by the Royal Canadian Orchestra—made for a bewitching evening. I hoped the music might lighten things up for the dower-faced cousins, but even sixteen musicians and the Australian nightingale and a young couple celebrating their first wedding anniversary failed to change the glum look on their faces. I worried they disapproved of me. They made me feel uncomfortable. I thought that this would be a very long evening, but I saw a chance to escape the dower-faced cousins.

The bandleader announced: "Ladies and gentlemen, let's give Elsa and Mike a round of applause, and please join them on the dance floor." More couples joined Elsa and Mike on the dance floor.

I leaned over to Moke Chee and whispered, "May I have the pleasure of this dance? Would your cousins mind?"

Moke Chee said, "Yes, you may," and started to push her chair from the table.

I scrambled to my feet, offered Moke Chee my hand, and said to the cousins with a smile, "With your permission, please excuse us."

The cousins didn't respond. Not even a blink of an eye. I didn't expect them to and thought my request was way too exaggerated, but like her cousins, Moke Chee didn't take notice of it, or if she did, she didn't make fun of it. It made me conscious of how socially awkward I was. It wasn't as if this were a date and I was courting Moke Chee or trying to make a good impression on her and her family. But I didn't want to make a complete fool of myself like a moonstruck rookie in front of Moke Chee, either. Moke Chee took my hand and rose from her chair.

I was taught in fraternity etiquette class that a gentleman offers a lady his arm or takes her hand when escorting her to and from the dance floor. Since Moke Chee took my hand getting up from her chair, I continued to hold her hand until we were in the center of the dance floor. The band continued playing "I Love You Truly," followed by "How Deep Is the Ocean," and then they played a swing tune and a cha-cha. You might ask me how I remember the name of that song after six-ty-plus years? The answer is: If you were dancing with Moke Chee under the stars on a dance floor that extended out into the Andaman Sea to "I Love You Truly" sung by the Australian nightingale with the Guy Lombardo and His Royal Canadian Orchestra just back from a two-month tour of Australia, you too would commit every heavenly moment to memory. Also, back when I was playing the trumpet, "I Love You Truly" and "Let Me Call You Sweetheart" were among the most frequently requested tunes.

When the music started, I recalled Sheridan's complaint about men who danced with her like she was a prune-eating spinster and tried to hold Moke Chee close, not body-pressed-to-body close but not like a prune-eating spinster either. Moke Chee must have had any number of wolves trying to hold her tight when dancing because she placed her hand on my shoulder, and her forearm came down the right side of my chest, preventing me from dancing close to her. I thought that was a clever and well-executed technique to keep men from holding her too close. I didn't mind it. Dancing like this, a half-arm's distance apart, enabled me to look into Moke Chee's face close up and to look into her soft inquisitive deep brown eyes as we talked while dancing. She was full of self-confidence and had a quick wit.

I said to Moke Chee, "This is the most beautiful night of my life."

"Thank you, I'm taking that as a compliment."

"It is. Thank you. I'll never forget this, but it doesn't appear your cousins are having a good time."

I looked over at the cousins, and they still had glum looks on their faces, and they weren't even talking to each other.

Moke Chee said, "They're having a wonderful time."

I stepped a half step further away from her and said, "How can you tell?"

"They're my older cousins. If they didn't like something,

they would say, and if they didn't want to be here, they would leave."

"But they have such glum looks on their faces, and even now, they aren't talking."

"That's how they look. They don't smile much and don't talk unless they have something important to say."

"I was worried that I did something to offend them. I'll apologize if I did."

Moke Chee playfully slapped my shoulder and said, "Don't be silly. If you did, they would not hesitate to give you a shelling. Sometimes you have to accept people just as they are." Now she laughed, "But if you feel a need to apologize, you can start with my feet."

I pulled further back, tried to make an apologetic expression with my face, and looked down to address Moke Chee's feet: "I am awfully sorry; please accept my sincere apology. Which of you did I abuse the most?"

Moke Chee replied, "Both of us."

Now I looked into Moke Chee's eyes and said, "I am sorry. I promise to try harder to dance on the floor rather than all over your feet."

"Apology accepted, and you've already improved. A little."

I moved back in as close as Moke Chee's stiff arm would allow and said: "But seriously, Sui Lay isn't dancing with his wife. Do you think she would like to dance? If it's alright with you and alright with him, I'll ask her for a dance."

Moke Chee burst out laughing. She nearly doubled over with laughter and said, "They're not husband and wife. They are sister and brother. This is the first time either of them have been to The Green Parrot. They are enjoying the experience and listening to the music and watching you. Gim Lan would be embarrassed if you asked her to dance. Besides, you're under no obligation to ensure the happiness of others."

"I'm glad to hear that, but as a Peace Corps Volunteer, I'm obligated to ensure all Malayans have a good time and not trample on a dance partner's feet while doing so."

"Now you're teasing me, or are you trying to be flirtatious?"

"How long do I have to answer?"

"I already know your answer."

"It's all of the above."

"That's what I thought."

"Are you being flirtatious now?"

"You'll never know. A lady is entitled to her secrets."

Our conversation ensued during slow numbers over the course of the evening. Moke Chee loved dancing, and we stayed on the floor for every dance, including swing numbers and Latin tunes. She particularly enjoyed the cha-cha. Moke Chee became animated, and her face lit up, smiling ear-to-ear, as she substituted three short bunny hops for the cha-cha-cha stutter steps. She was so adorable.

The band played two forty-five-minute sets while we were at The Green Parrot. At the end of the first set and beginning of the second, I escorted Moke Chee to and from the dance floor by holding her hand. By now, it felt so natural to hold her hand, as if we had been holding hands for years rather than just a little over an hour. By the time the second set started with the tune "My Funny Valentine," Moke Chee let me hold her close while dancing slow numbers. I thought "My Funny Valentine" must be a favorite of Australians because when The Posse of university students took me to two different clubs in Kuala Lumpur during Peace Corps training, the song was requested by an Australian at each club.

I always like to dance near the bandstand. Even more so now. It gave me the vicarious feeling of being a member of the Royal Canadian Orchestra while enjoying dancing with Moke Chee. The only disadvantage, if it was a disadvantage, was seeing the Australian nightingale up close. From our table, she had blonde hair and a white gown, but up close, her hair was rooted in gray, and her faded yellow gown had seen better years. The Australian nightingale's voice gave way and crackled when reaching for a high note. She must have been in her mid-sixties, but she was a wonderful performer and made me feel like she was singing to only Moke Chee and me. As the next to last number, three band members joined her in singing "Goodnight, Ladies," and then she got the entire house on their feet, including the glum-faced cousins, to sing "Auld Lang Syne" to close the evening. The evening was coming to an end. I couldn't believe it. Never had an evening passed so quickly.

I didn't realize it then, but years later when reflecting back on that night, I realized something happened to me, to our relationship, while dancing to Guy Lombardo and the Royal Canadian Orchestra over the two forty-five-minute sets. At the start of the evening, we were acquaintances who enjoyed each other's company. But by the end of that magical night, with Moke Chee's two older dower-faced cousins looking on, I felt I had known Moke Chee all my life and felt like I knew her better than anyone that I had ever met. I wanted to spend more time with her and get to know her even better.

True, the first time I laid eyes on Moke Chee, I thought she was physically the most beautiful woman I had ever seen, and then after talking with her, I discovered she was more than a pretty face. But at most, I thought of her as a kind person, maybe a potential friend, willing to help out a person who was a stranger to her country as payback for the kindness shown to her as a student in England. After all, she had a boyfriend completing an engineering degree in Australia, and I had a sort-of girlfriend back in Chicago, but by the end of the evening, I felt Moke Chee and I had just had our first date chaperoned by two older dower-faced cousins. During our last dance of the evening, "Goodnight, Ladies" was playing when Moke Chee told me she was staying with Joo Ee's family in a bungalow reserved for senior government officials on the top of Penang Hill.

"One of the things Joo Ee told me in Hokkien before she left us was that she approved of you and that, if I wanted, I could invite you to stay in the bungalow's extra room. Would you like to join us up the hill?"

"Yes. Of course. If I wouldn't be imposing. I'd love that."

Sui Lay dropped me at the Hotel Continental, and Moke Chee said, "Tell the desk clerk you're checking out tomorrow, and I'll be around to fetch you at nine o'clock."

I got out of the car, leaned back through the open door window, and said, "Good night and thank you for a wonderful evening," to each cousin while looking them in the eye.

To my surprise and pleasure, each cousin smiled and said, "Good night."

I looked at Moke Chee, trying to fix her beaming image in my mind until the morning, and said, "I look forward to seeing you at nine. I'll be waiting out front."

The car drove away, leaving me feeling as if I were floating above the pavement. My mind was so full of anticipation about meeting Moke Chee in the morning that I forgot to notify the clerk that I was checking out in the morning.

CHAPTER 14

The loud voices and laughter of revelers on the north end of Penang Road drifted in over the hum of my room's air conditioner at the Hotel Continental, but I fell asleep easily and slept soundly until morning. I rose before dawn, anticipating the day ahead. I showered and shaved and packed my bag and waited. Finally, the first light was emerging over Penang. It was only seven, but I was too excited to stay in my room, waiting for Moke Chee to call for me at nine. I went down to the lobby to tell the desk clerk that I was checking out at nine and asked where I could get something to eat.

The desk clerk said, "I understand many Europeans enjoy the Sunday Buffet at the E&O Hotel. It's just a short walk from here."

My first thought was: It's Sunday already. I had lost track of time. I tried to attend Mass every Sunday and thought about asking for directions to a Catholic church, but I recalled reading something in a tourist brochure about Somerset Maugham and other notable figures staying at the E&O. It was a place full of history, and I wanted to be part of it, so I walked there rather than to church. I entered the genteel lobby and asked the concierge where I could find something to eat. He escorted me to the veranda and told the waiter, "This gentleman desires something to eat."

The waiter said, "My apologies, Sir. The buffet isn't available yet. May I bring you morning tea?"

I had no idea what the cost was for the buffet or tea. I was too embarrassed to ask the price. I paused for a moment wishing I hadn't ventured into the E&O. Maybe I should use this as an opportunity to retreat by telling him that I would be back later. But then I figured I should go ahead and splurge because the opportunity to have morning tea with Somerset Maugham might never present itself again.

I said, "That will be fine. Thank you."

"Will you be taking tea alone this morning, and do you have a seating preference?"

"Yes, I'll be taking tea alone, and I would like to sit at Somerset Maugham's table."

The waiter gave me a strange look. "Sir, I'm sorry. No other guests have arrived yet. You are the only one here."

"I know, but I want to sit at the table where Somerset Maugham sat when he stayed here."

The waiter looked perplexed and sat me at a table off to the side, away from a long table covered in a white tablecloth that I presumed was the buffet table. It was perfect. I had a clear view of the doorway leading from the lobby to the veranda. After seating me, he disappeared and was back in a matter of minutes with a hot pot of tea, two thick slices of toast, butter, and preserves, and Sunday's *Strait Times* newspaper and asked, "Will that be all for now, Sir?"

"Yes. Thank you."

I felt like quite the aristocrat reading the newspaper with my morning tea on the E&O veranda, just as I imagined Somerset Maugham had done not too many years ago. Sitting at what I fantasized was Somerset Maugham's table, I observed other hotel guests and eavesdropped on their conversations.

The veranda suddenly became a beehive of activity with more people. The staff, a half-dozen men dressed all in white, began setting up the Sunday Buffet. It was nearly eight-thirty.

I had to get back to the Hotel Continental. I made a writing motion in the air to my waiter. He brought the bill on a silver platter.

I started counting out cash and continued counting even as he said, "Sir, your room number will do. We do not take cash here."

A look of anguish swept over his face when I told him my room was at the Hotel Continental. He said, "Please wait here, Sir. I need to call the manager."

The manager arrived and said, "Sir, please follow me."

I left ten one-dollar notes on the silver platter and followed the manager to the lobby, where he told me, "Dining on the veranda for Sunday buffet is reserved exclusively for E&O guests. May I suggest you leave the hotel discreetly?"

"Oh, I didn't know. I'm sorry."

He said, "If you please, Sir." He wasn't entertaining discussion from me and held his right arm out with his palm open, gesturing toward the front door.

I felt so embarrassed. I left as swiftly as possible. I just got kicked out of Penang's finest hotel. Too bad Somerset Maugham wasn't there to take in the morning drama.

Good Morning, Miss Fong

I walked back to the Hotel Continental, got my bag, checked out, and waited outside by the lobby door for Miss Fong. Moke Chee arrived in a trishaw before the appointed hour of nine. I saw her before she saw me. Seeing her made me appreciate Penang's trishaws, where the passengers ride in front of the driver. I had a full view of her as she arrived. She was back to wearing her natural look with her hair in a ponytail and no face makeup detracting from her natural beauty.

I waved both arms and called out to her before the trishaw

came to a stop, "Good morning, Miss Fong."

She responded, "Good morning, Mr. Wolter. Have you eaten?"

I replied, "Yes. The desk clerk directed me to the E&O for their renowned Sunday buffet." I thought the word "renowned" would make me sound sophisticated, but after the words "Sunday buffet" left my mouth, I thought I probably should have just answered yes, and I hoped she wouldn't ask me how I liked the Sunday buffet at the E&O.

She slid over to the far side of the trishaw, patted the seat next to her, and said, "Climb aboard."

It was a simple natural gesture that I found beguiling. I climbed in the trishaw beside her. It was a snug fit, so I draped my right arm across the seat's back behind Moke Chee after placing my bag on the floor. I was tempted to let my arm "accidentally" drop-down around her shoulders, especially when my blood-starved arm started to throb in pain and then turned numb. I didn't want to come across as just another man trying to be "funny" with her and risk losing her as a friend, so I kept my arm safely on the seat's back. It didn't seem like a long ride to the Macalister Road bus terminal, but by the time we got there, my arm was completely lifeless and my fingers were tingling with pain. It was worth it.

We boarded the Ayer Itam bus, and our conversation made the trip seem short. After exiting the bus, I saw a long queue, maybe thirty people deep, waiting to purchase tickets for the tram ride up Penang Hill. I tried to join the end of the queue, but Moke Chee took my arm and pulled me around to the front of it. I felt uncomfortable about butting in front of the others and said, "I'm OK with waiting my turn."

She said, "That's the queue for coach. We're going first class."

"Coach is OK with me. There's no need to go first class."

"I have first-class tickets. My cousin manages the tram, so his family and guests are entitled to ride first class as often as they desire. It's part of his compensation. Besides, nobody pays to ride first class. The seats will go up unoccupied if we aren't in them."

"Great," I said, "but I feel guilty." I didn't know what else to say. My preconceived image of self-sacrificing Peace Corps Volunteers living with the hungry, huddled masses was by now completely shattered. Dancing under a starry sky at The Green Parrot last night, having morning tea at the E&O, and now traveling first class on the tram up Penang Hill was far more luxurious than the initial image I had of a Peace Corps Volunteer's life and was, in fact, more luxurious than my life back in Chicago.

However, I learned, other than not having to wait in a long line, first class wasn't a whole lot different than coach. It comprised the first two benches on the tram. There was more legroom between the first-class benches, but that was it. The coach was packed, and every bench had people sitting shoulder to shoulder, while Moke Chee and I were the only ones in first class. We occupied less than half of one bench in the two-bench cabin.

Moke Chee said, "See, what did I tell you? These seats would be unoccupied if we weren't on board."

The tram stopped midway up the hill at a station. The sister tram came down to greet us at the midpoint just as we came up. We got out of our tram and hurried across the concrete platform, passing passengers who were hurrying to board our vacated tram to complete their downhill journey. At least three-quarters of the coach passengers from our tram didn't board the second uphill tram. Moke Chee told me they lived in the houses and farm plots that dotted the hillside and were returning home after delivering their produce to market or going home at the end of their night shift in Georgetown.

The tram ride up the hill was slow and smooth. Alone with Moke Chee in the front seat, I imagined us ascending in a huge colorful balloon lifting up and away from the noise and hustle and bustle of hawkers hawking their wares, the hubbub of the sweltering crowd, and the din of motorbikes, cars, and buses with reviving engines belching noxious fumes. All of that gave way to silence. Sweet air replaced exhaust fumes and the odor of decaying matter in storm drains. The air became thinner and cooler as we drifted toward the clouds. The momentum of the tram caused us to lurch forward as it bumped to a sudden stop at the hilltop station. It might have been 2,733 feet above Ayer Itam and Georgetown, but it was a world apart.

Stepping out of the tram, I felt I was entering a Garden of Eden. There were no hawkers, no traffic, no litter, no noxious odors, no stray dogs lazing in the shade, nor stray cats moving aimlessly in the blazing sun. Instead, the cool air was alive with the floral aroma of fresh green living plants and of flowers that lined the solitary and secluded meandering blacktop pathway that Moke Chee and I strolled on to the hilltop bungalow. At some point along the path, it struck me that we were alone. For the first time, Moke Chee and I were alone. Oh, we were alone before, on the dance floor and even sitting in the trishaw, but there were always other people around. Now, there wasn't a soul in sight. It was just the two of us, and I loved it. Moke Chee didn't seem to mind, or maybe it was that she didn't notice we were all alone, and that was OK with me because it meant she had trust in me as a friend and was comfortable being alone with me. Fortune was smiling on me. I was thinking that this would be the perfect path to walk hand in hand with a special somebody.

Then Moke Chee asked, "How was it?"

"How was what?"

"You know. Don't play coy. Sunday buffet at the E&O. How was it?"

"OK, I guess, if you like that sort of thing."

"And do you? Do you like that sort of thing?"

"The Sunday buffet opened at eight-thirty, and I didn't have time to wait."

"But you said you ate."

"Yes, the waiter served me tea."

"And?"

"Tea, two pieces of toast, butter, and preserves. It was delicious."

"Was it expensive?"

"Sort of."

"Why, all of a sudden, is getting you to answer a simple question like pulling teeth? What is it you're not telling me? Come on, out with it." Moke Chee was smiling when she stepped in front of me, blocking my way. She knew she caught me holding something back and was enjoying it too much to let it go.

"At the E&O, you pay by signing a chit with your room number."

"And?"

"They don't accept cash."

"And?"

"I got kicked out. They were polite about it, but I definitely was kicked out of the E&O."

Moke Chee was bent over in laughter, and by now, I was laughing, too. She said, "That's a good story. You should write it up and submit it to the 'People' section of the newspaper. They'll publish it, and you'll earn fifteen dollars."

"I'll leave that to Somerset Maugham."

"Out with it. What brings Somerset Maugham into the conversation? You're not going to make me pull teeth again."

"I was pretending I was him."

"Why on Earth would you do that?"

"I read in my hotel travel brochure that he stayed at the E&O while in Penang. Then I couldn't help observing a couple and their twin daughters sitting at a nearby table and listening in on their conversation. I tried to imagine what it would be like to be Somerset Maugham creating a story out of that."

"You're not playing Somerset Maugham now, are you?"

"What do you mean?"

"You're not making this up, just telling me a story, putting me on, are you?"

"No. It's wrong, I know, but I enjoy eavesdropping on people sitting at tables next to me in restaurants. I live vicariously through their conversations. Their lives are full of many more interesting events and people than mine."

"Well, thanks a lot."

The smile was gone from Moke Chee's face, and I didn't know if she was serious or teasing me. I felt it best to treat it as if she was serious and possibly insulted by my stupid comment. I said, "Oh no, I didn't mean now. I can explain."

"You don't have to. I know you're having the best time of your life." Now I could tell by the twinkle in her eyes that she was teasing.

I said, "Thanks to you. I am."

"You're a flatterer. Aren't you?"

"No, I'm serious."

"I know, but do you know that you don't have to be Somerset Maugham to write a story?"

I didn't know how to respond, and the quiet was making me uncomfortable. I was trying to formulate something to say. Then Moke Chee broke the silence. Her voice still sounded serious as she asked, "Will you write a story about your time in Malaya and your visit to Penang? And will you include me in your story? If you do, what will you say about me, and how will you describe me?"

"No. I'm not a writer. I couldn't, even if I were Somerset Maugham, possibly write about all of this, and there is no way I could describe you."

I felt my face turning warm, and I was relieved we were in a dark-shaded area and more relieved when Moke Chee said, "Then that's settled. This is it. This is our bungalow."

CHAPTER 15

Moke Chee and I followed the flat, stone path that led away from the blacktop pathway, and there, behind thick shrubbery in the middle of an expansive manicured lawn, was a huge bungalow, not as huge as the Trengganu Sultan's palace, but the grounds were far more beautiful with fragrant flowering shrubs and trees like the mansions my brother Bill and our friends, the Jones brothers, rode our bicycles by in suburban River Forest and Oak Park. We would stop and imagine what it must be like to live in one of those magnificent homes and whether, by living there, we, too, would magically become magnificent. Back then, our boyish voices filled with exuberant joy as we cycled up one street and down another, selecting which mansion we would live in when we grew up, but a silence grabbed us as we cycled back to our own neighborhood. I can't speak for the others, but the dream of living in a mansion dimmed as the reality that the best the future held out for me was a steady union job in a factory like my father and oldest brother. Never could I have dreamed of walking up a path to a mansion on Penang Hill where I would be staying for a couple of days with the most beautiful woman in the world and Joo Ee's family.

The bungalow imparted a sense of strength and power and importance with its massive three-foot-wide, one-and-a-half-foot-thick granite block walls and tall teak front door. Moke Chee knocked on the door using the six-inch round brass lion's head clapper and called out, "Joo-Jupes."

Joo Ee came to the door and said, "Welcome. Let's get you settled and then have tea." She looked up at me and batted her eyelids as she said, "By the way, did you, as I instructed, keep your mouth shut yesterday and let Mokes negotiate with the proprietor of the haberdashery?"

I replied, "I didn't utter a word." I made a gesture crossing my heart with my right hand.

Joo Ee opened her eyelids extra wide, and she spoke so emphatically I could see her tongue click against the roof of her mouth when she said in a long, drawn-out, "Annnnnd?"

"I felt sorry for the proprietor. He was no match for Moke Chee."

There were two teenagers hanging around. I think they were Joo Ee's brother and sister. She ignored them and didn't introduce me to them, but she did introduce me to her mother and three "aunties" who were her mother's friends up for the day to play mahjong. They stopped playing mahjong just momentarily to look up at me, flash a smile and say hello in English before settling back into the rhythm of constructing and reconstructing walls of peapod green-backed mahjong tiles with ivory-colored faces. Each tile was inscribed with black Chinese calligraphy except for a few with red calligraphy and various other tiles with red and green circles inscribed on the faces. After constructing their mahjong walls, the aunties tossed coins into an ever-expanding mound of coins.

After introducing me to her mother and the three aunties, Joo Ee showed me to my bedroom.

I turned to Joo Ee and said, "This room is huge. It's bigger than the living room of my quarters in Kuala Trengganu."

Joo Ee said, "We're also going to spoil you with your own bath. It has hot running water."

I placed my bag on a dresser and stuck my head in the bathroom for a peek. The bathroom featured a Western-style toilet, sink, shower, soaking tub, and bidet. I said, "This bathroom is larger than the bedroom I shared with my two older brothers growing up in Chicago."

Then Joo Ee said, "Please resist the urge to sleep in the bathroom and kindly sleep in the bed." Joo Ee turned to Moke Chee and said, "Mokes, I'll let Cook know if you're taking lunch with us."

Moke Chee replied, "Thank you, but I'm fetching tiffin back for my parents, and I haven't checked on Nanny yet. And last night, I promised 'The Barbarians' I'd let them meet a real American and then take them to the creameries. You're welcome to join us."

Joo Ee declined Moke Chee's invitation and asked, "How about dinner?"

"My father has been after me to take him to the padang to have rubbish for dinner."

Moke Chee and I walked to the tram and caught the bus back to the Macalister Road bus terminal.

Learning More About Miss Fong

At the bus terminal, Moke Chee bought fried chow fun with prawns to bring home to her parents for lunch. When we arrived at her house, Moke Chee's father was napping with the Sunday newspaper draped across his lap. Moke Chee's mother answered the door and then served me tea and a chocolate custard dish she had just made.

Moke Chee's father woke up, and in our conversation about how I spent Sundays back in America, I told him that I usually attended Catholic Mass on Sundays. He told me about the Lady of Sorrows Catholic Church just around the corner on Macalister Road. I heard the church bell calling worshipers to prayer. Moke Chee told me that she would wait at home for me while I went to church.

Mass had already started and was conducted in Mandarin.

My Mandarin lessons back in Kuala Trengganu enabled me to understand just a few words of the service. After Mass, I went back to Moke Chee's house. The same gaggle of kids recognized me by now and didn't bother shouting, "Where are you going?" But still, they followed me.

While I was at church, Bee Har, Moke Chee's neighborhood friend, dropped in to see Moke Chee and to give her two tickets to the Cathay movie theater, as well as to look over Moke Chee's American visitor. Moke Chee introduced us, and I learned that Bee Har had just returned from London, where she studied to become a dress designer. I also learned that Bee Har frequently had theater tickets to distribute because her father was the financial controller for the family who owned the theater. I was amazed at how fast news traveled in Malaya. It also amazed me how Moke Chee had access to free perks like first-class theater and tram tickets.

Bee Har asked me a question that made me feel very stupid. When she learned that I was in Penang to purchase new trousers because mine were too big after losing sixty pounds, she said, "Do you mind?"

She was looking at me, but I didn't know what she was talking about. Bee Har reached over and took the fold of fabric on my pant leg between her thumb and finger and rubbed it together, and said, "This fabric is perfectly fine. Why didn't you have your trousers taken in by a tailor in Kuala Trengganu?"

I had no response other than, "I never thought of that. Thank you. I'll do that as soon as I get back." That was my intention, but like so many of my intentions, I was unable to follow through on this one.

After Bee Har went home, Moke Chee and I left her house and walked to visit Nanny. Moke Chee invited Nanny to join us for lunch. She accepted without hesitation, and that made me happy because I felt she was accepting of Moke Chee's befriending me. We went to a coffee shop and had a steamed chicken dish from a stall famous for its Hainanese Chicken.

Nanny and Moke Chee talked throughout lunch, smiling and holding hands with their arms resting on the table when not eating. They talked as if I weren't there, which could have made me feel excluded, but instead made me feel welcome. I thought to myself: They're comfortable enough with me not to feel they have to include me in their conversation. For me, it was enough just to be with them, listening to the happy sounds of their words and watching the expressions on their faces without invading their privacy by trying to pick out words and follow what they were saying. It was like listening to music without having to pick out specific notes. It was pure enjoyment.

After lunch, Moke Chee and Nanny continued holding hands as we walked Nanny back to her quarters. Then Moke Chee and I headed for her maternal grandmother's house to pick up "The Barbarians," who turned out to be her nephews. Grandmother's house was on Macalister Road just across the back lane from Moke Chee's house, except it was located on a huge compound. The house was built on pillars similar to a Malay kampong house but much larger.

The family had just completed eating lunch, and a silence settled over the household. Grandmother, the dowager matriarch of the family and reportedly the granddaughter of the former king of Thailand, had settled down in her favorite inlaid mother-of-pearl reclining deck lounger on the front porch for her afternoon nap. I was still smiling from having lunch with Nanny when Moke Chee and I climbed the stairs to greet Grandmother. I don't know whether it was because we had interrupted Grandmother's nap or whether she was genuinely displeased with me, but when Moke Chee presented me to her, she made no attempt to disguise her displeasure. An angry look crossed her face. She scowled at me. Her brow furrowed and fierce bolts of anger were shooting from her eyes. She uttered a few words that I didn't understand, but from their sound, there was no mistaking her disgust. If Grandmother intended to make me feel uncomfortable and unwelcome, she succeeded.

Moke Chee didn't respond to Grandmother, and I followed her cue, but I picked up on the hurt in Moke Chee's voice when she whispered to me, "Don't mind her. Let's go inside."

We took our shoes off and went inside the house. Gim Lan and Sui Lay returned my greeting. The three Barbarians were seated at a table with a high school-aged boy who was tutoring Gim Lan's two sons in math while Sui Lay's son, Hock Tee, worked on an art project. Hock Tee, who had his arm in a cast, came over first and held Moke Chee's hand with his good hand. Ah Gay, Gim Lan's eldest son, came over to me and asked if I were a cowboy or knew any cowboys. Ah Soon, the youngest of the three, didn't look up but continued working with the math tutor. Gim Lan scolded Ah Gay and made him continue with tutoring.

Moke Chee asked, "What happened to Hock Tee's arm?"

Sui Lay laughed, "He thought he was Superman. He tied one of Grandmother's red sarongs around his neck last night to make a Superman cape and then tried to fly off the table."

Moke Chee asked, "Can he still go to the creameries?"

Sui Lay was still smiling as he said, "Yes, of course."

We went to the creameries. Hock Tee ordered what was called a "Merry Widow" on the menu, which was basically a banana split with four scoops of chocolate ice cream and was covered with chocolate syrup and a pile of whipped cream, as well as sprinkled with nuts and topped with a cherry. He ate it and was all smiles when we walked him home. Moke Chee led me through Grandmother's back gate, across the back lane, and into the back compound of her house.

My Conflicting Feelings

After a short visit with Moke Chee's father to let him know we would be back after the theater to take him to eat rubbish at the padang, Moke Chee and I headed for the Cathay Theatre on Penang Road. Outside the theater, vendors were selling movie treats like pickled mango and pickled shallots on thin bamboo squires. We purchased both, six to a squire, and went inside to take our seats in the first-class section of the theater. The theater was air-conditioned, and our plush padded seats were a pleasant contrast to the hard wooden seats of the Capitol Theatre back in Kuala Trengganu. Before the movie started, the audience was required to stand while the National Anthem played. Printed Malay words to the anthem were projected across the movie screen, and some people sang along with the recording. That was followed by about a dozen or so advertisements with primarily Australian and a few Asian actors. Smoking was permitted in the theater, and by the time the feature film *The Flower Drum Song* started, a haze steadily began filling the air, growing to a thick cloud by the film's end.

Going to a movie with Moke Chee was another new experience, and I enjoyed watching her reactions to the film more than the film itself. How ironic, I thought. The genesis of my becoming a Peace Corps Volunteer began by taking Lolly to see "The Flower Drum Song" on stage at the Shubert Theater in Chicago. On the way back to her house, while discussing the play, the conversation turned to the merits of arranged marriages versus love marriages, which resulted in Lolly's mother later interpreting this as our soon-to-be engagement. But that thought briefly flashed through my mind. My more persistent thought was: Should I hold Moke Chee's hand?

Back home, when taking a date to a movie, it was expected that the boy would hold the girl's hand. Holding hands wasn't a big deal. It was just something that was done without any thought or, for that matter, any commitment to go any further. But this wasn't back home, and this wasn't a date. My desires aside, I dared not hold Moke Chee's hand. I didn't want to take advantage of her hospitality and didn't know how she would take my advance or what it would signal to her. To me, it would be more than simply a boy holding a girl's hand in the movies. My feelings were starting to conflict with my plan to return home in August.

I couldn't help myself. Moke Chee was the kindest and most thoughtful, respectful, loving, and interesting person I had ever known. If I had met her back in Chicago, I would never have joined the Peace Corps. I would have pursued her romantically if she would have had me. But this wasn't back in Chicago, and that's where I was returning in just three months. In a day, I was leaving Penang. Once I collected my trousers and jacket and left Penang, I would likely never see Moke Chee again. It was better to keep my inclination in check. That made me think that I had better let April Jennings know that I'm exiting the Peace Corps early. It wasn't fair to let her think I was staying in Malaya and something could develop between us. But first, I wanted to let Moke Chee know. Other than the Peace Corps administration and Dr. Nickerson, my mentor at the medical school, I hadn't discussed exiting the Peace Corps early with anyone, not even Teh Eng.

I knew as soon as I exited Bankim's office that I was exiting the Peace Corps early. It was just a matter of when. I shouldn't have accepted April's invitation to spend my school holiday with her. I know this sounds conceited on my part, but I decided I would tell April that I was leaving Malaya in three months as soon as I saw her in Kota Bharu, to squash any romantic feelings she might harbor for me. Since nothing had transpired between us, it should be easy to tell her and easy for her to take. But before I told April, I wanted to tell Moke Chee.

There was no reason to tell Moke Chee I was leaving for home in three months, but I wanted her to know. We only spent a little more than a day and a half together at the Teacher's Union picnic on Pulau Perhentian, and now only about two more days in Penang, and we were just friends, certainly no more than that. But exiting the Peace Corps and returning home was a big decision, and for reasons I couldn't explain, I wanted Moke Chee to be the first person to know I was leaving. Sitting passively in the dark, air-conditioned theater allowed all those uninvited thoughts to worm their way through my mind. I didn't like it but was unable to stop it.

Atop Penang Hill at Night

It was late but not yet dark by the time Moke Chee and I fetched her father to go to the padang to eat rubbish. The padang was a field where soccer and cricket matches were held during daylight hours. It was within easy walking distance from Moke Chee's house. At the far end of the padang was a row of shade trees, and under the shade trees was a line of hawker stalls, maybe forty or more, each specializing in one dish. There were also a series of folding tables scattered among the hawker stalls. We found an empty table, and Moke Chee's father sat at it to reserve it as I followed Moke Chee, scurrying from hawker stall to hawker stall, ordering rubbish. I had chicken satay and wonton soup, while Moke Chee and her father had cuttlefish, periwinkles, soft-shelled crabs, and a few other things that I couldn't identify.

By the time we finished eating and paying the various hawkers, it was dark. It was pitch dark walking across the padang, and in that darkness, unable to see the turf, the padang ground felt very uneven. Then unexpectedly and without saying a word, Moke Chee's father clasped my left arm just above the elbow to steady himself as we walked him home. That gesture of trust from Moke Chee's father capped off a perfect day.

While riding in the tram up Penang Hill after dark, I thought Georgetown was beautiful. Looking over my shoulder, I saw the city aglow with multicolored twinkling glints of light. The tram ride, in fact the entire day, had been magical, and I didn't want to break the spell, but Grandmother's reaction when Moke Chee presented me to her was bothering me. It must have shown on my face or in my demeanor because Moke Chee asked with a note of earnestness in her voice and a serious look in her eyes: "You look lost in thought. Is something wrong?"

I didn't want to answer at first. I wasn't comfortable sharing personal thoughts, especially hurtful ones, but Moke Chee continued to look into my eyes, searching for an answer. I said, "I don't know how to put this. Your grandmother. She was so angry. What was it? I'm trying to figure out what I did wrong."

"It wasn't you specifically. Grandmother was angry with me for bringing a 'red-faced monkey' to her house. 'Red-faced monkey' is a derogatory term that Chinese people call Europeans. Grandmother has nothing against you specifically; it's simply that Grandmother dislikes and looks down on all white people."

"I knew whites were disliked, but it never occurred to me that we were looked down on by other races. I thought only whites looked down on other races. I really feel dumb."

"You're not dumb, just innocent."

I didn't know how to respond. This wasn't the discussion I anticipated having when we boarded the tram. Moke Chee was being kind to me. I should have thanked her but being an "innocent" wasn't in my concept of manliness. Is that how she saw me? An innocent? This was a much more serious and far too personal discussion than I had anticipated or wanted. The tram came to a stop with its usual thump at the hilltop station. We got out of the tram and, to my relief, left that conversation behind.

It was so dark atop the hill that the hilltop path to the bungalow would have been impossible to follow had it not been for quaint lamp posts guiding our way. It was a clear, beautiful evening, with stars seeming to wink at us from above. A serenade of crickets filled the cool, almost cold, air. Moke Chee and I made our way along the path, walking close to each other but not touching. She was so close to me that I could feel a gentle warmth radiate from her body. I thought that I should perhaps put my arm around her and tell her it's just to keep her warm. But that thought was short-lived because Moke Chee asked, "Did you bring swimming trunks with you?"

It seemed an odd question on such a romantic stroll. I answered, "Yes."

"Good. Tomorrow, after picking up your clothes, we'll go swimming, spend the day at the beach, and you can catch a taxi first thing the following morning, unless you have to leave town tomorrow."

"That sounds great. But I don't want to impose another day on you or Joo Ee or her family."

"That's very considerate of you, and that's why you're not imposing on us. Joo Ee and her family welcome you. So far, everyone does."

"Except Grandmother."

"You should be flattered that she even took notice of you. But enough about that. Penang is known as the 'Pearl of the Orient,' so you have to experience Penang's beautiful beaches and get a seaside view of the pinang trees, the trees that lent their name to my island in the sun."

We arrived at the bungalow, and again Joo Ee answered the door. Her mother and the two children were in front of the fireplace, where we joined them. Cook built a fire in the fireplace before retiring for the evening and left a stack of wood so we could keep the fire going. We roasted the marshmallows that Cook had set out for us. Something about gathering around a fire in the darkness of Malayan nights proved fertile ground for the telling of ghost stories.

On this night, as I found to be the case on subsequent

nights, Joo Ee's mother started the storytelling by sharing ghost stories she learned as a child from her granny in China and then sharing even more stories she learned from her early days in Penang. Places with rural populations like Penang in the early days and the east coast of Malaya were particularly fertile ground for stories of Chinese, Malay, and Indian ghosts and dozens of supernatural spirits. Moke Chee and Joo Ee took turns telling frightening stories of supernatural spirits who inhabited Kelantan. During story time with my Boy Scouts on overnight campouts, I took the opportunity to interject that there is no scientific evidence for the existence of ghosts or other supernatural spirits, but as a guest at the hilltop bungalow, I listened politely, quietly dismissing the stories to myself as mere superstition. Yet as the hours passed—well after sunset, with the night getting darker and the thin hilltop air growing colder—the dancing shadows cast by flickering flames took on a spine-chilling lifelike ghostly form. We, including Auntie and myself, inched closer together, closer to the light and warmth of the fireplace.

On that first night and each subsequent night, when Joo Ee's mother declared it was time to turn in, we went to our respective bedrooms. I went to my room and climbed into the most magnificently comfortable Goldilocks bed, not too soft and not too hard but just right. I cocooned myself under the warm billowy down comforter, savoring each recollection of the day. My reverie was interrupted by two quick raps on the bedroom door and Moke Chee calling out while opening the door: "Are you decent? Can we come in?"

"Yes and yes."

Moke Chee entered the room, followed by Joo Ee, who turned the ceiling light on and closed the door behind her. They were in their pajamas. Moke Chee looked so cute in her pajamas with a loose-fitting flower-print top hanging out over cream-colored knee-length shorts that I wanted to jump up and hug her, but I couldn't. I wouldn't have anyway because

I really couldn't. I wasn't wearing pajamas. Under the down comforter, I was naked. Why? To me, pajamas were superfluous, especially in Malaya's tropical climate, and pajamas were just one more item of clothing to wash. Moke Chee and Joo Ee sat on the edge of my bed to talk because, to them, the evening was still young, and Joo Ee wanted to know every detail of our day in town.

Moke Chee sat closest to me, that is closest to my face, and did most of the talking. Joo Ee got a kick out of Grandmother calling me a "red-faced monkey."

"I don't think your face is particularly red," Joo Ee said.

I asked, "What about the monkey part?"

She didn't answer, but she and Moke Chee laughed. They were having a grand time at my expense, and I was enjoying it. Then we engaged in Malaya's national pastime: we talked about people we knew. They knew everybody that I knew in Kuala Trengganu and many I didn't know. They had stories to tell about each person. Moke Chee and Joo Ee assured me that we were not gossiping but only sharing information. They also assured me that other people were talking about us this very instant and talking about my visit up Penang Hill.

I said, "How can they be talking about my visit up Penang Hill when I just got here?"

Joo Ee responded, "This is Malaya, lah."

Moke Chee said, "We should call it a day. Jim's had a full day, and he has a full day tomorrow. After picking up his clothes, we're going to the beach. Would you care to join us?"

"Thank you, no. I'm relaxing with a book in the cool hilltop air. You two go on without me. Good night, Jim."

Moke Chee added, "Pleasant dreams."

Then I started singing "Goodnight, Ladies."

They laughed and said, "Oh God," and closed the door.

I enjoyed their visit, but seeing the door close left me feeling doleful. I wished the night and that surprise visit didn't have to end and particularly that Moke Chee could have stayed bantering about nothing of particular seriousness or importance.

I fell asleep thinking the sooner the night passed, the sooner morning arrived, and the sooner I had another day with Moke Chee.

CHAPTER 16

It was Monday morning. Happily, it was another whole day with Moke Chee. This being our last day together—ever—I wanted to savor every minute of it and make it as memorable for her as for me. Following breakfast in town—hopefully, at her house or at a coffee shop with Nanny—I wanted to see the old folks one more time before departing. They were so much part of the Moke Chee who I discovered in Penang, and any memory of her would be incomplete without them. Then, it would be time to pick up my trousers and suit jacket from the haberdashery, book my seat on the Tuesday flight to Kota Bharu, and—best of all—spend the afternoon at the beach alone with Moke Chee. As it turned out, it was a day full of surprises.

Moke Chee and I went down the hill, and Moke Chee purchased some food for her parents and us—a rice porridge called chicken choke with a thousand-year-old egg. With the food in hand, we walked to her parents' home for breakfast. After arriving at the house, Moke Chee did something I never expected. She invited me to follow her into the kitchen, where I joined her and her father for breakfast at a little two-foot-square breakfast table. Moke Chee's mother served me a bowl of chocolate custard, so I helped myself to a small serving of choke and had only a sliver of the thousand-year-old egg.

Teh Eng, my housemate, had told me that being invited to a Chinese family's kitchen was a privilege only enjoyed by relatives and close friends. I said to Moke Chee's father. "Sir, thank you for allowing me to take breakfast with you."

He replied, "Don't mention it."

Then I turned to Moke Chee's mother. I motioned toward the empty custard bowl with my thumbs up and said, "Delicious." She smiled and said something I didn't catch.

On leaving the kitchen, I said, "Thank you," and repeated "thank you" several more times, bowing slightly with each "thank you" before leaving. Later I told Moke Chee how much I appreciated being invited to have breakfast with her and her parents. She smiled.

Moke Chee and I left to fetch my trousers and jacket. Nanny's house was only a five-minute walk from Moke Chee's parents' house, so we stopped to visit her. Nanny said to me, "Hello, Jim," and then she and Moke Chee held hands and talked and laughed in a world of their own.

I offered to walk the short distance to the haberdashery on my own so Moke Chee could have a half hour more to visit with Nanny, but Nanny said that she had chores she had to attend to. Moke Chee and I left and started walking to the haberdashery. I felt guilty about Moke Chee leaving with me and asked her if Nanny really had chores or did she say that because I offered to go to the shop alone. Moke Chee assured me that Nanny had chores to do, and our leaving together gave Nanny an excuse to get back to them. I felt better.

As soon as we entered the haberdashery, the proprietor bypassed other customers and came walking toward us with his hands held out toward me and an apologetic look on his face. He clasped my hand and said, "I'm so sorry. Your trousers and jacket are not ready. My tailor was unable to get to them. So many orders came in before yours. We will get your order soon." He tried bypassing Moke Chee by speaking directly to me.

Moke Chee was having none of that. She asked, "When will you have them ready?"

"In three days. I'm so sorry."

"That will be Wednesday morning."

"Thursday morning."

Moke Chee turned to me. "Four more days. Is that acceptable to you? You're welcome to continue your stay up the hill."

I said, "Yes. But I don't want to impose."

"You're not imposing. Joo-Jupes told me you 'bring a joyful mirth to the hilltop and are welcome to stay as long as you like.'"

I said, "What's a joyful mirth? Nothing bad, I hope."

Moke Chee said, "That's just Joo Ee playing with vocabulary. But we have to go back to my house. My bathing suit is there. I thought we'd drop your clothes off there before going to the beach."

"I thought we'd drop them off up the hill. My swimsuit is there."

"Then we'll skip the beach for today and go sightseeing."

Visiting the Sites with Moke Chee

Moke Chee and I walked to Fort Cornwallis at the northeast corner of Penang. The fort's star-shaped walls were much smaller and less intimidating than I had imagined. But in reading the brass placard near the main entrance stating the fort was built in 1810, I realized what a formidable structure it was back then.

I told Moke Chee, "I'm going to do something that I hope doesn't embarrass you." She had a look on her face that said: Do something wrong, buster, and I'll give you an earful.

I stepped over the low pipe-bar fence surrounding the fort's grounds, walked across the lawn, and hugged the wall with both arms and my whole body.

I called out, "I can't believe it. General Cornwallis surrendering to George Washington. I feel like I'm actually there at

Yorktown. I can't believe it."

Moke Chee said, "I don't want to burst your fantasy, but Cornwallis never stepped foot in Penang. The fort is just a relic from the colonial past. Let's walk the Esplanade. We'll have rubbish for lunch."

It was a pleasant walk. The cool sea breeze was refreshing. Trying to identify the flags of the ships at anchor gave me a sense of being at the hub of worldwide trade routes. It made me feel like I was a citizen of the world.

We escaped the heat of the noonday sun by sitting at a table under a shade tree. We ate light. The cendol with a glass of ice-cold, freshly squeezed sugarcane water was more like a sugary dessert than lunch but just the thing for a day of sight-seeing in Penang. It would have been easy to spend the whole afternoon sitting in the shade, talking. I don't recall what we talked about, but the time seemed to evaporate in thin air.

Moke Chee said, "We're going to the Hock Kin Keong temple next. Don't hug anything there."

The Hock Kin Keong temple was also known as the "snake temple" by the local people and tourists alike for good reason. I never saw so many snakes slithering around, uncaged, in one place. They were everywhere in the dense smoke-filled temple. I wondered why the snakes stayed in the temple and didn't slither away. Perhaps, I thought, the Buddhist Monks kept them well supplied with rodents, or maybe there was something in the smoke that they found addictive, or possibly it was, as the locals believe, something supernatural at the temple that called to them.

Meeting More Friends

We walked a few miles on Penang's commercial streets, where trishaw drivers called out, offering us rides. It was more interesting to walk among people at work. It was a pleasure walking on commercial streets, as opposed to the strictly residential streets, where local businesses of all sorts existed, and most people were too busy to stare at me or hurl insults at Moke Chee for walking with a European.

Moke Chee pointed to a building about four times larger than the rest and said, "There, that's the old Anglo Thai building where my father was the shopkeeper. And next to it is Uncle Hashim's print shop. He and my father are good friends. I haven't visited him yet this holiday. Do you mind if we stop by to say hello?"

I followed Moke Chee into the shop. The worker in the front of the store seemed to know Moke Chee and said, "Hello," as we walked past to the back of the shop. Moke Chee called out, "Uncle Hashim, hello, it's me."

Uncle Hashim was a broad-shouldered rotund man dressed in a white Arabic robe. He got up from behind his desk and greeted us with a broad smile. "Welcome, Moke Chee. It's been a while. And how is your father? Please sit."

"Uncle Hashim, Father's fine. I'd like you to meet my friend Jim."

"Welcome, Jim. How about a cup of tea and tell me, Jim, what brings you to Penang?"

We sat and had tea and talked about the Peace Corps and interspersed in a generally pleasant conversation, I realized afterward that Uncle Hashim managed to get me to tell him about my family, my education, and my aspirations. He was checking me out in a convivial manner with his disarming broad smile. I liked him, and I liked that he was checking me out. I sensed he had a protective paternal feeling for Moke Chee.

Moke Chee told me beforehand that Uncle Hashim provided her with school supplies when she was a student, and he still offers her supplies, which she accepts out of respect for him. She told me that if he offered me supplies, it indicated that he accepted me and that I should accept his gift out of respect for him. I didn't need school supplies, but when Uncle Hashim asked what school supplies I needed, I asked for a tablet of graph paper. He gave me two reams to take with me as we departed and thanked Moke Chee for visiting him.

It was close to dinner time, and Moke Chee suggested we go to a nearby Muslim Indian restaurant. She asked, "Can you take spicy-hot food?"

"I like hot food," I replied.

"Be warned, it runs from hot to extremely hot."

I thought it prudent to heed Moke Chee's warning and ordered a mild chicken curry dish. Moke Chee ordered a hot curry dish. My "mild" curry was so hot that my eyes teared up. Moke Chee called the waiter to bring a glass of yogurt to soothe the pain in my mouth.

We had just finished eating dinner and Moke Chee was standing at the counter, picking out food to take back to her parents and Nanny, when Choo Choo, another friend of Moke Chee, stopped by the restaurant to pick up food to take home. I wondered if there was any place in Penang where Moke Chee would not run into a friend or family member. Choo Choo said her brother, Henry, was waiting outside with a car and invited us to join her for dessert at her house. We agreed.

Moke Chee and Choo Choo sat in the back seat, catching up on what each of them had been doing since secondary school. Choo Choo had just returned from Australia, where she studied interior design, and was in the process of interviewing for a designer job in Kuala Lumpur with a Dutch firm. I sat in the front seat with Henry. He and I didn't talk. He seemed to have all he could handle driving the car. He meshed the gears, causing a harsh grinding sound when he shifted gears. He continually jerked the steering wheel from side-to-side, making for a harrowing herky-jerky ride on the way to delivering the food before going to Choo Choo's house.

We arrived at Choo Choo's house. It was an old colonial mansion with a compound so spacious that it easily could accommodate two more mansions. It was surrounded by a ten-foot-high fence and patrolled by two Doberman pinschers. Henry pulled the car under the front cupola, and Choo Choo told us, "Remain in the car until Henry gets the dogs under control."

When I entered the house, I saw a large foyer and marble columns lining a huge reception room with marble floors. One whole wall of the house was an ornate gold-leaf screen. It was a labyrinth of magnificently carved birds, shrubs, flowers, and trees. Choo Choo invited us to sit while she went to the back of the house. She returned with her mother and a servant carrying a tray full of colorful Malayan cakes and a pitcher of rose-colored water.

Moke Chee stood up, and I followed suit. Moke Chee said, "Hello, Auntie. I would like you to meet my friend Jim. He's an American Peace Corps Volunteer. Jim, this is Mrs. Gan."

Mrs. Gan said, "Hello, Moke Chee, and welcome, Jim. Have you eaten? Please sit, don't stand on ceremony."

I bowed slightly and said, "It's a pleasure to meet you, Auntie. We just ate some Indian food." Following Moke Chee's example, the word "auntie" just came out of my mouth. For an instant, I wondered if I was being too familiar, but Auntie's eyes brightened when I called her Auntie. Malayans my age called their elders Auntie or Uncle, so I adopted the custom.

"At Hameediyah?" Auntie asked.

Choo Choo said, "That's where I happened to meet Moke Chee and Jim."

"How did you find it?" Auntie asked. I assumed she was directing the question to me.

"Delicious but very spicy."

"You'll need a glass of iced rose water and some nyonya kuih. They're traditional Chinese-Malayan cakes. I hope you enjoy them."

Auntie and Choo Choo asked me the typical questions about Chicago, my family, how I found Malaya and Malayans, and, of course, why I joined the Peace Corps. What surprised me during our conversation was that Choo Choo openly expressed her critical opinion of Malayan politics when she came from an obviously prosperous and privileged family.

The sun was setting when Auntie asked where we were staying. Moke Chee told her we were staying with Joo Ee's family up the hill. Auntie said, "I know the family. I don't recall Joo Ee. She wasn't a St. George's girl, but I know of her father. He is very senior in the Ministry of Finance. It's getting late. Choo, call Henry and fetch Moke Chee and Jim to Ayer Itam."

Before we left, Auntie Gan asked how long I would be in Penang. Moke Chee replied for me, "Until at least Thursday."

Auntie said, "Then, how about coming over for lunch tomorrow at noon? I'm making popiah. You may bring Joo Ee as well."

We had planned on going to the beach, but Moke Chee said, "Auntie makes the best popiah. We look forward to it. Thank you."

Henry pulled the car around to the front portico. Moke Chee and Choo Choo got in the back seat and continued their conversation about where and what old classmates were doing while I got in front with Henry. I was glad Henry wasn't a talker. I didn't feel like talking. I was thinking about April and was feeling guilty. Her big smile and twinkling eyes and her saying, "I'm looking forward to seeing you the second week of May," became fixtures in my mind since the last time I saw her in Kuala Lumpur. Now instead of spending a week, it would be just a weekend.

After another harrowing herky-jerky ride, we arrived at the tram, and on the way up, I told Moke Chee, "I'm happy my trousers and jacket weren't ready." I surprised myself by that statement. It was true. I was happy to spend more time up on Penang Hill with Moke Chee. But I had to be honest with myself. I also felt sad and guilty that April would be waiting for me to visit. While riding on the tram in the dark, I realized that our time would never be. I had to let April know when I saw her. I didn't look forward to it.

Moke Chee remained silent. I worried that I came off as being too serious about her and added, "I'll never tire of looking out at the twinkling technicolor lights of Georgetown from the tram."

Moke Chee didn't respond, and I wondered if she had heard me. I was just making small talk, but I still thought of repeating my last comment. Then again, if she heard me the first time, repeating myself would make me look foolish. The tram thumped to a stop in the dark. I got out of the tram first and offered my hand to help Moke Chee out. Before accepting my hand, she said, "I hope you didn't mind my accepting Auntie's invitation to lunch. It would have been a 'loss of face' if we didn't accept her invitation."

"I look forward to it."

Moke Chee took my hand, got out of the tram, and then let go of my hand. The twinkling stars were blanketed from view by an overcast sky, but there was a bit of moonlit luminescence in the clouds. We walked back to the cottage at a slower pace this night than the previous night. Again we walked close enough without touching for me to feel the warmth radiating from her body as we followed the lantern-lit blacktop path back toward the cottage.

Another Night of Stories

We arrived in the middle of storytime. Auntie Khoo, Joo Ee, and Moke Chee retold variations of the stories they had told the night before. Even in their retelling in the cool darkness of night on the hilltop, they chilled the spine.

When we were finished, Auntie Khoo said, "It's time to go to bed." We each went to our respective rooms. I settled in bed and heard two raps at the door and Moke Chee saying, "Are you decent? May we come in?"

Moke Chee and Joo Ee took their usual seats on the edge of my bed, with Moke Chee describing our day in Georgetown. Joo Ee laughed when Moke Chee told her how I was hugging the outside wall of Fort Cornwallis. In my defense, I told Joo Ee that I had only read about Cornwallis and the British East India Company in school, and now I could wrap my arms around the fort named after Cornwallis. It made me feel like I was touching history.

When I gave my explanation to Moke Chee, she seemed sympathetic to my feelings. She was among the Malayans who appreciated Penang's status as a Crown Colony and being a British subject. Joo Ee was opposed to being a British subject and all the implications of second-class citizenry implicit in colonialism. Moke Chee and Joo Ee went back and forth on the topic of governance. Their discussion was very serious until Joo Ee said to me, "If you really want to hug the fort, you have to hug the entire fort. Tomorrow I expect you to walk around the entire outer perimeter, wrapping your arms around each meter."

Moke Chee and Joo Ee then shared hilarious stories and nicknames Malayans gave to Peace Corps Volunteers. Moke Chee said, "You know you're called 'Baggy Pants,' but other Volunteers have nicknames too. Victoria is called 'Queen Victoria' or 'Queenie' because she is so bossy, and Malayan teachers have placed bets on whether Queenie will catch Baggy Pants. She's trying so very hard."

I said, "She is?"

Joo Ee said: "Did you hear about 'Coconuts,' the surveyor in Kuantan? He plants two coconut trees in his compound each time he comes back from weeks of surveying in the jungle. Then, when he goes back out to survey again, the old granny who is his housekeeper tears the trees out of the ground because, in their kampong, it is customary for the man of the house to plant a coconut tree when the woman of the house becomes pregnant. The coconuts on the tree ensure the woman will deliver a son. The local people tease the old granny that not only is she carrying one son, but she is carrying two sons for Coconuts."

Moke Chee said, "What about 'Banana Man' in Besut? He only eats bananas because some of his fellow teachers told him there was a woman after him and she has tried to cast a spell on him by putting a potion in food served to him. Joo Ee, tell Jim about 'His Lordship' and 'Road Runner' and why 'Road Runner' should be a Thai Volunteer."

"Jaron invited four of us, all teachers at the same school, another Chinese woman, me, and 'Road Runner' to his house for dinner. I don't know if he does this all the time or if he was trying to impress us, but when we were seated for dinner, he had a little dinner bell that he rang for his houseman to come and serve us. It was so ridiculous. All of us were younger than the houseman. We could have served him. Thereafter, Jaron has been called 'His Lordship.'"

"Tell Jim about 'Road Runner.'"

"He's disgusting. Every weekend he and whatever lowlifes he can round up head across the border to Songkhla to visit the Thai night spots and ladies of the night. He spends so much time in Thailand that he should be a Volunteer there."

I said, "Do Malayans have nicknames for all of us?"

Moke Chee replied, "Of course, and we hear all the stories."

Joo Ee added, "This is Malaya, lah."

I said, "Then you'll have to give me a new name when I get my new trousers."

Moke Chee and Joo Ee both said, "Oh no. You'll be 'Baggy Pants' forever."

Moke Chee said, "Jupes, Choo Choo's mother invited you to join us for lunch at her house. She's making popiah."

"Thank her for me, but I need to be up here and sit in on the mahjong game for one of the aunties who will be absent tomorrow." Joo Ee scrunched up her face and rolled her eyes back into her head.

Moke Chee said, "Then we'll be back right after lunch, and I'll relieve you."

Moke Chee then turned to me and said, "Is that alright with you?"

I nodded my head in the affirmative and said, "Yes." What else could I say? I figured it would be good to just rest for a day.

With that, Moke Chee and Joo Ee said, "Well, Baggy Pants, pleasant dreams."

I started singing "Goodnight, Ladies" and thought after they left: Malayans have each of us pegged, and being known as "Baggy Pants" is not all that bad.

CHAPTER 17

The Penang Road haberdasher did not have my trousers and jacket ready on Monday as promised. I was pissed. But Moke Chee's invitation to stay up Penang Hill for the three extra days eased the situation. She said, "You'll have three more days to learn why Penang is known as the 'Pearl of the Orient.' " I enjoyed Moke Chee's company, particularly her straightforward, no-pretense attitude. And more importantly, she accepted me as me, as a friend named Jim. I didn't have to work at impressing her. Besides, my hilltop accommodations were far better than sleeping on the floor of another Volunteer's house. I will never live in such luxury again.

On Tuesday morning, my first extra day in Penang, Moke Chee and I followed the same morning routine that we had followed the previous day by taking the tram down the hill and then the bus to the Macalister Road bus terminal—with Moke Chee purchasing breakfast treats from hawkers to share with her parents and then visiting Nanny. After visiting Nanny, we went back to Moke Chee's house, where her father entertained me while Moke Chee went down the street to visit a friend called Annie. Mr. Fong was a marvelous storyteller, giving details about growing up as a child in Penang. He grew up in the Penang household of a prosperous tin miner father, his mother, nine siblings, and his father's mother, who was a medium. As a medium, she could foretell the future and command spirits.

Lunch with Auntie Gan

Moke Chee and I had accepted Auntie Gan's invitation to lunch today, so we walked to her house. We rang the house from the front gate and waited for Henry to get the guard dogs under control before entering. Auntie Gan served popiah for lunch in her greenhouse. The approximately twenty-by-forty-foot structure was a bit humid but not uncomfortably so. As a matter of fact, it was surprisingly cool and was decorated floor to ceiling, and across the ceiling, with countless varieties of orchids, which emitted a delightfully intoxicating aroma throughout the room. Auntie belonged to the Malaya Orchid Society. After learning I was a biologist, she took pleasure in giving me a tour of her greenhouse while the ingredients for popiah were arranged on the serving table. Popiah was a meal assembled at the dining table by each person. It was a seven-inch rice paper crepe slathered with plum sauce and then filled with various parboiled thinly sliced vegetables and shrimp or other protein of choice, and then wrapped like a tortilla.

Auntie hand-wrapped extra popiah for Moke Chee to take home to her parents. Moke Chee and I walked back to her parents' house after lunch and delivered the food. Then we walked to the Macalister bus terminal, stopping along the way to buy some kuih.

When we arrived back at the cottage, Moke Chee shared credit for the kuih with me, saying, "I hope we're not too late. Jim and I stopped to pick up some kuih for tea."

By the way the aunties, Joo Ee, and the children dug into the kuih, lavishing praise and thanks on Moke Chee and me, it was obvious they appreciated the tea-time treats Moke Chee brought for them. Tea time for the aunties was not a leisurely break but just a short pause before getting back to their mahjong game. To me, mahjong seemed more an addiction than a game.

After the tea break, the aunties resumed playing mahjong and allowed Moke Chee and Joo Ee to join them at the table. They tolerated Moke Chee's and Joo Ee's slow pace of play and gleefully separated them from their coins. Moke Chee and Joo Ee willingly paid the price for the privilege of playing mahjong with the aunties. It seemed, to me, to be some sort of unwritten rite of passage.

I sat on the floor and played Monopoly with the children until my legs ached and Moke Chee rescued me. Moke Chee and I then spent the afternoon wandering the hilltop pathways, following them to their dead ends before doubling back.

Spending an afternoon at the hilltop enabled me to learn about the rhythm of life at the cottage with its own set of rules. Each day the same aunties took the early morning tram up the hill to play mahjong. They played intently into the late afternoon when they would make their way back down the hill in time for dinner with their families. Each auntie occupied their favorite seat at the mahjong table. I was amazed at their fast pace of play.

Hilltop Life at the Bungalow

The bungalow came with its own staff: a husband who was the cook and a wife who was the housekeeper. While showing us around the residence, Joo Ee took Moke Chee and me to the kitchen, where the cook was busy inspecting vegetables. The kitchen was his domain, and we just peeked in from the doorway. His wife served the meals. Moke Chee and I ate in town, so I never got to experience his cooking or her serving meals. But I was the beneficiary of her housekeeping. Specifically, she turned down my covers in the evening and picked up the clothes I left outside my bedroom door each night and had them completely laundered and ironed by the next morning.

I told Moke Chee that I'd like to do my own laundry and prepare my own bed at night. She told me I was a guest, and it would be an insult to everyone, especially the housekeeper, if I disrupted the order of how things were done.

"If you insist on changing things, discreetly tuck a five-dollar note in your laundry on the last day of your stay and leave another on the bed. No one needs to know, and the housekeeper will appreciate it."

Moke Chee went on to explain the bungalows and the rules governing their operation were established by the British to enable senior British civil servants to take a holiday away from the Malayan heat and Malayan people during the British Colonial days. For better or for worse, the British bungalows, their rules, and class distinction remained in place after Malayan independence. Moke Chee concluded by telling me: "You don't have to like everything. You change what you can and learn to live with what you can't. Remember, you're here for only two years, but the rest of us will spend the rest of our lives here."

Life in the hilltop cottage was luxurious beyond imagination. I felt guilty adjusting to it so freely. It was a treat taking a hot shower and shaving with hot water in the morning and then again in the evening, or anytime I desired.

My bedroom was princely with a king-sized bed, a thick billowy down comforter, and equally billowy down pillows. When I first saw the down comforter, I questioned why one needed a comforter in Malaya. I learned my first night up the hill that it got unpleasantly chilly once the sun went down.

I appreciated spending the afternoon getting a fuller understanding of actually living up the hill rather than just sleeping there at night. But dinner time was approaching, and Moke Chee and I joined the mahjong aunties on the tram back down the hill.

Having seen me every day, the aunties were used to me now. So much so that they spoke and acted without any inhibitions when I was present. I enjoyed my status of being a fixture in their lives and listened to their chatter as we rode the tram down the hill. Moke Chee told me they were reliving the hands they played that afternoon. She explained that playing the game and then reliving it afterward was all part of mahjong's attraction.

The aunties, Moke Chee, and I took the bus to the Macalister Road terminal and then dispersed. Moke Chee and I found Choo Choo and Henry waiting at Moke Chee's house to take us to Coast Road to have rubbish for dinner. As we got out of Henry's car on Coast Road, the mouthwatering aroma and sizzling sound of garlic and onions frying in woks over open fires washed over us. Loud Chinese music was broadcast from each hawker stall. Scores of fluorescent lights illuminated dozens of hawker stalls. We found a table away from the dizzying clamor of competing loudspeakers blasting Chinese music and the people jockeying for position at hawker stalls.

Moke Chee and Choo Choo did most of the talking. Occasionally, I added to the conversation. Henry remained silent the whole time, but he smiled when one of us said something humorous, so I was pretty sure he was enjoying the evening. We spent the whole night sitting there without being pestered by waitstaff asking us to purchase more drinks or to move on. It was a laid-back, comfortable atmosphere, and I could see why it was so popular with local people.

It was time for Moke Chee and me to catch the tram up the hill. Henry drove us in his herky-jerky way to Ayer Itam.

Back to the Hilltop

Henry got us to the tram station just in time to catch the last tram up the hill. As far as I could tell, Moke Chee and I were the only passengers on the tram. The sun had set, and night was upon us as we changed trams at the midpoint station. I gave Moke Chee my hand to help her change cars. I continued holding her hand until the second tram started up the hill, then she let go of my hand. I enjoyed being alone riding with Moke Chee in the quiet privacy of the tram. There was a chill in the night air, but we walked slowly along the dark lamp-lit path to the cottage. Again we walked close together but not touching. I could feel the warmth emanating from her body. I could smell the aroma of logs burning in the fireplace as we approached the cottage door.

When we arrived at the cottage, Auntie Khoo was already in the middle of telling a story about the ghost inhabiting Penang Hill's Crag Hotel. As the days passed, I found myself looking forward to evening story time before turning in for the night. It was a time when all of us, including me, suspended reality and huddled close together around the fireplace in fear.

Lovers' Isle Beach Picnic

On Wednesday, Moke Chee and I had a picnic at the beach. As usual, we stopped by her house first to check on her parents and then went to see Nanny before walking to the Macalister Road bus terminal. We caught a bus to Lovers' Isle Beach. I asked Moke Chee how Lovers' Isle Beach came by that name. She told me that opposite the beach is a little rocky isle called Lovers' Isle. There, according to local folklore, a tragic Malayan Romeo and Juliet story unfolded when two lovers of different ethnicities committed suicide because their parents refused to grant them permission to marry. Moke Chee said it is rumored that local couples who seek privacy still wade out to the isle at low tide.

Why couples had to wade out to the isle for privacy was

beyond me because the beach was absolutely devoid of people when Moke Chee and I arrived. We settled in a shaded little sandy cove sheltered by a rock outcropping that stretched into the sea. Something that amazed me about Malayans was their seeming aversion to swimming. The beach was exquisitely beautiful but completely empty. Since it was the school holiday, I thought the beach would be swarming with children. But we had the entire beach to ourselves. Malayans were surrounded by beautiful beaches, and they seldom went to the beach. And equally amazing was how few Malayans, even how few fishermen who made their living at sea, knew how to swim. I was told that many women in Kuala Trengganu became widowed when their fishermen husbands were lost at sea.

Moke Chee was different. She enjoyed going to the seaside. She liked to walk the shoreline and search for seashells. She wasn't concerned in the least about the sun turning her complexion dark. However, like other Malayans, Moke Chee didn't know how to swim, but at least she wanted to learn.

Moke Chee started unpacking the bag she had brought from home. She laid a sarong on the sand. "This will be our beach blanket. Our things will be safe here." We were wearing our swimsuits under our clothes, so we slipped out of our street clothes and folded them in a pile on the sarong. Moke Chee dashed toward the water with me close behind. We plunged into the water and played there, in waist-high water, splashing about. I dove underwater and swam further out to sea.

Moke Chee said, "I wish I could swim."

I swam back to her and said, "I'll teach you. Let's start with learning to float."

I held my arms out just below the surface of the water and said, "Lean back. I'll hold you. I won't let you sink."

Moke Chee laid back on my arms. I turned her so that my body was shading her eyes from the sun and waited until she was confident I wouldn't let her sink under the water.

"Keep breathing normally. I'm going to drop my arms a

bit. You may drop a little further into the water, but you won't sink. You'll still feel my arms there to support you, but you will be floating on your own."

After Moke Chee mastered that, I said, "When you are ready, you can tell me to drop my arms further. They'll be there but just not touching you."

She said, "OK. Arms away."

I lowered my arms, and Moke Chee's arms started flailing. "I'm sinking. I can't do it." She grabbed hold of me and then stood up and splashed water at me and said, "That's enough for now. I'll try again after lunch."

I held Moke Chee's hand and walked back to where we left our clothes. We dried off and sat on the sarong. I watched Moke Chee comb her hair and fasten it into a ponytail with a red band before she unpacked fried rice and juicy slices of mango from a cream-colored metal tiffin carrier and poured hot Chinese tea from a green metal thermos.

She said, "What's going to happen now?"

"Happen?" I repeated.

"You were supposed to visit the Peace Corps nurses in Alor Star and Kota Bharu."

"I'll skip Alor Star. After picking up my clothes tomorrow, I'll take the afternoon flight to Kota Bharu."

"I'm sorry your holiday plans were ruined."

"Changed, not ruined. Made better, actually." I said that in a more serious tone than intended. I think Moke Chee caught the seriousness of my comment, and a disquieting silence followed. I didn't know what to say, so I joined Moke Chee's silence as we sat in the shade of the rock with the sea breeze washing over us—listening to the shrieks from the shore birds skirting the sky above and the hum of the waves churning against the rocks that surrounded our very own private cove.

It seemed like a half hour, maybe more, passed without either one of us talking. This was unusual because conversation between us was easy and free-flowing at all times. Moke

Chee seemed comfortable, not needing to talk. The thought that kept tumbling around in my mind was how unselfish she was to invest so much of her school holiday in me and how much I treasured these last several days.

Finally, I said, "I wish I could stay here, like this, forever."

"You can't. You promised to teach me to swim." With that, Moke Chee got up and raced toward the sea.

I was glad Moke Chee came up with a light-hearted comment because, in short order, I was about to come down with a case of melancholy, and there was no telling what would come tumbling out of my mouth.

I ran after her, and when we got in the water, she splashed me. I enjoyed water fights and was capable of unleashing a torrent of water on my opponent, but with Moke Chee I only splashed back soft and playful. I held out both hands. Moke Chee took my hands, and I said, "Now kick." She did, and I walked backward and said, "See, you're swimming." She smiled.

A wave caught her as she was taking a breath, and she got a mouth full of water. She grabbed me around the neck and coughed out the water and said, "That didn't go too well."

Moke Chee held onto my neck and continued kicking. I turned on my side and started swimming, towing her along with me. I could feel her upper body and her bare legs against mine. She felt so soft and smooth. Once again, I wished we were dolphins and could swim together like this forever, but this time I kept that wish to myself. She's engaged, I told myself, and you're going home in a few months. We played like that and then walked the beach searching for shells until the sun rested low on the horizon.

Moke Chee said, "We should change out of our wet clothes and into our street clothes before going back."

There were no buildings on the beach. There was a large rock, almost waist high, that would serve as a place for me to change without too much difficulty, but it wasn't nearly tall enough to provide Moke Chee with adequate privacy. Of course,

I would turn my back to her, but people passing by on the road would have a full view of her. If she trusted me, I could screen her from people on the road by standing between her and the road.

Moke Chee pulled a second sarong from her bag, stepped through it, and then stepped over to her clothes lying on the first sarong. The next thing she did both stunned me and filled me with a sense of trustworthiness. Moke Chee gathered the top of the sarong and held it just under her chin while the sarong unfurled down to her knees and then said to me, "Hold this right here."

Then I saw her swimsuit drop to the ground. I couldn't believe it. Behind the sarong, Moke Chee had absolutely nothing on. Trust—and a thin veil of cloth—were the only things that stood between her naked body and me. She trusted me not to drop the sarong or not to try to peek over it. And, of course, I didn't betray her trust.

Then Moke Chee stepped over her street clothes and bent down—with the sarong's movements indicating her arms pulling and her body wiggling—and in a minute or two, or three, Moke Chee was fully clothed. Then she handed the sarong to me and said, "Your turn."

I already had my shirt on and took the sarong. I gathered the top like she had and then held it with my teeth.

She said, "Don't you want me to hold the sarong for you?"

I replied, speaking through clenched teeth, "It's OK. I got it."

She laughed, "What's the matter? Don't you trust me?"

I tried explaining as best I could with a mouth full of sarong, "You've got things to pack," and finished dressing.

She was enjoying this too much, teasing, "Maybe, if you don't trust me, that means I can't trust you."

"I promise. I didn't try to sneak a peek at you or anything."

"I know." She paused and then added, "You're not the type."

"Are you sure?"

"A woman knows."

"Is that good or bad?

"That a woman knows?"

"No. That I'm not the type."

"That depends."

"Depends on what?"

"Did you enjoy your time at the beach with me?"

"Yes. Absolutely. Thank you. I had a wonderful time."

"Then it's a good thing; otherwise, you would never have been invited."

We took the bus back to the Macalister Road bus terminal and then walked to Irving Road. Along the way, Moke Chee asked, "Do you know how to take a bucket bath?"

"Yes."

"You don't mind it?"

"I love them."

"Good. We'll rinse the saltwater from our swimsuits and wash the saltwater from ourselves."

Showering with Oscars

Moke Chee's mother opened the front door for us when we returned. We slipped off our shoes, and Moke Chee led me through the living quarters and the kitchen to the back courtyard, where the washing, showering, and toileting facilities were located.

Moke Chee handed me a fresh towel and said, "You shower first while I rinse the swimsuits."

I entered the shower room. It was a structure constructed of vertical wood planks enclosing a three-foot-cubed concrete cistern. The wood door came up to my forehead and had a six-inch opening at the bottom. I noticed two large oscar fish swimming in the cistern. I said, "There are fishes in the water. Will they be OK?"

"Don't mind them. My father thinks they keep the cistern

clean. And they think you are there to feed them. They'll swim out of the way when you dip the bucket in the water."

Sure enough, the oscars swam out of the way when I dipped the bucket in the water. By the time I was dried and dressed, Moke Chee had the swimsuits rinsed and hanging on a clothesline to dry.

Moke Chee entered the shower room. All but her feet and ankles vanished from view. From the opening at the bottom of the door, I could see that she had the cutest adorable tiny feet, and the backs of her heels were perfectly sculpted. Moke Chee came out of the shower room, dried and dressed, and threw two more buckets of water across the pavement to chase the remaining soapsuds into the drain. After combing her hair, she said, "Let's walk to town for something to eat."

After dinner, we went to visit Nanny. She was sitting on a stone step outside the front door of her residence when we arrived. She started getting up, and Moke Chee motioned to her to remain sitting and then sat next to her. Moke Chee motioned for me to sit, and I sat on the other side of Nanny. The three of us sitting on the stoop, Moke Chee on one side of Nanny and me on the other, must have been quite a sight for the local people because we garnered stares from everyone passing by, and some even stopped to stare at us. I understood that it was not uncommon nor considered rude for Malayans to openly stare at others. I tried to shrug it off but have to admit there was something about being blatantly stared at by people with their mouths agape that crinkled my spine. I didn't like it.

I was stared at all the time in Kuala Trengganu, and I felt the stares violated my privacy. I knew some people viewed me as a celebrity. But at times, I also felt I was being viewed as some sort of oddity in a freak show. I was stared at because I appeared different and, therefore, in their minds, was different. There was no escaping staring eyes. I sympathized with rock stars who couldn't escape their fans. Being constantly watched and stared at was irritating. I longed to be anonymous.

But strangely, on this evening, sitting on that stone stoop with Moke Chee and Nanny in the cool evening air, the stares didn't bother me too much. Rather, I oddly found myself savoring every minute of it. Nanny, I was sure, in the coming days, would be a celebrity in her own right for having a European visitor keeping her company on her front stoop. Once again, I found the day passing too fast.

An Evening Walking Hand-in-Hand

It was evening, and the evening chill filled the air by the time the tram stopped with its usual thump atop Penang Hill. As before, I gave Moke Chee my hand to help her out of the tram. It was necessary earlier in the day for her to hold my hand while I was teaching her to swim. It was the natural thing to do. Nothing out of the ordinary. But now, atop Penang Hill, it was different. Yes, I offered her my hand to exit the tram, but this time I didn't release her hand, nor did she mine.

We followed the meandering lamp-lit pathway back to the cottage holding hands all along the way. Back home in the States, holding hands with a girl was no big deal, but in Malaya, Moke Chee allowing me to hold her hand was something special. Yet, it felt so comfortable and so natural, as if we had been holding hands for years rather than just the past few minutes.

That evening at the cottage, as with previous evenings, the routine was to tell ghost stories until Auntie Khoo said it was time to turn in. Since this was my last night up the hill, I folded a five-dollar note in my laundry and placed the laundry outside my bedroom door. Moke Chee and Joo Ee, clad in pajamas, knocked on my door, entered my room, and sat on the edge of the bed for more conversation. I didn't want the night to end. I wished I could grab onto it with both hands and not let go. But the night did end with me singing "Goodnight,

Ladies" as Moke Chee and Joo Ee exited my room.

They closed the door laughing and said, "Oh no, not again!"

I laid in bed, amused at how pissed I was the previous Monday when the haberdasher told me he didn't have my clothes completed as promised. Being delayed in Penang for three more days forced me to change my holiday plans to visit Regina in Alor Star and April in Kota Bharu. But nothing could have equaled those extra three days with Moke Chee in Penang. She allowed me to share in her daily life—introducing me to her parents and Nanny and friends and the things she loved to do and the places she loved to go.

That over-promising haberdasher on Penang Road turned out to be a blessing. If he knew how grateful I was, he would have charged me an extra five dollars, and I would have gladly paid double or more. The extra three days—in total, five days—were priceless.

CHAPTER 18

It was Thursday morning. I woke before sunrise and was feeling down. I showered and shaved, hoping that would wash my glumness away. It didn't. I told myself: You should feel happy and excited. This afternoon you will be with April in Kota Bharu. Her invitation to visit was something special. She's interested in you.

Visiting Kota Bharu and spending a week with April to see if something more than a casual admiration of each other developed was something I had been looking forward to for weeks, but now I didn't want to leave Penang. More accurately, I didn't want to leave Moke Chee. But after tonight, Moke Chee and I would be living miles apart, and it was unlikely I would ever see her again. That was a miserable thought that permeated into the marrow of my bones.

I packed my bag and made the bed as I had every morning, but this morning I left a five-dollar note on the pillow. Moke Chee also rose before sunrise and knocked on my door. She also seemed more somber than usual, if not sad. We heard Auntie Khoo's voice coming from the kitchen where she was talking to Cook. I went to the kitchen doorway and waited for a pause in Auntie and Cook's conversation to call out, "Excuse me, Auntie."

Auntie looked my way, and I continued in a softer voice,

"I'm leaving now. Thank you for allowing me to spend the holiday with you and your family. I will treasure it for the rest of my life, especially the ghost stories."

Auntie's response, graciousness mixed with practical advice, was typical of people from her generation, "Don't mention it. But if the tailor disappoints you again, you are welcome back for another night."

I threw my bag over my shoulder and said, "Thank you. I may have to take you up on that," and headed for the tram with Moke Chee, hoping that the tailor did disappoint and make me stay in Penang with Moke Chee longer. We didn't chat much going down the tram or on the bus ride to Macalister Road. Moke Chee's mood reflected mine. I hoped my glumness wasn't rubbing off on her.

Moke Chee did not follow her usual daily routine of checking in on her parents and visiting Nanny before doing anything else. Instead, we went straight to the tailor shop. I was worried that her somber mood and change of routine indicated that she had grown tired of me and that she was anxious to get rid of me. But as it turned out, Auntie Khoo must have had a premonition of what would happen.

Delayed in Paradise

Once again, the haberdasher came to me all apologetic, "My sincerest apology. The tailor wasn't able to complete your order, but you have my solemn promise it will be ready by tomorrow afternoon."

Moke Chee said in an angry voice: "You've broken promises twice before. Why should we believe you now?"

He replied, "The pattern is cut. All that remains is the stitching."

Moke Chee said, "Why can't that be done now while we wait?" I was sure now that she wanted to be rid of me.

The haberdasher replied, "There are orders before yours. Orders that pay full price. In fairness, they must be served first." Moke Chee said, "So that's your game." Then she turned to me, "What do you want to do? Do you want your refund back and do as Bee Har suggests and have your trousers altered by a tailor back in Kuala Trengganu?"

I instantly thought: another day with Moke Chee in Penang. Thank you, Jesus.

My mood was so buoyant I could have hugged the haberdasher. I tried to act nonchalant but figured this was no time for pretense, so I replied, "Actually, if it's OK with you, I'll pick the clothes up tomorrow."

Moke Chee said, "Your friend April is expecting you."

I replied, "John, another Peace Corps teacher, is cycling from Ipoh to Kota Bharu to visit her. She may be so impressed with his heroics that she'll forget about me. I'll write and explain what happened." When John first announced his long-distance cycling adventure from Ipoh to Kota Bharu, I was pleased that April didn't seem very impressed, but now I was hoping she would be.

Moke Chee's spirits seemed buoyant now. She smiled and said: "Then, let's make the best of it. You still owe me a swimming lesson. We'll picnic at Lone Pine Beach."

"First, I better cancel my flight reservation for this afternoon. The next flight is Sunday afternoon. Do you mind if I fly back with you?"

"Of course not. Spa Er will be waiting in his taxi to take me to Pasir Puteh. You can join me, and with luck, he'll be able to get you to the Trengganu River ferry before it stops running for the night."

Moke Chee and I walked to the Malayan Airways office on Penang Road. I canceled my reservation for the afternoon flight and tried to make a reservation for Sunday afternoon. The young woman at the reservation desk said, "I'm sorry, Sir. All the seats are booked for the Sunday flight. There are seats available on the Tuesday flight."

"Thank you. That will be too late."

Moke Chee turned to me and said. "We better go to the taxi stand and book you on a taxi to Kuala Lumpur first thing Saturday morning."

We walked to the taxi dispatch stand, and Moke Chee booked me on the first taxi leaving for Kuala Lumpur on Saturday morning. She asked that the taxi pick me up at her house, and she insisted that they reserve the front passenger seat, the most comfortable of the four passenger seats, for me.

With that taken care of, we went to a coffee shop where we had a hot cup of Malayan coffee loaded with sweetened condensed milk and a thick slice of buttered toast while waiting for the food—fried noodles with clams, which Moke Chee ordered to bring to her parents and Nanny. We stopped to see Nanny first, and instead of visiting with Moke Chee, which I know she loved to do, she shooed us along to deliver the noodle dish to Moke Chee's parents while it was still hot.

We got to Moke Chee's house, where we changed into our swimsuits. Moke Chee's mother insisted that I have a bowl of her chocolate custard pudding before leaving. After finishing the custard, Moke Chee and I went back up the hill to let Auntie Khoo know I was staying for another night. On the walk from the tram to the cottage, Moke Chee and I held hands again. This time in broad daylight. That isolated meandering blacktop pathway, where we were alone, where no one else existed, where there was no past, no future, only the present in the clear light of day, was, for us, the perfect place to walk with Moke Chee's hand in mine.

After entering the cottage, Auntie Khoo was most gracious and said, "I've been expecting you. The shops are always busy during the holidays, and they always take care of their regular customers first. We're pleased to have you extend your stay with us."

Back to the Beach

We invited Joo Ee and the little ones to join us at the beach. The little ones wanted to join us, but Joo Ee declined for everyone. I admit that I was pleased she did. I wanted to spend more time alone with Moke Chee, and I also wanted to ask her about some sites I noticed while riding the bus.

Moke Chee's father told me about a Chinese cemetery and a rambutan estate on the hillside on the way to the beach that, according to Mr. Fong, was owned by his father and that was still held in the Fong Family Trust, but neither he nor his brothers desired to develop the land. He said it was up to Moke Chee and her cousins to develop the land. He also told me about a property that his father donated to the missionaries to build St. Nicholas' Home for the blind across from the rambutan estate. Mr. Fong told me that his father died young from diabetes and that his father's mother was blind. He presumed her blindness was caused by diabetes. He also presumed that his father donated land for the missionaries to build a facility for the blind because of his grandmother's blindness.

I told Moke Chee that Malaya's home for the blind and special school for children with visual deficiencies intrigued me, and I asked her if the Sisters would allow us to visit on Friday.

Moke Chee responded, "There's no harm asking. We can stop by tomorrow. All they can say is yes or no."

The director of St. Nicholas' Home was another one of Moke Chee's St. George's classmates, and she said we could visit the school.

The bus also drove by The Green Parrot. It was attractive in the daylight but not anywhere as enchanting as it was in the evening. It was closed during the day. Now, the road was getting narrower. The bus drove past Lovers' Isle Beach, which was as desolate as the day before, and then on to Lone Pine Beach.

The bus rolled to a stop. A broad flat beach with a few

clumps of pinang trees faced the Andaman Sea. The low-slung modest looking two-story white building stood out in a grove of casuarina trees. A white sign with black letters proclaimed it the Lone Pine Hotel.

After first hearing the words "Lone Pine Beach," I felt an immediate affinity to it. I don't know—was it the way the words came off Moke Chee's lips, puckering as if kissing the air with each symbol, or was it the conjured image of a single pine tree standing tall, standing strong, by itself, in command, firmly planted on the ground? I don't know. But immediately after leaving the bus, the longing I felt in my soul eased. I felt I was where I was meant to be. I felt at home. Moke Chee and I rested at a place on the sand at the edge of the hotel's grassy realm shaded by a grove of casuarina trees. I wiggled my toes in the sand. The pure fine white powdery sand, unlike the coarse, grainy khaki-colored sand of other Malayan beaches, tickled my toes. It was a sensual feeling that I repeated with my hands as I sat on the sarong and scooped handfuls of sand—watching the fine grains slip through my fingers and then ride away on the wind.

Moke Chee and I walked the water's edge searching for shells to no avail. We had better luck at the previous night's high water mark. There we found, cradled in the tangle of seaweed, whole and unbroken shells with beautiful mahogany patterns of dots and dashes and swirls drawn by an unseen hand on creamy calcium backgrounds. Spoiled by the bounty, Moke Chee selected only eight of the most exquisite shells to add to her collection at home; of those, only two actually made it home with her. Now it was time to swim.

I held Moke Chee's hand as we dashed to the water. I held both her hands and walked backward as she kicked with her smiling face out of the water. Lone Pine Beach waves were long soft rolling waves. They posed no threat of plunging a mouth full of water down Moke Chee's throat. I continued back until my feet no longer touched the bottom.

I started treading water and said, "I'll put my arm around you, and we'll swim together. Keep kicking."

I put my right arm around Moke Chee's back just under her armpit, which made her face meet my face. We swam like that for several minutes. We practiced floating, and of course, being in the water meant we had to have a water fight. I let her get the better of me. After a couple hours, we took a tea break.

We toweled off. Moke Chee tied a sarong over her swimsuit, and I put a shirt on and let it hang out over my trunks. We walked over to a table in the hotel's grassy area. I didn't bother to wear my flip-flops and paid the price. Hidden in the grass were a host of spiky casuarina tree cones. Tiny little nuggets about the size of almond shells with tough, sharp spikes raised havoc with my feet. I brushed casuarina tree leaves, which resembled the pines of pine trees, off the table and the accompanying metal folding chairs before we sat.

The staff left us unattended until I waved a waiter over. We ordered afternoon tea, which consisted of a pot of English tea, toast, marmalade, butter, and one orange sliced into wedges. A woman and two small children—a boy and a girl about three or four years old—came out of the hotel carrying beach pails and shovels and walked to the beach. A man came out later and joined them. They were Europeans and the only people, aside from us, on the beach.

Spilling My Woes

Moke Chee and I sat and talked for hours. This time it was me doing most of the talking. It started with her asking,

"What do you plan to do after your two-year tour with the Peace Corps is over?"

I had wanted to tell Moke Chee that I was leaving the Peace Corps and going home. This was the perfect opportunity to tell her. I replied: "For me, my Peace Corps tour ended last March, and I'm returning home in August. I haven't told anyone other than the Peace Corps administration in Kuala Lumpur."

"I thought Peace Corps Volunteers served for two years."

"They do, but I don't have a job."

"I thought you were teaching at Tengku Bariah."

"It's a long story."

"I'm listening."

I didn't feel like rehashing the whole saga and was trying to figure out how to tell her that when she said, "We have until Saturday. I'll wait," and smiled.

There was something about her smile. It was kind and welcoming. That and her brown eyes. They, too, were soft and inquiring. I couldn't believe that sitting across the table from me was the most beautiful woman in the world who wanted to listen to my story—without judgment. I couldn't help but start: "The whole thing makes no sense, and I'm embarrassed by it." I started telling her my story. At one point, I stopped and told Moke Chee, "If this is boring you, just say."

Moke Chee said, "I'm still listening."

As I was telling her about my transfer to a new school in need of a new teacher, Moke Chee interrupted and asked, "Since you were already established at your school, why didn't they send the new teacher to the new school?"

"I asked them the same question."

"And?"

"The Headmaster told me that Tengku Bariah needs a science and math teacher, and the Ministry transferred me. That's it."

Moke Chee said, "The Peace Corps sanctioned that?"

"I turned to Norb and said, 'Why did you approve of this?' And he replied: 'This is the first I've learned of it.' "

Moke Chee said, "What a lame response. It sounds like your Peace Corps is run by a bunch of incompetent eunuchs."

"I don't think they ever considered what an untenable position they put me in and what a disaster it would have been if I hadn't worked things out. To make matters worse, my new Headmaster assigned me to provide the Ugama classes with supervised study periods. They still refuse to acknowledge that the whole situation may yet blow up. But come August, I will be out of there, and the Peace Corps will give me the airfare home. Thank you very much."

"What then?"

"I'll get a master's degree in biology and then apply for a research fellowship leading to a doctorate in genetics."

"If you wanted to go back to school, why didn't you leave right away?"

"I'm ashamed to face my mother and some others, but mostly her. She vehemently opposed my joining the Peace Corps. Also, now, believe it or not, I've found a way to help my students prepare for the LCE. So I've decided to stick it out to August for their sake."

Moke Chee said, "Just about every school in Malaya needs a math and science teacher. My Headmaster would give anything to have you teach science and math at my school. Assigning you to provide a supervised study period for Ugama classes is so stupid."

"I agree. But it's me; I'm the stupid one. I left medical school thinking I was going to make the world a better place by teaching needy kids science and math. I thought I would be making Malaya a stronger country by improving the lives of my students. What a pompous gullible fool I was. Now, the hardest part will be facing my mother and others who told me this would happen."

"You'd be a wonderful doctor. If that was your dream, why not go back to medical school?"

"Too many strings attached to my attending medical school. I'll find a way to become a genetics professor and do research."

"I don't know whether to cry or scold someone. I feel so angry and so helpless. I wish I could do something."

I could see Moke Chee's eyes turning red. I was afraid she would cry, so I said, "You have. I didn't realize how much I needed someone to listen to me and you listened."

"I was angry at the tailor for not having your clothes done on time. I didn't want you to have a bad opinion of Malaya. All that seems like such a small matter now."

"Truthfully, I'm glad the tailor didn't have my clothes done on time, and I'm glad you have been willing to take me around, introducing me to your family, to Nanny, and to all of your friends. You let me enter your world. That has made everything worthwhile."

"Are you intentionally trying to make me blush by flattering me?"

"No, this past week, I don't know how to put it, but I've never felt, never experienced, anything like it before, and I'll never forget the time you spent with me."

"Now you are trying to make me blush. I had a wonderful time with you too. Now shall we change the topic and decide where we'll eat tonight?"

"Do you think your father will be up for rubbish at the padang?"

"Will the sun rise in the morning? Of course he will. He loves going to the padang and enjoys your company. You're the only one who listens to his endless stories."

Moke Chee and I changed out of our swimsuits, but this time we used the ladies' and men's rooms at the hotel to change and shower. We weren't guests at the hotel, but the staff still allowed us to use their facilities and even offered us towels to dry off. We didn't need any because Moke Chee brought towels from home.

At the Padang with Mr. Fong

After reaching Moke Chee's house, Mr. Fong was eager to join us at the padang. During our meal, he asked, "Jim, do you believe in the supernatural?"

"I believe in God, but other than that, I don't believe in anything that cannot be scientifically verified. As a science teacher, I spend a lot of effort debunking superstitions. Sometimes I'm not sure I'm doing the right thing. In Kuala Trengganu, when an unmarried woman gets pregnant, she will blame the 'Oily Man' or say she slept wearing a sarong previously worn by her father or brother. I, of course, explain how that is scientifically impossible. In doing so, I may be ruining a local woman's reputation. So, I wonder if I'm doing the right thing."

"Don't you think they know? It's a folklore that serves its purpose. You can't impose your views on them. The best you can do is introduce them to the merit of fact-based conclusions. Isn't the goal of education to provide students with the tools to think for themselves and to draw their own conclusions?"

"You should be a professor."

"I thought of becoming a teacher for a brief period in my youth. The Lasallian Brothers at St. Xavier Secondary School encouraged me, but my father passed, and my father's younger brother confiscated all of my father's property and wealth. I had responsibilities to support my mother, who now was a penniless widow without standing in the Chinese community. She lost everything except the house she was living in. I was offered an accountant position tracking tin production by the British Government in Kuala Lumpur. At that time, Kuala Lumpur was a muddy place plagued by malaria. My living conditions were worse than Georgetown. I moved back to care for my mother and became the shopkeeper for Anglo Thai, the company that bought out my father's import business."

As always, while talking, the time passed too quickly. Moke Chee and I walked her father back to her house. In the pitch blackness of crossing the padang at night, Mr. Fong again held my arm to steady himself walking over the rough turf. The turf appeared relatively smooth in full daylight, but once the sun set, in the absolute blackness of night, I could imagine polo pony hooves gnashing the turf in the heat of competition.

And now we had to negotiate that tattered turf in the blackness of night.

When we got to the house, Moke Chee asked, "Pa, is it alright if Jim stays here tomorrow night? He has to catch an early taxi to Kuala Lumpur on Saturday morning."

Mr. Fong said, "Of course," and turned to me and said, "Our accommodations are modest, but you are welcome to them."

I said, "Thank you, Sir."

First Kiss

It was dark—a time when street hooligans grew brave—so Moke Chee hailed a trishaw to take us to the Macalister Road bus terminal, and we then took the Ayer Itam bus to the tram. This would be our last night up the hill and our last tram ride. Riding the quaint green cars up Penang Hill was dreamlike in and of itself, but riding alongside Moke Chee made the dream complete. The only drawback, from my perspective, was this was our last trip up the hill, and the dream was coming to an end.

We exited the car. The night was clear, free of clouds, the clearest of all the nights. Sparkling stars blanketed the inky black sky above. They seemed close enough to reach out and grab. Moke Chee and I held hands, walking at a pace barely beyond still, and if we were talking, the conversation wasn't registering. There was a bend in the path that, in my mind, was our bend, Moke Chee's and mine, secluded but offering the best view of Georgetown's tiny twinkling technicolored lights below. We paused there as we had nights before. And like nights before, I didn't want this night, this moment, to end.

I desperately wanted to hold on to the magic of the night and delay going back to the cottage. It was a lovely cottage. Lovelier than I had ever stayed in before and lovelier than any home I was likely to stay in again. But it was a cottage filled with people, and I would have to share Moke Chee with those people. I wanted her alone all to myself on this last night until forever.

I started pointing out the constellations to Moke Chee. My favorite, Orion, was relatively easy to see. Moke Chee loved reading myths and legends and told me about the Greek myth of Orion, the son of a poor shepherd called Hyrieus, having designs on the seven daughters of the Titan god Atlas. Moke Chee asked me to point out Pleiades, the seven sisters turned into stars by Zeus to protect them from Orion. I was enlightened and pleased with Moke Chee's telling of the Greek legends associated with the constellations—pleased because it stalled our return to the cottage.

I knew the constellation but not the myths associated with them. So I told Moke Chee that I didn't know Orion was such a rough figure in mythology, but he was my favorite because he was so easy to find in the sky. In the States, when helping to point out the constellations to new stargazers, I had the benefit of using a flashlight's beam to direct the viewer, but here I didn't have a flashlight, so I put my left arm around Moke Chee's back and put my head next to her head and pointed at the Pleiades with my right arm. I glanced over at Moke Chee to make sure she was looking in the right direction.

Moke Chee had such an earnest look on her face as she struggled to find the Seven Sisters frozen in the sky. I looked at the profile of her lips. They looked as puffy and temptingly kissable as the first time I saw her from the bus at the Teacher's Union picnic in Besut. I couldn't help it. I didn't even think, but intuitively I knew I shouldn't. In America, a kiss on the second date is no big thing. Girls kissed all sorts of boys and moved on to another and likewise kissed the new boys. But in Malaya, a kiss was more than just a kiss, and I knew it. But my heart—which had admirably been held in check by my mind until now—had the better of me. And there—in that secluded bend along the quiet blacktop footpath, suspended between the star-strewn inky-blue sky above and the twinkling technicolored lights dancing in distant Georgetown below—we had our first kiss. I leaned over and gave her just a brief and admittedly clumsy peck. I wasn't thinking. She could have slapped my face or walked off in disgust—or worse—laughed at me. I wasn't thinking. I just gave in to impulse and kissed her and was absolutely thrilled she kissed me back. There was no long, passionate follow-up kiss. None was needed. It was just a brief and admittedly clumsy peck, but enough to ignite a lifelong courtship. Moke Chee turned and buried her face in my chest while I wrapped both arms around her and held her tight. And in that instant, with the two of us alone atop Penang Hill, I felt that my life was complete.

I held Moke Chee like that, both arms wrapped around her waist and her arms around my neck. I pulled her in tight against me. She was soft and warm. I could feel her chest surge taking in the night air, and I synchronized my breathing with hers. Holding her in the still cool hilltop air, her head buried in my chest and my cheek against her head, I wondered where this romance would lead and wondered if she wondered, too. And I worried.

I felt Moke Chee's arms loosen around my neck, and I loosened my arms around her waist, but only enough for her to look up at me. Her brown almond eyes were soft and warm and loving, and we kissed again, but this time it was a long hold-your-breath kiss.

We then turned to return to the cottage, walking slower than slow. I don't recall whether we talked or not or whether my feet touched the pavement of that meandering path. I felt like we had floated back toward the cottage, each grasping at air, trying to hold on to that moment forever as time—like so many grains of sand—slipped through our fingers and was carried away in the wind.

We were late getting back to the cottage. Auntie wasn't wearing her usual welcoming smile when she said, "I thought you decided not to return tonight. I'm afraid you missed storytelling tonight. It is time to go to bed."

Moke Chee and I both said we were sorry for being late, and Moke Chee said, "Jim was pointing out the constellations to me."

With that explanation, Auntie smiled, and Joo Ee said, "And do you both have stars in your eyes?"

Moke Chee and Joo Ee again knocked at my bedroom door and sat at the edge of the bed for more conversation as they had every night. This was a bedtime ritual that I would miss when I was back in Kuala Trengganu. Joo Ee, like the previous nights, wanted to know every detail of every minute of our day. I let Moke Chee do the talking, and she related every detail except the kiss. I was embarrassed by my first clumsy attempt to kiss Moke Chee and was glad she didn't mention it. I found sleep difficult, wondering and worrying what the next day and the days after would bring.

CHAPTER 19

Morning came. Moke Chee was already up, as well as Joo Ee and Auntie. Again, I thanked Auntie and Joo Ee. Moke Chee also had her bag, which I picked up and then slung my bag over my shoulder. We exited the cottage.

Joo Ee called out after Moke Chee as we approached the end of the cottage's stone walk, "I'll fetch you to the airport Sunday."

Moke Chee and I turned around. Joo Ee was standing on the front porch waving, and we waved back. Moke Chee replied, "I'll be waiting."

I said to Moke Chee, taking in the magnificence of the stone bungalow on its expansive manicured lawn bounded by the beautiful landscape, "Can you imagine people actually living like this?"

Moke Chee said, "It must get boring."

I didn't know how to respond at first, and then we both burst into laughter. I took Moke Chee's hand in mine, and we held hands until we reached the secluded bend in the path that was our bend. The bend where there was a clear view of Georgetown below, the bend where we had our first kiss. I put the bags down. We didn't bother to view Georgetown below. I leaned over and put my arms around Moke Chee's waist. She reached up and put her arms around my neck, and we kissed again. How long? I don't know. While kissing the One-Meant-to-Be, time stands still, and the rest of the world moves on. We missed the early tram. That early in the morning, no one else was at the hilltop station. We had it all to ourselves and sat on a green park bench holding hands until the next tram arrived.

We exchanged greetings with the mahjong aunties as we boarded the tram. We were the only passengers until we switched trams at the midpoint station, where we were joined by farmers taking produce to the market and day laborers heading to jobs in the city.

Holding Moke Chee's hand dulled the sadness that I felt creeping over me as the tram slowly lowered us down the hill for the last time. Yesterday, I felt misery oozing from every pore, thinking that would be my last downhill tram with Moke Chee. Now, I was miserable thinking this would be the last time I would see her.

After our first kiss last night and then again this morning, I should have felt jubilant, but I felt conflicted and confused and worried. My plan was to return home in three months' time, but I wanted to see more of Moke Chee. I didn't want to leave her, not tomorrow, not in three months, not ever. She obviously had feelings for me, and I was worried for her. It was one thing for me to push all my fears and reservations aside and live for the moment and deal with tomorrow when tomorrow comes and not worry about the future when I had no obligations. But for Moke Chee, it was a different matter. Her future entailed taking care of three elderly people who couldn't care for themselves—and a likely marriage to a man studying engineering in Australia. All that was incompatible with a casual flirtation with me. But we kissed last night and again this morning, which, by Malayan norms, meant that our relationship had moved beyond a casual flirtation.

We reached the Macalister Road bus exchange, and Moke Chee purchased her father's favorite bolsambor from a hawker stand. The ever-present cluster of Irving Road kids shouted at us, "Is he your boyfriend?" as we walked to Moke Chee's house. Her mother opened the front door for us and insisted we have tea before settling in. Mrs. Fong again served me her special chocolate custard. Various street hawkers pushed their carts down the street, shouting out their wares. Moke Chee ordered barbecue chee cheong fun for us.

Moke Chee's Memento-filled Room

After eating, Moke Chee took me upstairs to my room and said, "This is your room for tonight. I hope you'll find it comfortable."

I looked around the room, taking in its decorations and furnishings, and said, "This is beautiful, but it looks like it is your room. Where will you sleep?"

"I'll be fine. There's a mat in Nanny's old room."

"Let me sleep there."

"No, I'll be fine."

"I can't let you give up your room. It's ungentlemanly. If there's such a word."

"No. Nanny is very proper. She wouldn't approve."

"I don't want to cross Nanny. Your room is beautiful. Did you do the decorating by yourself?"

"Yes, I collected the hats and fans from Kelantan."

Moke Chee's room was about seven feet wide and ten feet long. Two walls were plastered over the brick outer walls of the house. Those walls were painted powder blue. The narrower wall had a window that faced east and overlooked the kitchen and wash area while framing the view of a coconut tree in the distance. The other two walls were made of vertical plank boards. Moke Chee painted the narrow wall red and the other wall yellow. Straw hats of various sizes, colors, and patterns decorated the narrow wall. Straw fans decorating the long wall, while of similar size, had weave patterns and color combinations unique to each one.

There was also a dressing table with a lamp and a mirror and a cane back chair. Moke Chee stored her treasures in her dresser. She sat on the bed, and I sat on the chair. She showed me the scrapbooks she made as a child. She shared one book filled with photos of Hollywood stars clipped from magazines. Another book contained cutouts of women's fashions. They portrayed women in elaborate evening gowns and less ornate party dresses. Still another book contained Moke Chee's sketches of evening and party dresses. She even had a sketch of the sack dress she wore. She said that the sack dress is an ideal dress for Malaya's climate because the simple loose-fitting lines made it a cool dress that could be worn daily.

Moke Chee had a box filled with mementos from her trips to Europe as a student. They were mostly postcards and a few pins. She had some college photos of her bundled up in a winter coat. She said, "I put on a lot of weight eating English potatoes and cabbage. We had a cook from Poland using English ingredients to cook Malayan food. It was awful, but I was always hungry and ate a lot of potatoes and bread and butter. My face had broken out something awful. My housemates called me 'cactus face.' "

Moke Chee shared other college experiences: "On school holidays, most of the students traveled through Europe. I had limited funds and hitchhiked. We were given a ride by a distinguished older man who warned us not to hitchhike because it was dangerous. Once, we were chased by a bunch of hooligans in Ireland. But most of the time, we were treated well."

I had never been to Europe and enjoyed learning about her experiences. She continued: "My college was in a working-class area where people were less worldly, and once on a bus, Joo Ee and I were mistaken for Japanese by an English man who had fought in the Pacific and treated us rudely until we told him we were from Malaya. Then there was another bus incident when an English woman told us to go back to where we came from. But not everyone we met was bigoted. Some Europeans took us into their homes and understood how difficult it was for us to be so far away from home and our families. It's them, their kindness, I try to remember. I wish I could erase the hurtful incidents from my memory, but they're there, and they pop up now and again when I encounter a white person."

"Is that what you thought when you first met me?"

"I met Peace Corps people before you and was not favorably impressed. And, like I told you on the boat, you looked ridiculous wearing a sweatshirt with Greek lettering on it in Malaya, and your beard and that ridiculous pipe. And you were so quiet, not talking to anyone but Teh Eng. I thought you were the most stuck-up, ugliest, conceited man I had ever seen."

"And now?"

"You shaved and got rid of that pipe."

"Thanks."

"Let me show you this. I haven't looked at it in years." Moke Chee had a shoebox full of mementos, spoons and pins and postcards memorializing various events of the British Royal Family. As the shopkeeper for Anglo Thai Imports, Moke Chee's father had several British friends. He could be considered an Anglophile, so it was natural for him to bring back souvenirs and samples carried by his shop. Moke Chee also had a collection of French perfumes, and she had access to Western canned foods, all carried by her father's import-export company. One of her favorite Western foods was canned Spam, which her mother fried for breakfast.

Moke Chee kept her collection of seashells in a cardboard shoe box and arranged a few on a plate for display. She told me that as a child, every so often, she rearranged and replaced the shells with new ones from the box as a way of entertaining herself. I enjoyed the escorted trip Moke Chee gave me through her childhood and college days, and then she said, "It's time we go for lunch and pick up your clothes. If they aren't ready today, you should insist on getting your refund back. This stalling tactic has gotten beyond ridiculous."

We stopped at Nanny's house to invite her to join us. She was busy and unable to join us for lunch, so we went to a coffee shop on Penang Road and had a bowl of chicken noodle soup. I had hot coffee, and Moke Chee had her favorite iced sugarcane water.

Back to the Haberdashery

It was time to go to the haberdashery and see if my clothes were ready as promised. This time, the proprietor approached me with a big smile. "They turned out handsomely. Please try them on, and you will be very happy with the fit and the look."

I tried one pair on and came out for Moke Chee's approval. I said, "What do you think?"

"They look good, but how do they fit? Are they comfortable?"

I said yes. But even if they didn't fit, I'd say yes after Moke Chee said they looked good. That was more than enough for me.

I tried the other two pairs, and Moke Chee approved, so all was good as far as my new trousers. Then Moke Chee said, "What about the coat? Let him try that on."

The proprietor said, "You see the quality of the workmanship. Rather than rush and do poor work, it was worth the wait. You will be very happy with your coat, but I'm afraid it will not be ready until tomorrow afternoon. I can assure you that it will be of the same high quality as your trousers."

I said, "But I won't be here tomorrow afternoon. I'm leaving in the morning. Is there any way you can have it ready tonight?"

He said, "I'm so sorry, Sir. If it were possible. It would be of such poor quality that I wouldn't let it out of my shop. Tomorrow afternoon is the earliest."

I said, "I don't know what to do."

He said, "We can hold it for you, for your next visit to Penang."

I said, "That won't work."

Then Moke Chee said, "I'll pick it up for you and carry it in my luggage. I may have to rub a little of my face powder on the shoulder, so if the customs officials ask me about the coat, I can say that I'm carrying it in for my husband, and I'll bring it to Kuala Trengganu next Friday. I can stay with my cousin Peggy. Is that OK with you?"

I was beside myself. I tried to act cool. I could have kissed the proprietor. I told Moke Chee, "I don't want to put you through so much trouble, but I would appreciate that very much."

Then I reached out my hand to the proprietor and said, "I appreciate all you have done for me."

He replied, "It's my pleasure entirely."

They both asked me if I wanted my old baggy trousers. My duffle bag was packed full. I wore a pair of the new trousers and left the old ones at the haberdashery. I was no longer "Mr. Baggy Pants" and was a new man. I said, "Please donate them to someone in need."

We went back to Moke Chee's house, and I packed my bag and set it aside for my trip tomorrow. Then we went across the back lane to Grandmother's house to fetch The Barbarians to go to the creameries for ice cream. Grandmother was her usual grumpy self and said to Moke Chee something to the effect of: "You're still with that 'red-faced monkey.' "

I knew enough Hokkien to understand what she said, but I smiled, bowed slightly, and said, "Good afternoon, Grandmother," in Mandarin. The little Barbarians laughed at that. Again only Hock Tee was allowed to go with us. He held Moke Chee's hand and my hand as we were off to the creameries on Penang Road. He danced and skipped and sometimes swung from our hands. He was a joy, and I fantasized about him being my son with Moke Chee.

After the creameries, we brought Hock Tee back to Grandmother's house and then walked about six blocks to Moke Chee's paternal sixth uncle's house. Moke Chee wanted to ask her cousin Peggy if she could stay with her when she brought my coat to Kuala Trengganu next weekend.

Visit to Sixth Uncle

Moke Chee introduced me to Sixth Uncle; Peggy; Peggy's elder sister Leng Chee, who the family called Ah Lian; and her fiancé, Chang What, who was quiet and reserved. Then there was their brother Ah Chai, who talked to me nonstop even while Sixth Uncle was talking to me. Sixth Uncle's second wife and their two young children were also in the house but stayed in the background. All ten of us were clustered together in Sixth Uncle's fifteen-by-twenty-foot sitting room, which was kept surprisingly cool by a ceiling fan with four long broad blades rotating slowly overhead.

Sixth Uncle, after making Ah Chai give up his seat, said, "Jim, sit here next to me. I heard about you being Moke Chee's guest, and I want to know what kind of man she has been spending time with."

I sat in the cane chair next to Sixth Uncle. I would never have guessed that he was the brother of Moke Chee's father, who was refined in the way that he dressed, spoke, and carried himself. Moke Chee's father looked more elegant. Her father was tall, as tall as me, and slender with fine facial features accentuated by a thin aquiline nose. His looks and the way he carried himself, and his British accent caused numerous people to mistake him for an Englishman. Not so, Sixth Uncle.

Sixth Uncle was shorter with a thick and broad muscular body. His face was broad and flat with thick features. He had a booming voice. His gregariousness bordered on obnoxiousness. I found him coarse and blunt and unpleasant. He said to me, "Are you one of those European men who sweeps our local girls off their feet for a brief fling and then leaves them crying or worse, and then goes home?"

Never mind that when Sixth Uncle's wife died, he fathered four children with their teenage girl servant, who was not much older than Ah Lian at the time. I was stunned by his question but didn't want to let on that I was.

While talking to Sixth Uncle, I also was observing and trying to listen in to Moke Chee asking Peggy if she could stay with her when she came to Kuala Trengganu the following Friday. Forget my suit coat. Seeing Moke Chee again hinged on Peggy's answer. I could tell by Peggy's facial expression and her pause in responding to Moke Chee's request that she was trying to find a face-saving way to decline.

Sixth Uncle apparently was observing his daughter and Moke Chee and came to the same conclusion. He bellowed so loud that he made me jump, "Of course you can. You're family. Isn't she Tim Chee?" Sixth Uncle made it a point to call Peggy by her Chinese name as a reminder, I thought, that she was Chinese, not European, and of the same generation as Moke Chee and belonged to the Chinese culture, where family helps family. Way to go, Sixth Uncle, I thought. To my surprise, I was beginning to like him. He might be a bit indelicate, but his heart was in the right place.

I decided to have a little fun with him to see if he caught it, so I said, "If I am the kind of European man who plays the fool with your niece and abandons her, I will submit to your flogging since Moke Chee's father is too much of a gentleman to do so."

Sixth Uncle burst out laughing and slapped my leg hard. He said, "By God, I like you, Mr. Jim." The others in the room, except for Peggy, joined in the laughter. Peggy left the room wearing a sourpuss face, but not before Sixth Uncle forced her to accept Moke Chee's request. Peggy's jealousy of Moke Chee was palpable. Her rudeness made my blood boil. Moke Chee ignored it.

I hoped Sixth Uncle found me as good an audience as I

found him a fascinating storyteller and a fountain of information. He was the owner-operator of a ship tender. He supplied merchant ships and an occasional war vessel with supplies. He had to anticipate what the ships required and then compete with other tender operators to get to a ship first. The agreement among ship tenders was that the first tender to get to a ship—if they had the merchandise required by the ship—got the job. He specialized in American cigarettes, alcohol, and undergarments. I thought that was an odd combination, but he told me the cigarettes and alcohol were for the ship's consumption, but the undergarments were made in Malaya and for trade. He added that none of the items were perishable, reducing his risk of waste. He invited us to stay for dinner, but Moke Chee told him we had a previous engagement. His response was to wink at me and say, "I understand. It was not that long ago that I was young."

Chang What said, "I'm also leaving. May I offer you a ride home?"

We accepted Chang What's ride, and Ah Lian came along and sat in the back seat with Moke Chee. I thought Ah Lian was prettier and certainly more tenderhearted than her young sister. When we arrived back at Moke Chee's house, Moke Chee asked her father if he wanted to join us for rubbish at the padang. He said, "Not tonight. You go ahead without me."

Moke Chee said, "Pa, what would you like us to bring back for you?"

He replied, "Nothing; I've had enough to suffice for the night."

I enjoyed going to the padang with Mr. Fong and listening to his stories and then helping him negotiate the rough terrain of the padang in the dark. But on my last night in Penang, I was glad I would spend it alone with Moke Chee.

Over dinner, we talked about the upcoming school term. Moke Chee said she escaped her miserable living conditions in Pasir Puteh with no running water or electricity by spending weekends with Joo Ee in Kota Bharu. I told her that I thought I would be living in conditions like hers when I joined the Peace Corps and that there were three male art teachers in Kuala Trengganu. One was from Kelantan, so I asked her why one of them wasn't sent to Pasir Puteh.

Moke Chee said, "The same reason you are assigned to Ugama classes. But I've been promised a hardship transfer back to Penang at the end of the school year because I'm an only child and have to care for my elderly parents."

We settled up our bills with the various hawkers and made our way back across the padang. In the darkness, it was literally impossible to see anything more than six feet away. In other words, walking across the padang, we were alone, and it was safe for us to hold hands without eliciting the scornful gazes of others. Cloaked in the protective blanket of darkness, the world was ours alone. We could hold hands and stop and linger. We could hug. We could kiss a long breathless kiss—and we did. It was bliss.

By the time Moke Chee and I reached her home, her father and mother were waiting to start securing the house for the night.

Mr. Fong said, "If you need to use the toilet out back, you had better do so before I lock up."

I used the toilet while Mr. Fong set up an ingenious alarm system of empty tin cans hanging from the lintels of each door.

Book of Fate

With the house secured, it was time for the parents to turn in, but for Moke Chee and me, it was still early. Moke Chee went to her father's library and came back with an ancient-looking book with a well-worn red cover that appeared to have been devoured by bookworms, both invertebrate and human, over the years. She sat next to me on the floor. Most of the title's gold lettering had worn away, but it was still legible. Moke Chee said, "As children, my friends and my cousins and I played using *Napoleon's Book of Fate* to tell our fortunes."

Moke Chee handed the book to me and said, "Search through it and find a question you want answered, or if you can't find one, think up a question you want answered and let me know when you have a question."

I thumbed through the book. It was so ancient that the pages had come loose from their binding. I had to be careful not to let the pages fall out.

I said, "I have two questions."

"Are they from the book?"

"They're my own questions."

"Do they require sentences or yes-no responses?"

"Yes-no."

"Then, for the first question, write a single line of circles, as many as you like."

I bent over, placed a piece of paper on the floor, and drew a line of small circles across the page. When I finished, Moke Chee asked, "What is your question?"

"Will my school have an Ustaz when I get back?"

Moke Chee began counting the number of circles. She counted twice to make sure she had the correct number of circles and then turned to a matrix in the book and said, "I'm sorry. No is the answer."

I replied, "What does a book know?"

"OK, write another line of circles. Do it at random while thinking of the question. Maybe I didn't tell you that the first time."

Again, I did as instructed and handed Moke Chee the sheet of paper with a line of random little circles that would tell my fate. She asked, "What is your question?"

I said, "I'd like to keep that to myself if that's OK."

Moke Chee said, "Ah, a secret question. That makes it all that much more mysterious." Then she proceeded to count and recount and then counted once more for good measure. She once again turned to the well-worn, red-covered book. I didn't like the sad expression on her face. She said, "I'm afraid it's no again."

I had hoped, for Moke Chee's sake, that the answer would be "yes," even though that answer would make me feel sad. Maybe I shouldn't have had the compound question: Will Moke Chee and I go our separate ways tomorrow? Will her plan to marry her engineer boyfriend and take care of her parents and Nanny happen?

I said to myself: Well, it's only a book. As a schoolboy, the nuns at St. Celestine school taught me that "love is the wishing of the good for the other." I wanted to wish the best for Moke Chee, but I was no longer a young schoolboy. I found that love had a romantic side, and for me, romantic love had a selfish side that conflicted with the love taught to me by the nuns over the years. The competitive, selfish side of romantic love was consuming me.

Moke Chee said, "Now it's my turn," and started writing down two lines of circles.

I said, "Aren't you going to look in the book for a question?"

"No, I know the question, and I know what the answer will be. It's always the same. You count the number of circles on each line and write them down."

I did and came up with the numbers seventeen and twenty-three. Moke Chee said, "Those numbers correspond to letters L and W, and the answer from the matrix will direct us to a line on a page that reads 'a stranger from abroad.' "

Sure enough, the matrix directed us to a specific line on a specific page that read "a stranger from abroad."

"OK, what's the trick?"

"There's no trick. I'll do it again."

Moke Chee again wrote out a series of numbers. This time only six on the top line and fifteen on the second line, and again just as she predicted, the corresponding answer was "a stranger from abroad." Moke Chee paused. I didn't know if she expected me to respond, and if she did, I didn't know what to say. She seemed to be weighing her next words, which was unusual for her. She was a spontaneous person.

Then she said, "When I ask, 'who will I marry,' the answer is always 'a stranger from abroad.' But you don't believe in such things. Do you?"

I said, "I'm from abroad, and no one is stranger than me."

Moke Chee slapped my shoulder playfully and said, "You're making fun of me now."

She continued, "When I was a child, my cousins teased me, and my girlfriends envied me because they thought marrying a stranger from abroad was so romantic. As a child, I also thought it romantic, but it's frightening, too. Match-made marriages can be frightening. Which do you favor, match-made marriages or love marriages?"

"Definitely love marriages. If we had match-made marriages, my mother would have married me off right out of high school."

"What is it you're looking for in a wife? That is, if you want to marry."

I thought that I had better be careful how I answered this, but then I answered without thinking: "Somebody who is thoughtful and kind and generous. Somebody who knows things, non-science things, that I don't know. Somebody who will be a friend and listen to me. Somebody who loves me like I love her and wants to be with me as much as I want to be with her, and who, when I'm with her, makes time fly by."

"That's an awful lot, but you said nothing about her looks. Do you want a tall or short wife? Or do you want a wife with blonde or dark hair, or blue eyes or dark eyes or what? Surely, you have some ideal woman in mind."

"Well, unfortunately, you have spoiled me. I can only hope she is half as beautiful as you, and then I will be married to the second most beautiful wife in the world. That is, if she'll have me."

"Are you teasing me again? Have you found her yet?"

"Yes."

"That's the saddest yes that I ever heard. Why so sad?"

"She's unattainable."

"I thought Americans never said never."

"Only in movies."

"We had better say good night. You have a long journey ahead of you tomorrow. You better get some sleep."

I leaned over and kissed Moke Chee good night. It was again just a short peck, and again it was significant. It was our first kiss in her parents' house and in her bedroom—the room that she slept in and kept her treasures in since childhood. Then she said, "I'll be right back," and left the room.

She came right back carrying a yellow porcelain pot. She said, "This is a chamber pot. If you need to go to the toilet, go in this and leave it outside your door, and I will clean it in the morning."

I stood up and hugged her, and whispered, "That's the most romantic thing that has ever been said to me."

We kissed again, and Moke Chee said, "You pathetic thing. You must have lived an awfully unromantic life."

"Now it's you who's teasing me."

"Would I be that errant? Don't answer that. Your taxi will be here early tomorrow, so you had better sleep now, and that's not teasing."

One more kiss and we said good night.

The moon was up and shining through the bedroom window as I lay down in Moke Chee's bed, surrounded by her treasures. I loved the warm feeling that filled my heart. I had to admit that I also was hoping I wouldn't need to use the chamber pot that night. I didn't want to wrestle Moke Chee over the cleaning of it. Of course, I'd clean it myself, but Moke Chee offering to clean it for me when I was perfectly capable of cleaning it myself was so typically thoughtful of her.

CHAPTER 20

The early morning light woke the entire household. It was Saturday. My day of departure. What was it—just a week ago when I had left a message for Miss Fong with her mother. And now, just seven days later, I'm waking up in her room. The week, each day and night, no matter how hard I tried to hold on to each one, flew by. We spent every waking minute of those seven days together. In those days, Moke Chee so filled my life that I couldn't imagine a time when she wasn't in my life. Until now, I didn't realize how empty my life was and how lonely I felt before meeting her. I assumed that was the natural state of living and that was the way everyone felt. That had all changed. Now, for the first time after finding my lovely Miss Fong, she and I would be separated. I would be separated from not just the unattainable, physically beautiful, and exquisite Miss Fong, but also the warm, thoughtful, and loving Fong Moke Chee. I wouldn't see her again until Friday. That seemed like an unbearably long time.

I made the bed, and as I smoothed the top sheet, I thought that Moke Chee would sleep here tonight and hoped that she would think of me when she did.

While sitting on a stool waiting for my turn to shower, Mrs. Fong brought out a small aluminum bowl of hot water and placed it in front of Mr. Fong's shaving mirror—motioning me to shave. That was so thoughtful and sweet of her. She made me feel very welcome and cared for. After I showered and dressed, Mrs. Fong said, "Eat breakfast." She set out a fried egg, a fried slice of Spam, and toast for me on the kitchen table. Moke Chee was seated at the table. Mr. Fong had already eaten and was in the sitting room reading the paper. Mrs. Fong stood over Moke Chee and me while we ate, smiling an admiring smile.

The taxi arrived. Moke Chee and her father and mother stood at the front door to see me off. The driver, a Chinese man perhaps a few years older than me, addressed Moke Chee's father and mother: "Good morning, Uncle. Good morning, Auntie." I was his first passenger. The driver put my bag in the boot while I climbed into the front passenger seat. Moke Chee and I couldn't kiss goodbye or give each other a hug or even hold hands. Not in public. Not yet. But we did exchange smiles. I felt the familiar glum feeling sweeping over me again, but I smiled, forcing myself to think about seeing Moke Chee again in Kuala Trengganu in six days.

The driver started pulling away. I leaned my head out the window to hold on to Moke Chee as long as possible. She held me with her eyes, and I her, while the ever-present little Irving Road street urchins waved at the passing taxi and shouted, "Bye!" I felt like I belonged. I waved back.

First Separation

The taxi picked up three more passengers waiting at the taxi stand near the ferry dock, including an elderly couple and a teenager. We were the first car on the ferry, and as we exited the ferry, a customs inspector waved our taxi over. I thought perhaps that I would have to pay an import tax on my trousers. The taxi driver handed the customs inspector something and said, "Nothing to declare." It happened so quickly and was so well choreographed that I would not have noticed had I not been sitting next to the driver. The customs inspector waved us through without further delay.

I bent over to look out the driver's side window to watch Penang Hill disappear from view. My heart sank. I didn't want to leave Penang, or more precisely, Moke Chee, her parents, Nanny, and grumpy Grandmother. Nor did I want to leave Moke Chee's warm and wonderful home and the ritual of securing the house at night and setting up the ingenious tin can burglar alarm system. I was already missing Moke Chee. Kuala Trengganu had nothing for me.

We arrived at the taxi stand in Kuala Lumpur in time for me to catch a taxi to Kuala Trengganu. It was a flat-out race now to Kuala Trengganu, stopping only to wait at the Kelantan, Kemaman, Dugong, and Merang River ferry crossings, where we could get out and stretch our legs. The ferry crossings slowed our progress and reintroduced the slowed-down pace of Kuala Trengganu life. Time was moving forward, and the life I lived in Penang was miles behind me. By returning to Kuala Trengganu, instead of moving forward, I felt like I was traveling backward to a place and time where I didn't belong and didn't want to be. The reality of my Peace Corps assignment in Kuala Trengganu was nearing.

It was still light out when I arrived at the house, where Boon and Teh Eng were standing outside. "Welcome back," said Teh Eng. "Are you ready for the new term?"

I replied, "I'll try my hardest," and then asked Boon, "What will I teach?"

Boon simply replied, "Jim, I'm sorry to tell you there are no changes."

I said, "Then I'll carry on as before." After Boon left, Teh Eng and I went to our favorite, "The Green Door Restaurant." I told him about getting stuck in Penang because my pants weren't ready on time and that Moke Chee invited me to stay up Penang Hill with friends for the week.

Teh Eng asked, "Did your friendship turn into a budding romance?"

I replied, "Moke Chee is an only child with responsibilities here. I'm afraid there's no way this ends well for her."

Teh Eng asked, "Have you had this discussion with Moke Chee?"

I said, "No, not really. It's an internal battle I've been waging with myself."

He said, "Isn't that being rather selfish? Isn't that something you should be discussing with Moke Chee? You might tell her when she comes down on Friday."

I was stunned and asked, "How do you know Moke Chee is coming here on Friday?"

Teh Eng laughed and spoke in a voice an octave higher when he was amused. "This is Malaya, and in Penang, news travels even faster," he said, and he laughed some more.

On Sunday evening, after preparing for Monday's classes and before going to sleep, I sat down to write April a letter explaining why I didn't visit her the prior week but ended up writing Moke Chee a letter instead. I thanked her for the time she spent with me and told her how much I enjoyed being in Penang with her. After much debate with myself, I signed it with *Sincerely, Jim*, and then worried that it was too formal and cold. I also wrote in words far too constrained: *I look forward to seeing you soon.* But what I wanted to say was, *With every breath I take, my very being thinks only of you and when we'll be together again.*

I was pleased to receive a letter back from Moke Chee on Tuesday that said she had no problem taking my coat through customs and, more importantly, that she too enjoyed my visit to Penang and looked forward to seeing me between four and five o'clock on Friday.

Tuesday's mail also brought a letter from April. It read: *Jim, You dog! You said you would visit me. I waited and worried and prayed, and not one word from you. Now I'm angry.*

Who do you think you are standing me up like that? I never want to see you again! Not ever, but if I do, you better have a darn good excuse. It was simply signed *April.*

I responded to Moke Chee's letter with another letter but didn't respond to April. Her letter showed that she assumed the worst in me. Maybe I should have written to explain, but it seemed she was trying to make me feel guilty and ask for her forgiveness. Head games and guilt trips. That was so not for me, especially after meeting Moke Chee, who was so straightforward. Anyway, I planned to attend a dance sponsored by the Kota Bharu nurses in two weeks and hoped to see April then and explain what happened.

I missed Miss Fong more than ever and couldn't wait to see her on Friday. I didn't know it then, but each Monday, for the rest of the school term, I would have that same longing for Friday to come.

Friday, at Last

I thought Friday would never come, but it finally did. I was anxious all day in class, and my mind wandered. I doubt my teaching that Friday was very effective. I was a clock-watcher that day. Time seemed to drag on. After my classes and the Boxing Club meeting finally ended, I rushed to my motorbike, got on it, and raced home. Even though Moke Chee's letter said that she wouldn't be at my house until four o'clock, I wanted to be home before that just in case she was early. So, as it happens, did Teh Eng.

Teh Eng was already home when I arrived and had the tea kettle ready. We usually took our tea at the dining room table after school, but this afternoon we took it in the sitting room. I tried to act nonchalant in front of Teh Eng. I didn't want to appear like a moonstruck schoolboy, but that's exactly how I felt. I was anxious and wanted to get up and pace the floor but forced myself to sit in a chair. Teh Eng was hard to read. His face, with a smile always at the ready, seemed unchanging, so I couldn't tell if he was as anxious as I was waiting for Moke Chee to arrive. But he did ask more than once, "What time do you expect Miss Fong?"

Suddenly Teh Eng stood up and said, "Ah, I hear something. Miss Fong has arrived."

I heard the rattling of a diesel engine in front of our house. I got up and quickly went out to the front lawn with Teh Eng close behind. Moke Chee was in the backseat of a taxi, looking out the window and smiling. I had missed her but didn't realize how much until I saw her.

I said, "You found us. You remember Teh Eng, don't you?"

Moke Chee said, "Yes, of course. The famous Free School geography master."

Teh Eng said, "Oh really? Well, welcome to Kuala Trengganu. While you grace us with your company, may I prepare a cup of tea for you?"

Moke Chee said, "Yes, please." She handed me my jacket and said, "Try it on and see how it fits."

I put the jacket on. It was perfect. I asked, "Do you approve?"

Moke Chee said, "I approve. It looks very nice on you. I had to rub a little of my powder on the shoulder so it didn't look new. I hope you don't mind."

Teh Eng said, "He doesn't mind at all. Believe me."

Moke Chee, fortunately, changed the topic and said to Teh Eng, "A number of your students were disappointed when you were transferred from the Free School. Why did you accept a transfer?"

Teh Eng responded, "That's a long story, but the simple answer was to get promoted. I was told the only way for me to become a Headmaster and earn more money was to accept a teaching assignment on the east coast. I've reached the top of the teacher pay scale and will never earn more unless I become a Headmaster. So here I am, waiting for a promotion in January."

Teh Eng and I had talked about how and why he accepted a post in Kuala Trengganu, but it didn't register with me. Now, while listening to him describe his plan to be at Sultan Sulaiman for just one year, I realized that Malayan schools were like a mahjong table—with the teacher as the mahjong tile constantly being shuffled about. How could a school establish a culture with its faculty constantly turning over? By Teh Eng's smile and banter, I could tell he enjoyed talking to Moke Chee as much as I did, and that pleased me.

Moke Chee and Teh Eng were talking about all of Teh Eng's former students that she knew and where they were and what they were doing. I was impressed with Teh Eng's memory of his former students and his genuine interest in what Moke Chee said about them.

After an appropriate amount of time, maybe twenty minutes, Teh Eng said, "If you'll excuse me, I have a few errands to run in town. Shall we meet at 'The Green Door Restaurant' in about an hour?"

I said, "Yes," and Moke Chee said, "I have to be back at the women teachers' quarters before ten."

Teh Eng said, "We'll fetch you back in plenty of time."

Moke Chee said, "That won't be necessary. I have a taxi picking me up here at nine."

Teh Eng said, "It's set then. I hope you can take Chinese food," and chuckled to himself at his humor.

Teh Eng had no errands to run in town. He knew Moke Chee and I needed time alone. We walked with him to the front lawn, watched him ride off on his motor scooter, and returned to the house. I played a Mario Lanza tape on my tape recorder, and while listening to music, we sat and picked up the conversation that we had started in Penang as if no days had separated us.

It was time to meet Teh Eng. Moke Chee got on the back of my motorbike. She wrapped both arms around my body, and I was in heaven. Teh Eng was waiting for us along with Lee Ma Chow, a fellow teacher, when we arrived. The three men split the tab, and I got Moke Chee back to my house in time for her to be at the women teacher's quarters by curfew.

The next morning, Saturday, I met with my Boy Scouts for two hours and then went to fetch Moke Chee at the teachers' quarters. Moke Chee and I went to town for tea, and then I took her sightseeing on my motorbike. We drove to the top of Bukit Besar, a high hill that overlooks all of Kuala Trengganu, and went back to town for lunch and then to my house to spend the afternoon visiting with Teh Eng.

The primary source of entertainment in Kuala Trengganu was visiting and talking about other people. So it was not unusual for Teh Eng and I to have visitors drop by when we were home. With Moke Chee visiting, we had even more visitors, many who knew Moke Chee from Penang or college. Victoria came by but was uncharacteristically quiet. We shared tea and biscuits and conversation with all of our visitors through the afternoon into the evening.

Moke Chee, Teh Eng, and I went to "The Green Door Restaurant" for dinner, and after dark, Moke Chee and I went for a walk along the beach.

We had the beach all to ourselves and found a place to sit and talk. We had been holding hands while walking the beach. Now, I put my arm around her and reached over and kissed her.

I said, "I missed you."

"I missed you too."

"I learned there's a dance in Kota Bharu next Saturday. Would you like to go with me? I'm staying at Jaron's house."

"Yes, I can stay with Joo Ee."

"Great, let's plan on meeting at Jaron's house. I'm sure he'd like to escort Joo Ee."

Moke Chee agreed. And I said, "I hate for this night to end, but I'm looking forward to seeing you next week, and that will occupy my mind all week until I see you again."

Moke Chee said, "I'm looking forward to seeing you again, too."

We kissed, and I said, "I want to see you and be with you every day, but I'm also worried about where our relationship is going. You have responsibilities here in Malaya, and I'm just passing through and will be gone in three months. I'm afraid this isn't good for you."

"I'll be the judge of what's good for me. I'm an adult. My eyes are wide open. I know what I'm getting into. Let's live for today and worry about tomorrow when tomorrow comes."

"It's late. Do you want me to take you back to the teachers' quarters?"

"Spa Er is coming to fetch me back to Tim Chee's place. He'll be taking me back to Pasir Puteh first thing Sunday morning."

Moke Chee and I walked back to my house holding hands. Spa Er's taxi was in front of the house, and Teh Eng was waiting on the front lawn.

Teh Eng greeted us, "I was wondering where you were. Moke Chee, it was a delight having you visit. Please come again."

Moke Chee replied, "Thank you. I will."

Teh Eng's invitation and Moke Chee's acceptance made my heart sing.

She got in the taxi, and I said, "See you next week."

Moke Chee waved as the taxi pulled away. Teh Eng asked, "Moke Chee will be back next week?"

I said, "We're meeting in Kota Bharu to go to a dance. Do you want to join us?"

He replied, "You go on your own. I will only be in the way."

The Dance

The following week passed as the previous week, with me looking forward to seeing Moke Chee and writing her a letter every day and receiving a letter from her every day. Receiving and sending letters each day made being apart from Moke Chee bearable. Back in those days, teachers wanting to leave the State of Trengganu had to obtain permission from their Headmaster and the Chief Education Officer of the State to do so. So I went to the Chief Education Officer's office to file a "Permission to Leave the State" form. I asked Boon and Teh Eng why teachers had to file the form, and the only reason they could give me was that it has always been that way. I learned some teachers ignored the requirement, but since the requests were always granted, I complied with the request.

My school let out early on Friday. I canceled the Boxing Club meeting and took a taxi to Pasir Puteh to pick up Moke Chee. Her school was still in session when I arrived. I heard her voice, so I waited outside her classroom. Her school was located in a kampong. I followed her along a dirt path through an area with thick brush on either side to a house she shared with another young and fairly attractive Chinese teacher. The house had a sitting room and two bedrooms. There was no furniture. Moke Chee's room had a camp cot, mosquito net, chamber pot, and kerosene lamp. It was the primitive type of housing I had expected to live in when I joined the Peace Corps. I felt guilty that I lived in such luxurious lodgings while Moke Chee had to live in such primitive conditions. Besides being primitive, the house was isolated, away from other houses. I thought that it was no place for two young women to be staying. It was dangerous.

I said to Moke Chee, "You and your housemate live here alone. What is your plan if someone tries to break in?"

Moke Chee said, "Our landlord is the Head Man in the

village and said no one will dare bother us. And I showed the men teachers this." Moke Chee pulled a long knife almost as long as a machete that she kept in her bed at night. "I told them if any of them disturb us, I will cut them to pieces. And I have this to club them with." Moke Chee showed me one of those long six-battery flashlights. "If anyone tries something, they will find I am not an easy pushover."

Moke Chee had arranged for Spa Er to drive us to Kota Bharu, where we met Joo Ee and had dinner. After that, we walked to Jaron Knight's house. He had a crush on Joo Ee and was delighted that I had arranged for him to escort her to the dance. He shared his house with Jasper Turner—the Volunteer who Moke Chee and Joo Ee told me the Malayans nicknamed the "Road Runner" for his running across the border to visit the Thai night spots and ladies. The five of us walked to the dance hall. Jasper was the odd man out, but he was intent on changing that.

Jasper said to Moke Chee, "You are the most beautiful woman I've ever seen."

Moke Chee didn't respond, so he said, "Perhaps you didn't hear me. I said that you are the most beautiful woman I've ever seen."

Moke Chee said, "I heard you," in a tone of voice that should have put him off but didn't.

There were more men than women at the dance. It was customary for one man to tap another man dancing with a woman and say, "May I cut in?" and then dance with the woman. Jasper did that when Moke Chee and I were dancing, and I gave way. I looked around for April so I could explain why I didn't make it to Kota Bharu during the May holiday, but she wasn't at the dance.

Jasper tried to hold Moke Chee close, and I saw her put up her arm to hold him off. It was obvious that she was intentionally stepping on his feet, but he continued to try to pull her in against his body. It was more a wrestling match than a dance, so I cut back in on him, and Moke Chee said, "He is a disgusting, lecherous man. Keep him away from me."

Jasper tried to cut in on two more occasions, and I told him that Moke Chee and I wanted to dance with each other and no one else. Another man, a handsome, well-dressed Malay man about my height, which was tall for Malay men, tried to cut in. This time Moke Chee said, "No, thank you. I have my partner." She later told me that the man was an official in the State government and had been after her. She was glad I was with her, so he knew she had a man friend. It made my heart sing to hear Moke Chee call me her man friend.

I slept on the floor at Jaron's house that night. Jasper didn't come home that night or the next day. I thought he might be angry with me, but Jaron assured me that Jasper likely joined some friends and went to Songkla for the girls.

The next day, Moke Chee and Joo Ee came over to Jaron's house, and the four of us talked about the dance and the people we knew. The following morning, Sunday morning, Moke Chee came by in Spa Er's taxi, and we drove back to Pasir Puteh, where Moke Chee got out, and I continued on to Kuala Trengganu.

It was then, after leaving Moke Chee in Pasir Puteh, that I knew I couldn't leave her in August and that I would remain in the Peace Corps for my full term.

The following weekend, Moke Chee came down to Kuala Trengganu, and we did much the same thing as the first weekend, except we went to the market. Moke Chee made a curry dinner Saturday night, and a few of the male teachers came over and joined us for dinner. In Malaya, there was always room for one more when it came to mealtime. And that's how the following weekends went, with a few exceptions.

It was about the fourth weekend when Moke Chee came over and I noticed her eyes were red. I asked her if something was wrong.

Moke Chee said, "Tim Chee got all the women to call me

'Christopher Columbus' and tease me by saying that 'I discovered America.' Why is it anyone's business what I do?"

Boon's View of My Relationship

That evening, Boon and Nina invited us to their house for evening tea. Boon had talked to me earlier after playing tennis about my relationship with Moke Chee. He said, "I want to talk to you as a friend. I want you to consider what your intentions are with Moke Chee. When your Peace Corps term is over, you'll be going home. Have you thought about what will happen to her? Some Chinese men are very conservative and will want nothing to do with a woman who dated a European. No matter how beautiful she is, Moke Chee will be considered damaged goods for having dated you. If she goes back with you, what will happen to her family, and how will she be accepted in America? And if you stay here, what will you do for a living? I know you haven't been happy teaching here, and even if you taught, the Ministry would not give you a permanent assignment. If you have children, what will be their future? I bring this up as your friend and as someone who has experienced the stigma of a mixed marriage. Both Nina's family and mine disowned us when we married outside our race. It was very hard on us, particularly Nina. We got married by an American Evangelical minister with no family in attendance. I don't expect you to answer these questions now, but as your friend, if you care anything for Moke Chee, I expect you to think them over and discuss them with her."

I said, "Thank you. That's something that has been bothering me."

Boon said, "Why don't the two of you come over after dinner?"

Moke Chee and I went to Boon's house after dinner. After the customary pleasantries, Boon started the conversation about his marriage to Nina and the difficulties, hurt feelings, and resentments of their marrying outside their race. He also repeated much of what he said to me earlier in the week.

Moke Chee's response was, "If a Chinaman is so conservative and insecure that he wouldn't be interested in a woman who dated a European, I wouldn't want anything to do with him anyway."

As the evening winded down, Nina said, "You will be told you are young and you will meet someone of your kind and marry them. But love, true love, is not something that is easy to find, and is it fair to marry someone you don't love just because they're of your kind? I want you to know that if you decide after all this that you want to marry, I am an Evangelical minister, and I'm willing to marry you."

I said, "Thank you. We haven't discussed marriage yet."

Moke Chee said, "Thank you. It's too soon for that. I don't want to get married without my father's blessing."

Nina said, "I understand, and you are right to obtain your father's blessing, but I am here to help if you need me."

Moke Chee and I had talked about everything except our relationship up to that point. We walked to the beach, and I told her that I loved her and wanted to be with her every minute. But I worried about her reputation and it being ruined because of me. I worried about what would happen to her when I went home. She said that she loved me and knew what she was doing. That she would return to Penang in December. "Let's enjoy today and take care of tomorrow when tomorrow comes," she said.

After Moke Chee went back to Pasir Puteh, I talked to Teh Eng about what had transpired. His counsel was similar to Moke Chee's: "The rational mind and the heart are often not in sync. Moke Chee is an adult. It is no more appropriate for you to decide what is right for her than for her to decide what is right for you. It's something only the two of you can decide for yourselves, but hopefully together."

I felt better that Moke Chee and I finally talked about our relationship and that we declared our love for each other. But I couldn't believe that because of Boon, I actually was thinking about marriage. The last time I discussed the topic of marriage was with Lolly and her overly eager mother, Irma, and I was miserable. This time, I found in Moke Chee a person who made me feel whole, complete. I had never felt this way before. I found someone who I loved fully and who loved me in return. I wanted to be with her always and forever. Our friends—hers and mine—accepted us as a couple, but there were others, for reasons I couldn't understand, who were opposed to our relationship. To me, all that mattered was how Moke Chee felt.

CHAPTER 21

My relationship with Moke Chee continued to deepen. I wrote to her every night just before going to bed. Sunday night, I started each letter recounting the things we shared during her visit to Kuala Trengganu and telling her how much I missed her and what I had planned for the week until I saw her again on Friday. On other nights, I described what I did and who I saw during each day and ended each letter with the number of days it would be before we were together again. On Fridays, I wrote a letter during lunch break and posted it on my way home, so she would have a letter waiting for her on Monday when she got back to Pasir Puteh. After Moke Chee's first visit, I signed my letters *Love, Jim*. I looked forward to getting on my motorbike and stopping by the post office on the way to school to send my love to Moke Chee first thing each morning.

Moke Chee also wrote to me every day. I received my mail at school and looked for the postman's arrival at about ten o'clock. I read Moke Chee's letters while having a mid-morning cup of tea and again at home in the afternoon. Every Monday, I received two letters: one that Moke Chee wrote on Thursday and the other that she sent me on Friday in anticipation of her visit. That way, I received a letter or saw her in person every day. In addition to the letters, I looked forward to hearing the sound of Spa Er's taxi in front of my house every Friday afternoon and seeing Moke Chee's smiling face.

I think Teh Eng looked forward to Moke Chee's visits and her home cooking on the weekends almost as much as I did. My male friends at school enjoyed Moke Chee's company when they dropped by my house, as well as Tiong Kooi and Amy when we visited their house. Even Roy Masters supported my relationship with Moke Chee by inviting us to a dinner with Peace Corps nurse Eva and a cocktail party with his British friends. But it wasn't that way at first.

Expats React to My Relationship

While walking along the beach one evening, Geoffrey Lord called out, "Wolter, come join us for a drink."

The British expatriates had invited me for a drink once before and then tried to stick me with their bar bill, so I called back, "Thank you, but no thanks."

Lord said, "Oh, come on. Be sociable. This time, it's our treat."

I joined them and ordered a local beer, and Lord started with, "We see you have a lady friend." He had a smile on his face. Dr. Holmes shifted in his chair as if he wanted to get away, and Roy Masters looked at me with sad eyes.

He went on, "She's a looker; I'll give you that. Anyone we know? Where's she from, and what does she do?"

"She has a name, Miss Fong, and is a teacher from Penang who was trained in England. I would guess you don't know her; otherwise, you wouldn't be asking."

"Sorry, old chap, we didn't mean to put you off. A young fellow like you should sow his oats but mind you don't get yourself in a situation you can't readily get out of. It's alright to have a sip of wine without buying the whole bottle. If you know what I mean."

"I do and don't like it. What I do and who I see is my business."

Masters said, "Geoffrey, this is a delicate matter, and you

should have prefaced your reason for calling Jim over. Jim, it may not sound like it, but Lord and all of us are trying to be helpful. Certainly, matters of the heart between you and Miss Fong are none of our business, but you are one of us. We care for you and don't want you to get yourself in a fix. We would be remiss not to share from our experience that marrying a local woman is a career ender. For example ..."

I interrupted: "Stop. You're going to tell me about Red McClure, the Scotsman who threw away his career with the Ministry of Education to marry a local Chinese woman."

Masters said, "Precisely. Then you've heard about him and his sorry fate. Never accepted by the European or the Chinese communities."

"Yes, Bankim bought me a beer a week before you got around to it."

Masters said: "Then that puts the matter to rest." He raised his glass and said, "To the Queen."

A few weeks later, Masters invited Moke Chee and me to join him and Eva for dinner at his house. He was most gracious to Moke Chee and engaged her in a discussion of the Impressionist movement in painting and the Romantic era in poetry. Eva and I were out of our depth in those discussions and simply listened.

At another cocktail party, Masters introduced Moke Chee to his other guests, all Europeans, and engaged her in conversation. I enjoyed these parties because they gave me a different perspective on living in Malaya. At this particular party, the discussion was whether Singapore and Malaya could come together as one country—Malaysia—and the merits of permanent residents—like themselves and possibly Peace Corps Volunteers— applying for Malaysian citizenship.

Curiously, a few weeks later, Masters telephoned me at school and said, "I'm having a small dinner party in a fortnight, and Eva suggested I invite you. Are you available?

I said, "Moke Chee is coming to visit me then. May I bring her?"

He replied, "I'm so sorry. It's a dinner for six, and you would be the sixth guest. I have a young cousin, a teacher on holiday, visiting, and Eva and I thought you and she would make excellent dinner partners."

I replied: "I'm sorry, I can't make it."

Eva's reaction to my relationship with Moke Chee was one of gracious acceptance. She was gracious to Moke Chee as she was to all people. However, she did say to me, "Remember, Jim, just because you have fun with a girl doesn't mean you have to marry her. She's having as much fun with you as you with her."

I responded: "I enjoy Moke Chee's company, and she enjoys mine, but we're not having fun with each other. But if we were, that would be between us and no one else's business."

Donna, another Peace Corps nurse, tried to fix me up with her best Malayan friend, a Chinese nurse at the hospital, who reportedly had a crush on me. Donna said, "Chua wants to go out with you. Since you're into Chinese chicks, how about I fix you up?"

I said, "Thanks, but Moke Chee's the only one for me."

Donna said, "For a man, aren't you the provincial one?" She persisted in trying to convince me to go out with Chua, and I continued to insist that I wasn't interested in other women.

Ruth, a Peace Corps nurse, met Moke Chee once and asked Moke Chee about various Malayan recipes. She didn't get caught up in my relationship with Moke Chee, other than to say: "The two of you are adults. It's hard—impossible for some—to find love. When you do, if you do, don't be bothered by what other people think."

Victoria had the most difficult time accepting Moke Chee, right from the start at the NUT picnic on Pulau Perhentian. In many ways, it was understandable. Norb had asked me to mentor her, look out for her welfare, and introduce her to the community. We should have known better, but we didn't. It was natural back then for the Malayan teachers to assume that the only American woman teacher and the only American man teacher in Kuala Trengganu would become a couple. By paying so much attention to Victoria, I saw with the benefit of hindsight how she and her housemates would have interpreted that as courtship. In 1962, I was living away from home in beautiful Kuala Trengganu, where palm trees dotted the beach, waves rolled up the shore, and lush paddy fields shimmered across the road. It was the perfect setting for romance. When I started spending weekends with Moke Chee instead of going cycling with Victoria or playing tennis or hanging out at my house with her, it had to be more than what the Malayans called a "loss of face."

CHAPTER 22

In 1962 there were few telephones. Telephones were expensive, and people didn't use or need telephones to talk to each other. Instead, they went to see each other in person or wrote letters. For example, my school compound only had two telephones, one in the Headmaster's office at school and the other at the house of Mr. Khoo, the Chief Education Officer. Telephones were intended for official business only or for emergencies. That was it.

On a Monday at about three-thirty in the afternoon, I had just returned home and was taking a shower when I heard a frantic pounding on my front door. I quickly dressed and went downstairs to the door and found Mrs. Khoo's amah there. She was panting out of breath and barely able to say, "Mr. Jim, come quick. You have an important telephone call."

Naturally, I assumed the worst and sprinted the hundred or so yards to Mr. and Mrs. Khoo's residence. Mrs. Khoo was waiting in the doorway and directed me to the telephone.

I picked up the phone, and it was Norb on the other end. He didn't even say hello or ask how I was. He spoke rapidly in an anxious-sounding whisper, "Jim, I'm so glad I got you. Listen, I'm in a pickle. I know this is short notice, but I need your help."

I was relieved. Nothing was wrong with my family in Chicago. I wondered what he had in store for me now and said, "Yes?"

Norb said, "I'm in Alor Star with Sargent Shriver and his entourage. When we arrived here this morning, there was no one at the airport to greet him, no dignitaries, no Volunteers, no one. Sarge was perturbed. He traveled halfway around the world, and not one dignitary or a single Volunteer was at the airport to greet him. That was a major oversight by my office. We'll be flying into Kuala Trengganu this time tomorrow. I need you to arrange to have some dignitaries and whatever Volunteers you can round up to be at the airport to greet him. If we have another debacle like Alor Star, Sarge is going to give me you-know-what."

Sarge Shriver was the director of the Peace Corps and the brother-in-law of President John F. Kennedy. During Peace Corps training, he came to DeKalb and met with all the Trainees. I remembered he had told us that the success or failure of the Peace Corps as an idea and a program was dependent on each of us.

I told Norb: "I'll do my best. What time will the plane touch down?"

He replied, "At four, but can you have them there earlier in case we arrive early. Jim, you have to come through for me. I'm counting on you."

I said, "Consider it done. I'd better get going. See you tomorrow at four."

Norb said, "One more thing, while you're at it. Sarge wants to meet with all the Volunteers tomorrow night for dinner and afterward for a Q and A session. I know I can count on you to take care of the arrangements. And while you're at it, there will be eight of us. Jack chartered two taxis and made reservations for us at the Resthouse under my name. Double-check to make sure the taxis will be at the airport and that the Resthouse has our reservations."

I said, "I'll take care of it."

I hung up the telephone and turned to Mrs. Khoo, who was standing at my side with a worried look on her face. She

216

asked, "Is there any problem?"

I smiled and said, "There's no problem. I'm going to Mr. Khoo's office now, but if I miss him, will you please let him know that Sargent Shriver, the Director of the Peace Corps, is coming from Washington, D.C., to visit tomorrow, and if it is possible, could he be at the airfield at three-thirty to meet Mr. Shriver?"

President Kennedy's Brother-in-Law Is Coming

Mrs. Khoo had a pencil and a pad of paper in her hand and a confused expression on her face. She said, "Who is coming?"

After a few attempts of not being able to explain who Sargent Shriver was, I said, "President Kennedy's brother-in-law is coming."

A smile swept over her face, and she said, "Ah, President Kennedy's brother-in-law. May I come, too?"

I said, "Yes, and your friends, too, if they wish." Mrs. Khoo had three lady friends who were in the sitting room, and I could see out of the corner of my eye that they were physically leaning toward me, trying to hear what we were saying. When I said President Kennedy's brother-in-law and that they could come too, they became animated and almost giggling while whispering to one another.

Mrs. Khoo said, "Thank you. Thank you. I will tell my husband, and we will be there at three-thirty."

I thanked Mrs. Khoo and her amah, ran back to my house, jumped on my motorbike, and headed to Dr. Holmes' house. He wasn't home, but Mrs. Holmes was. I went through the same process of explaining that Sargent Shriver was coming to town and asked if it would be possible for Dr. Holmes to greet him at the airfield at three-thirty? Mrs. Holmes didn't know who Sargent Shriver was, so I explained that he was

President Kennedy's brother-in-law. She also asked if she could join Dr. Holmes at the airfield. I told her yes and that she could bring her friends. She usually wore a placid expression on her face with a blank empty stare, but by the time I left, her face had brightened with a hint of a smile, and her eyes seemed to lighten with anticipation.

I then drove my motorbike to Mr. Khoo's office. He was expecting me because Mrs. Khoo had already reached him and assured me that he would be there. I asked if he and Mrs. Khoo could give Victoria a ride to the airfield. That was bold of me, but I had been looking for a way to introduce Victoria to Mrs. Khoo. I had heard Mrs. Khoo was a tennis player but couldn't play because she couldn't find another woman who played tennis in Kuala Trengganu. I said to Mr. Khoo, "I've heard Mrs. Khoo enjoys tennis. Mrs. Khoo might be interested to learn that Victoria is keen on tennis and would like to find another woman to play tennis with."

Mr. Khoo said, "It will be our pleasure to have Miss Victoria join us, and I will inform my wife of Miss Victoria's interest in playing tennis."

I was quite pleased with myself and went to the hospital to talk to the Head of Nursing, Sister Katiejah. Luckily, I found her in the nurses' quarters. She was packing to go on holiday to visit her family in Kuala Lumpur. She was a short, jolly rotund woman, and as usual, she greeted me with a smile and a hug and said, "Jimmy, how thoughtful, you came to see me off."

I said, "Sister Katiejah, of course I wish you 'selamat jalan.' But honestly, I've come to invite you to greet Sargent Shriver, our big boss visiting from Washington, D.C., and to ask if the nurses' schedules could be adjusted, so they could have dinner with him and meet with him for a discussion session after dinner. He's arriving at the airfield at about three-thirty." I didn't have to go through who Sargent Shriver was. Sister Katiejah accepted my word that he was an important person, and that was good enough for her.

Sister Katiejah said, "Yes, of course. I'm scheduled to leave for Kuala Lumpur with Sister Sing tomorrow, but I'll postpone my holiday to give him a proper greeting and thank him for sending staff nurses to Kuala Trengganu. Where are you planning to take dinner?"

I said, "I haven't planned that yet, but I'll let you know; I hope you can join us."

Sister Katiejah said, "Good. We'll give him a genuine Malayan curry dinner at the nurses' quarters. He should experience our culture while he is here. How many are in his party?"

I said, "Eight."

Sister Katiejah, "You and Victoria, and the nurses, and Dr. and Mrs. Holmes and I make fourteen. Will there be anybody else?"

I said, "Maybe Mr. and Mrs. Khoo."

Sister Katiejah said, "I'll tell Cook to plan for twenty."

I said, "Sister Katiejah, I don't know how to begin to thank you. My Peace Corps boss, Norb Patton, will want to pay for the cost of the dinner."

Sister Katiejah said, "You're in Malaya. You're our guests. I'll hear none of that talk."

Sister Katiejah was from Kuala Lumpur and, having traveled in Asia and Europe, was the most cosmopolitan person in Kuala Trengganu. She had a sharp, inquisitive mind, a ready smile, and a raucous laugh. I counted Sister Katiejah as one of my friends and said to her, "Are you and I going to argue over this?"

She replied, "My Jimmy, you know we will, and we'll both enjoy it, but I'll enjoy it more because I'm going to win."

I said, "I know, but you have to let me reciprocate."

She said, "Off with you. I've got work to do."

With that taken care of, I told the nurses and Victoria about Sarge's arrival and the dinner and meeting afterward. I told Victoria that the Khoos would drive her to the airfield and that I told Mr. Khoo that she might be a possible tennis partner for Mrs. Khoo. I was a little afraid that Victoria might not like my being so intrusive in her life, but she welcomed it, to my great relief. Next, I went to tell Boon and Bankim. They had already heard that President Kennedy's brother-in-law was coming. Finally, I checked to ensure there would be two taxis standing by for Sarge's entourage, as well as reservations for them at the Resthouse.

I swung by the taxi stand to see Rahiem, the taxi dispatcher. Rahiem assured me that two taxis would be at the airport and standing by for the rest of that day and at the Resthouse at seven the following morning.

My last stop was to see George, the Resthouse manager, to make sure they had eight rooms reserved for Norb. George said that he had set aside a wing of rooms and asked who was in the group. I tried to explain who Sargent Shriver was and how he and the others were related to me and finally said, "He's President Kennedy's brother-in-law." George usually had an expressionless face, but after hearing the news, his face lit up. I could tell the wheels were turning in his head, figuring out how he could market the room as "the room President Kennedy's Brother-in-Law stayed in."

The next day, the faculty room was abuzz with the news that President Kennedy's brother-in-law was coming to Kuala Trengganu and that I was his host. The students were so excited that they required much refocusing during class time. Some wanted to know if they could ask for his autograph. A celebrity coming to a small town like Kuala Trengganu was a huge event. The atmosphere was electric with excitement as we waited for the bell to dismiss school for the day.

As soon as I heard the dismissal bell, I walked briskly to my motorbike and went to see Rahiem to check on the taxis. Rahiem assured me that they would be at the airfield on time. I rode my motorbike to the ferry crossing and crossed the Trengganu River and then drove to the airfield. I wanted to be at the airfield before three-thirty to gather the dignitaries who would be in the receiving line to welcome Sarge. When I arrived, no one was there. The ticket office, an eight-by-eight-foot cinder block structure with a corrugated metal roof and one window, was locked. It was just a few cows and a dozen goats grazing on the airfield grass and me. I was nervous.

To my relief, people started showing up. First, the ticket office manager, dressed in a white shirt and black slacks, came with two ground crew dressed in blue shirts and blue slacks. Then some teenagers and some women with smaller children arrived. Finally, I saw Sister Katiejah's Land Rover, and she arrived with three nurses. Dr. and Mrs. Holmes arrived next. They were closely followed by Mr. and Mrs. Khoo and Victoria. Boon and Bankim arrived, and I felt that we had a receiving party in size and diversity that would be to Sarge's satisfaction. But there was more.

While I focused on gathering the reception party under the shade of a tree just inside the gateway to the field, more villagers had gathered along the fence line. I'm not good at estimating crowd size, but using the number of students in my class as a gauge, which was forty, I would say the crowd was easily four times the size of that, so there were more than one hundred and sixty people waiting at the airfield.

The plane was a DC 3. A hush came over the crowd as the sound of the engine reached us. Soon the plane dropped under the clouds and made a low pass over the airfield scattering the cows and goats. Then it climbed and banked to come back around to land. The gathered crowd started applauding when the plane made its first pass over the field, and the applause grew louder as the plane landed and rolled to a stop. The ground crew pushed the portable stairs to the plane, and Sarge stepped out. Sarge gave the crowd a broad sweeping wave. He looked as handsome and as energetic as I remembered from his visits to DeKalb during Peace Corps training.

Sarge wore a broad smile as he exchanged greetings with the Volunteers and the dignitaries and signed autographs as he made his way to the waiting taxis. I overheard him say to Norb, "This is more like it."

Norb was smiling, and his face, which looked ashen when he got off the plane, had turned back to its usual rosy pink. Norb slapped me on the back and said, "I knew I could count on you."

A police Land Rover had arrived without my noticing or knowing and escorted the parade of Sarge's two taxis, Sister Katiejah's Land Rover, the Holmes' car, Khoo's car, Bankim's car, Boon's TR3, and my motorbike to the Resthouse. The police arranged to have a ferry waiting for our crossing. People lined Kampung Cina Road waving as we raced through Kuala Trengganu to the Resthouse. It was quite a scene. I was embarrassed, but nonetheless, I waved back.

The Jellyfish Incident

I followed Sarge's entourage to the Resthouse. Along the way, all the streets were lined with clusters of children and adults, waving and shouting greetings. Sarge looked ecstatic by the time we got to the Resthouse, which was nestled among casuarina trees adjacent to the pristine beach lined with palm trees. He said, "Look at that beach. Do we have time to go for a swim? Where are the Volunteers? I want to go for a swim with the Volunteers."

Sarge said, "Jim, can you gather the rest of the volunteers?"

I said, "Sure. The hospital is right next door. I'll let the nurses know, and I'll go to the school and get Victoria."

The nurses, Victoria, and I joined Sarge and two members of Sarge's entourage in going into the water. Norb and the rest of the entourage, along with Dr. Holmes, stayed on the beach watching us frolic in the sea.

It was jellyfish season. The waters were calm, and it was

late enough for the onshore wind to blow the floating globules toward the beach. As tempting as the warm, calm water was, I avoided swimming during jellyfish season. I shared this information with Sarge and the group. Sarge asked: "What are jellyfish? Do they bite?"

I said, "They are innocent-looking gelatinous globules floating on the water, but they have long, almost invisible tentacles under the water that sting."

One of Sarge's aides suggested Sarge pose for a photograph with the Volunteers. The aide had us gather around Sarge and took several photos while directing us to various locations on the beach.

Finally, Sarge said, "What are we waiting for? Enough photos." He plunged into the water, and the rest of us followed. Sarge swam way out into the sea. Then he came back and joined us, standing in waist-high water to talk. Suddenly, he shouted, "Ouch. What was that?"

I said, "You've been stung by a jellyfish." We all got out of the water.

Sarge was holding his wrist and asked, "Is it dangerous?"

I said, "It's not life-threatening, but you'll have a swelling about the size of a golf ball on your wrist for a few days."

Fortunately, Dr. Holmes followed us to the beach. He said, "If you will, please follow me. I will give you an injection that will ameliorate the jellyfish toxin."

Sarge said, "Absolutely, yes. I'm meeting with the Ambassador in two days. I can't see him with a swollen wrist. Are there any adverse side effects I should know about?"

Dr. Holmes said, "It will reduce the swelling and itching, and it may make you a little drowsy, but after a good night's sleep, you will be good to go. Until then, it would be advisable not to make any important decisions."

I looked at poor old Norb. He had an expression on his face that said, "Of all people, why did that blasted jellyfish have to sting Sarge?" I wasn't sure whether it was the right time to tell

Norb that I had changed my plan to exit the Peace Corps early, but we were here, and nobody was around. I went up to him and said, "Norb, I've changed my mind about going home this August. Is there anything I have to do?"

He said, "Just keep doing the fine job you're doing. Have you set up dinner and a place Sarge can meet with Volunteers afterward?"

Norb added, "Jim, Volunteer Ladd is traveling with us because he has had a difficult time adjusting in Alor Star. The psychiatrist thinks it would be better for him to stay with you for the rest of the week than travel with us."

"Of course," I said.

I told Norb that Sister Katiejah was providing us with a traditional Malay curry dinner and making her sitting room available to us after dinner. I also told him that she postponed her holiday to visit family in Kuala Lumpur so she could welcome Sarge and serve dinner—and that she refused to accept any reimbursement for the dinner.

Norb said, "That's Malaysian hospitality. I'll make sure Sarge hears about it."

Once Sarge went to hospital with Dr. Holmes, the impromptu beach party broke up, and we went to our respective quarters to clean up and returned to the nurses' quarters for dinner at seven.

Sarge was back to his energetic self. He sampled every dish, including spicy-hot curry, and praised Sister Katiejah. As dinner wound down at about nine o'clock, Sister Katiejah said it was time to take her leave. Sarge got up and thanked her and extolled her Malaysian hospitality, and said: "Sister, I understand you are traveling to Kuala Lumpur to visit family tomorrow. It would give me great pleasure if you would join us on our flight to Kuala Lumpur tomorrow morning."

Sister Katiejah said, "I would be glad to accept, but I'm traveling with Sister Sing."

Sarge said, "I don't want to disrupt the taxi service economy to Kuala Lumpur, but we have plenty of room for Sister Sing."

Sister Katiejah said, "Both Sister Sing and I are bringing Kuala Trengganu's famous salt fish back for family and friends. It's quite smelly. Ordinarily, it is prohibited on commercial flights."

Sarge said, "You may bring all the salt fish your heart desires."

Sister Katiejah said, "Mr. Shriver, you are very convincing. What time do we depart?"

Sarge said, "My friends call me Sarge. Meet us at the Resthouse at seven."

The following morning, which was Wednesday, Ladd and I stopped by the Resthouse on our way to school to see Sarge and Norb off. Sarge, Sister Katiejah, Sister Sing, Norb, and Sarge's entourage were loading their baggage along with the salt fish in the two taxis. They were getting in when they realized the two taxis carried only four passengers each, and there were nine of them. I suggested that Ladd wait at the Resthouse while I took the extra passenger to the airfield on my motorbike. Sarge's party looked around at each other to see who would take me up on my offer. Finally, Norb said, "I'll ride with Jim."

Then Sarge came forward before Norb could get on the back of my motorbike and said, "Norb, let me."

Sarge swung his leg over the back of my motorbike, and we departed for the airfield.

While riding to the airfield on my motorbike, Sarge asked me if there was anything he could do for me when he got back to Washington. I flippantly told him if he happened to run into my mother back in Chicago, he could let her know that I was behaving myself, eating regularly, and wearing clean clothes. He asked about my family, and when I told him where my mother worked, I was surprised he knew the location of the Chicago Zenith plant on Austin Avenue.

Sarge thanked me for the ride and added: "Jim, that ride was fun. If Eunice doesn't object, I'm going to get my kids one of these bikes when I get home."

As a side note, I gave our conversation no further thought until an unusually long letter arrived from my mother. She wrote that she was called off the assembly line to the front office to take a long-distance call from Washington, D.C. Like any mother with a child overseas, she thought she was about to hear news no mother should ever hear. Sarge introduced himself and quickly put her mind to rest—telling her that he had visited me earlier in the week and that I was healthy, happy, doing a terrific job and had asked him to send her my love. Before saying goodbye, he thanked her for raising such a fine son. For the remainder of her life, my mother never got tired of retelling the story of Sargent Shriver telephoning her long distance from Washington, D.C.

Teachers Must Find Work

For my holiday extra duty project, I wrote to Norb that I wanted to work with blind orphans at St. Nicholas' Home in Penang over the August holiday. I received a letter back. My request to work at St. Nicholas' Home was rejected, and I was assigned to work in Ipoh at the day camp that John was setting up for the first week of the holiday. The letter didn't give a reason for rejecting my request, but I was told later that it was because the Peace Corps wanted to remain secular. Never mind that I was teaching two hundred students in my five Ugama classes. It didn't make sense that I couldn't provide blind orphans at St. Nicholas' Home with day outings over the holiday but was assigned to work at a day camp in Ipoh. Moke Chee volunteered to teach art at John's day camp and stay with another cousin who lived in Ipoh, so at least she and I would work together.

I wrote John and told him about my assignment and that Moke Chee also had volunteered to teach art. He said I could stay with him and that he had more teachers than classes. Moke Chee could assist one of the women Volunteers who taught art, and I could be his assistant—running errands and helping out in classes as needed. He also included a tease: "I have news to share with you about Regina and me." That sure piqued my curiosity. I wanted to hear all about it, and I also wanted to share with him the development of my relationship with Moke Chee.

The rest of the school term went well. My students were learning. Moke Chee and I saw each other every weekend, mostly in Kuala Trengganu and sometimes in Kota Bharu, and we wrote to each other every day. My teacher friends and my friends in town accepted our relationship and socialized with us at my house and invited us to their homes. We were accepted as a couple, and except for Victoria and Tim Chee, people seemed happy for us. We wanted to marry and decided we would ask Moke Chee's father for his blessing when we got back to Penang for the August holiday. In one of my letters to Moke Chee, I wrote that I wished I was addressing the letter to Mrs. Moke Chee Wolter rather than Miss Fong Moke Chee. After that, Moke Chee wrote her return address as Mrs. Moke Chee Wolter, and I then started addressing my letters to her as Mrs. Moke Chee Wolter.

Telling of My Plans to Marry

Norb and Betty planned a Fourth of July party for all Peace Corps Volunteers for the Saturday after the Fourth of July to accommodate all the Volunteers with assignments in places outside of the Kuala Lumpur area. I was happy because I had accepted Roy Masters' invitation to celebrate the Fourth of July on the fourth with the British expatriates, the Peace Corps nurses, and Victoria.

I wrote to Norb and asked for an hour of his time to discuss a private matter.

I arrived at Betty and Norb's house at about eleven in the morning. A few Volunteers were already there. Norb was all smiles when he greeted me. He gave me an ice-cold bottle of beer and brought me to his home office. He thanked me again for providing Sarge with such a wonderful welcome and dinner. He asked me how I arranged to have so many people and dignitaries and their wives at the airfield to greet Sarge in such a short time. He said that the people lining the street to wave at Sarge absolutely surprised and delighted Sarge so much that it was all he talked about on his flight back to Kuala Lumpur.

I said: "I have a confession. When I told all the people that Sargent Shriver, Director of the Peace Corps, was coming from Washington, D.C., they didn't understand who Sargent Shriver was. I told them that he was President Kennedy's brother-in-in-law. When I went to school the next day, my students commented that Peter Lawford looks different in person."

Norb was one of those people who laughed with his whole body. He said, "It's best we not share that with Sarge." Then he asked why I wanted to see him.

I said, "I found someone I want to marry. Is that a problem as far as the Peace Corps is concerned?"

Norb said, "No, but you have to obtain permission from the State Department. You can obtain a permission form from the U.S. Embassy. Can you tell me about the lucky young lady, how you met, what you know about her, and if you've told your parents?"

I told Norb how we met, about the time we spent together, and about our correspondence. And that my parents know about Moke Chee and that I sent them photos of us, but haven't told them that we want to get married. We want to ask her father's permission first.

He asked, "Do you have a photo of Miss Fong with you?"

I said, "Yes," and shared a photo of her.

He said, "She's very handsome. Is there anything else?"

I said, "Do you know of any biracial marriages and how their marriages worked out and how their children have fared?"

Norb said, "Betty and I have several friends in happy, successful biracial marriages. You understand getting married is not a marriage. A marriage is ongoing over a number of years that two people continue to work at to make it thrive. All marriages have their rewards and challenges. A biracial marriage—particularly one where the parties are from different countries, much less continents—likely has additional challenges. In your case, Moke Chee is an only child. Have you thought about where you will live?"

I said, "We both assumed we'll live in the United States. We haven't had a discussion of which country would be best to raise our children. I'm worried about the problems our biracial children will encounter. The biracial teachers I have met seem to be struggling to find themselves and a place to fit in. Do you think our children will be confronted with discrimination? I'd hate to bring a child into the world who will face discrimination just because his mother and I love each other."

Norb said, "Well, I'm not an expert on childrearing and certainly have no crystal ball, but the children of biracial couples Betty and I know are beautiful, wonderful, and intelligent children who seem to have no problems socially, and the older ones have grown up to be very successful young adults. It's more a matter of the culture of the community they live in than race. Being educated, you and Moke Chee will likely be happier living and socializing in a better-educated cosmopolitan community, and your children will likely be happier in such a community."

A gathering of Peace Corps Volunteers partying creates a distinctive rustle of joyous and harmonious voices. I said, "It sounds like the other Volunteers have arrived. Thank you, Norb. You probably need to get out there."

As we walked to the office door, Norb said, "An astute observation, but have I answered all of your questions, or at least given you something to think about? Getting married is the most important decision you'll make in your life. You know, Jim, that Betty and I are one hundred percent behind you and will help and support whatever decision you and Moke Chee make."

I saw John. He was talking to Luke. I joined in, and when Luke moved to another gaggle of Volunteers, I said, "Did you make it all the way to Kota Bharu?"

John said, "I did. A bunch of us slept on the floor at Jaron's place."

I said, "Did you happen to see April?"

John said, "I did. She was waiting for you and worried when you didn't show up. She even had me call the Peace Corps Office to find out if anything happened to you. I guess you got diverted by Moke Chee."

I said, "I had every intention of visiting April. But I went to Penang to get some trousers that would fit me. The tailor didn't complete my trousers on time, so I got stuck and was invited to stay up on Penang Hill with the family of Moke Chee's friend and ended up spending the week with Moke Chee. We've been seeing each other, and I'm going to ask her father for permission to marry her in August."

John said, "Good luck and much happiness with Moke Chee. Now, I've got one for you. Regina and I told Norb and Luke that we are getting married once she completes her Peace Corps term."

I said, "Congratulations, I'll buy you a beer."

John said, "The beer's free."

I said, "In that case, I'll buy you two."

I thanked Betty for hosting the party and slipped away quietly to fly to Kota Bharu.

When I met with Moke Chee, I said: "Norb supports us getting married, but I have to get the State Department's permission to marry you as long as I'm a Peace Corps Volunteer. I resent having some bureaucrats determine whether I can marry you or not. Norb said, and I agree, that getting married is the most important decision that I will make in life. If your father approves of our marriage, I want to wait until I exit the Peace Corps, but only if you agree."

Moke Chee agreed.

CHAPTER 23

The August 1962 school holiday arrived. Riding in the front window seat of the taxi from Kuala Trengganu to Kuala Lumpur, watching the scenery and the mileposts stream by, I pondered about the change my life had taken because of an extremely inefficient Penang haberdasher. I wasn't heading back to Kuala Lumpur to catch a flight to Chicago and back to the life I left behind only ten months ago as a person who I no longer wanted to be. Back then, I didn't know what I wanted. I only knew that I didn't want a life governed by others' expectations and transitory romantic encounters. Now, I was on my way to meet Moke Chee, the person whom I wanted to spend the rest of my life with and build a future with—if her father granted us his blessing. But first, I had to report to John's day camp for a week to stand by and assist if needed.

I arrived at John's house on Saturday a short time before Regina. We were both staying with John—Regina for the weekend and me for the week. The Peace Corps had given John a motor scooter to use because his bicycle was inadequate for the amount of running around required to set up the school. That freed up his bicycle for me to use to visit Moke Chee, who was staying with Gim Lan's family in Ipoh. Gim Lan's husband, Boon Haw, was the Chief Internal Revenue officer for the State of Perak, and they lived in one of the hugest old colonial government houses in Ipoh.

The first day of camp, I cycled to Gim Lan's house, and after breakfast, Gim Lan's driver drove Moke Chee and me to the elementary school where the day camp was held. The Peace Corps assigning me to the camp was another blunder, and my encouraging Moke Chee to volunteer to teach art there also was a blunder.

First, there was nothing for me to do. Things weren't any better for Moke Chee.

John assigned Moke Chee to assist a Peace Corps teacher who was teaching watercolor painting, but Moke Chee was told by the Peace Corps teacher to leave because she preferred to teach alone. With nothing for either of us to do except hang out together, we made the mistake of holding hands. That generated hostile stares from the women Volunteers. I told John about their reaction to Moke Chee. John was already aware of it, and he agreed with me that it would be better for all concerned if Moke Chee didn't participate in the day camp. I suggested to Moke Chee that she remain at her cousin's house. Moke Chee was very happy because Nanny was now taking care of Lay Chin, Gim Lan's adopted baby. I fulfilled my assignment for the week, hanging around the camp with nothing to do except wait to see if I was needed. I wasn't.

Each day after camp, I cycled to Gim Lan's house and had lunch and played with Ah Seng and Lay See, Gim Lan's two primary-school-aged children. We played board games like "Snakes 'n Ladders" and read stories indoors during the heat of the day for about two hours, and then as the sun dropped lower in the sky, we played outdoor games like badminton and kickball until dinner time. I cycled back to John's house after dinner as the sun was setting.

JAMES A. WOLTER

Nanny's Approval

About mid-week, I was invited to stay overnight at Gim Lan's house. That saved me a lot of cycling, particularly on a highway as the sun was setting, and enabled me to spend more time with Moke Chee. I found that it was an unexpected treat to live with a family. I didn't have the feeling of living with a family since my brothers and sister left home, and now I was living with a mother, father, two primary-aged children, the baby, Nanny, and Moke Chee. I became very fond of Lay See and Ah Seng. At bedtime, I read Lay See and Ah Seng bedtime stories, and in the morning, the two of them rushed to my room saying, "Wake up, Uncle Jim!" We wrestled around in bed for a few minutes, then I showered and had breakfast with the family.

In the evening, Moke Chee and I found time for ourselves by walking to a nearby park. One evening, Nanny joined us for a walk to the park. When we found a place to rest, Moke Chee said to Nanny, "Yea Chae, Jim has asked me to marry him. I love him and want to accept his proposal, but before I accept, I wish to have your blessing."

A sad look swept over Nanny's face, and her body seemed to slump. Nanny seemed to age ten years right before my eyes. Nanny said, "What does your father say?"

Moke Chee said, "We haven't asked him yet. We wanted your blessing first."

Nanny remained silent for a while, and I thought she might cry, but she gathered herself, stiffened her back, and responded as I would have responded if I were her: "You are both young. You are in love. Jim is a good man. But he will go back to America. If you go to America and need help, you will be too far away. I will not be able to help you. You are an only child, and your parents are elderly; who will take care of them? No, you are both young, it is natural you want to marry, but you will meet other people. It is better if you wait."

Moke Chee started to weep and said, "Please, Yea Chae, please give us your blessing. I have met other people. I don't want any other man. Jim is the one I want. I trust him. He will take care of me, and we will find a way to take care of you and my parents. Please give us your blessing."

Nanny put her palms to the side of Moke Chee's cheeks and wiped away her tears with her thumbs the way she must have done dozens of times when Moke Chee was in her care as a child and said, "Now don't cry. You have my blessing if your father gives you his blessing."

Moke Chee wrapped her arms around Nanny and clung to her and said, "Thank you, thank you, thank you. I promise to care for you and for them."

Nanny said, "I know you will. You are a good daughter. Now no more talk of this until you speak to your father."

Nanny reached over, took my hand, looked into my eyes, and said in a combination of Hokkien and English: "You are a good man. I will be too far away to help my daughter. I trust you to care for her." Her eyes contained a look of desperation as if pleading for life itself.

I felt overwhelmed by Nanny's love for Moke Chee and said, "I solemnly promise you I will take good care of her."

I suddenly didn't like myself. I felt selfish. I felt small and inadequate in the presence of this frail old woman's unselfishness. I was taking from this frail old woman all that she lived for. It was an awful feeling that went to the marrow of my bones.

Nanny patted my hand twice and smiled at me and said, "I know you will."

I wanted to tell Nanny that I loved her, too, and would also take care of her but thought that might embarrass her and just said, "Thank you. I will take care of you, too." She smiled and patted my hand two more times.

Before going to sleep that night, I gave thanks for Nanny's

blessing and prayed that our request to marry would go as well with Moke Chee's parents the following day.

Seeking the Blessing of Moke Chee's Parents

The following morning, that would be Saturday morning, Lay See and Ah Seng jumped on top of me while I was still in bed, and we wrestled for a while before breakfast. When the taxi arrived to take Moke Chee and me to Penang, Lay See and Ah Seng each grabbed one of my hands and said, "Please, Uncle Jim, stay. Don't go. Please."

Gim Lan scolded her children, and they let go of my hands. The taxi driver loaded our luggage and some fruit that Moke Chee was bringing to her parents into the boot. Moke Chee sat in the front seat, and I sat immediately behind her. The driver picked up two more passengers at the taxi stand, and we were off to Penang.

We arrived in Penang slightly before noon. Moke Chee's mother was home, but her father was at the Georgetown dispensary to have a checkup with Dr. Wilson. Moke Chee said to her mother, "Ah Ma, we have something very important to ask you."

Her mother smiled and said, "I know."

Moke Chee said, "Jim has asked me to marry him. I want to accept, but before I do, I want your blessing."

Moke Chee's mother said: "Jim is a good man. He loves you and will take good care of you. You are an only child, your father and I are old, but you are young. Now it is your time to seek your own happiness and have a family with Jim. You have my blessing as long as your father gives you his blessing."

"Thank you, Ah Ma," Moke Chee said.

I followed by saying, "Thank you, Ah Ma. I promise I will do everything I can to care for Moke Chee and you."

Moke Chee's mother took my hand and, with a broad smile, said, "I know you will. Come, sit and eat."

I followed Moke Chee's mother to the kitchen and sat at the kitchen table and had tea and biscuits while Moke Chee went to take a bucket bath. When Moke Chee finished, I went to take a bucket bath. Taking three or four bucket baths a day was a way to cool off in Malaya.

Moke Chee and I went to Grandmother's house to take Hock Tee with us to the creameries for lunch. This was my lucky day because when I said, "Good afternoon, Grandmother," all she did was nod her head and say, "Ah." She didn't scold Moke Chee for keeping the company of a "red-faced monkey."

After having lunch at the creameries, Moke Chee and I stopped by Annie's house to visit. Annie was a longtime Irving Road friend. Annie was several years older than Moke Chee and unmarried. She was a superb cook and had a joyous outlook on life. She lived with her elderly mother, whom I called Auntie; Ah Hum, her youngest brother; Francisca, his wife; their baby son, Johnny; and Amy, a single female cousin. Annie's other brothers, Gee Kor and See Kor, which is Hokkien for "second brother" and "fourth brother," visited every day. I didn't know their given names, so I also called them Second Brother and Fourth Brother. Because I called them "brother," I think the family accepted me as an extended family member. I sat and drank iced coffee and read the newspaper and magazines while Moke Chee played mahjong with Annie, her mother, and others.

It was near dinner time, and typical of Malayan hospitality, Annie invited us to stay for dinner. I don't know what she had prepared, but it smelled absolutely delicious. We declined and walked down the block to Moke Chee's house. Moke Chee's father was home, and I thought she would do as she had with Nanny and her mother, but she surprised me and instead went in the back for another bucket bath, as did I.

After taking our bucket baths, Moke Chee and I went to

the sitting room, and Moke Chee said, "Ah Pa, Jim and I ..." A thought flashed through my mind: Now, she's going to ask for his blessing. But she continued with: "... are going to the padang for rubbish. Do you care to join us, or do you want us to bring something back for you?"

He said, "It's been a trying day, but I'll join you."

The three of us went to the padang and did our usual padang routine. Mr. Fong reserved a table while Moke Chee and I went from stall to stall, ordering food for the three of us. After a pleasant dinner of Penang favorites and Mr. Fong telling us tales of old Penang, we vanished into the black of night, walking back across the padang. Mr. Fong again held my arm to steady himself, navigating the padang's uncertain terrain. I thought: I hope this will be my future father-in-law and not just his daughter's friend that he is placing his trust in.

We got home after a very pleasant evening eating Mr. Fong's favorite padang rubbish and listening to his stories about the old days in Penang. It was the perfect time, I thought, for Moke Chee to work the same magic on her father that she had worked on her mother and Nanny and ask for his blessing as he settled in his favorite recliner. Instead, Moke Chee said, "Pa, Jim has something very important to ask you," and disappeared into the kitchen. Mrs. Fong followed her, leaving Mr. Fong and me alone in the sitting room.

Mr. Fong reclined in his favorite chair and said, "What is it you wish to ask?" I was still standing and wanted to speak to him at eye level, so I pulled a stool out from under the large round marble-top table, placed the stool to the side of Mr. Fong's chair, and sat down.

I said: "I love Moke Chee and want to marry her. She loves me and wants to marry me, but we won't marry without your blessing. May we have your blessing?"

I couldn't believe his response. He started talking about his new part-time job of fattening up pigs for market and having to lift heavy sacks of grain to feed them. Then, he asked me to hand him the evening newspaper that was on the table. He opened the paper to find the weather forecast and said: "The work is too heavy for me. I'm giving management notice first thing tomorrow."

His response made my head spin. I was momentarily disoriented. He totally ignored my question. I thought he must not have heard it or had misinterpreted it, but I concluded that he was too intelligent to miss what I asked. Perhaps he was testing me to see how determined I was to marry his daughter.

I decided not to let his response put me off and became more direct. I asked again: "Sir, may Moke Chee and I have your blessing to marry?"

He said, "You are a good man. I could tell, and I was afraid this moment would come. I have welcomed you into my home, and I still welcome you in my home, but you are not welcome to my daughter. I have only one daughter, but you have many women to take as a wife. You are young. Oil and water don't mix. You will go back to America and find an American wife. My daughter will stay here and find a Chinese husband. It is best if you stick with your own kind. No, you do not have, you will not have my blessing. I forbid this marriage."

I blurted out: "But we love each other. I don't want anyone else for a wife. I promise to take good care of Moke Chee and to take care of you."

He responded, "This is a matter not open for discussion in my home. I will hear no more of it. Don't force me to be impolite."

I said, "Thank you for hearing me out. I understand." I didn't understand, not fully at that time, but I understood he wasn't giving us permission to marry—yet, he didn't forbid us from seeing each other. Maybe he would change his mind by the time I left the Peace Corps, which was still a year away.

I went back to the kitchen to tell Moke Chee the bad news. I didn't have to say a word. She read the stunned expression on my face and said, "Father refused to give us his blessing, didn't he?"

I said, "Yes. When he turned me down at first, I pleaded with him, and he said the matter was not open for discussion and we should marry our own kind."

Moke Chee said, "Didn't you tell him we are each other's own kind?"

I said, "I tried, but he wasn't open to listening. I don't know what to do."

Moke Chee said, "Let him think about it for a while, and we'll see if he softens toward you. Maybe ask again before you leave for Kuala Trengganu. Nothing has changed about how I feel about you."

I said, "Or I about you. At least he didn't forbid us from seeing each other, and he didn't tell me to pack my bags and get out. Maybe that's a good sign."

Family Visits

The rest of the week, Mr. Fong acted as if I had not asked him for permission to marry his daughter. When we went to the padang, he still gripped my arm when walking across the uneven turf in the dark. I thought to myself: Good. The more we do that, the more you will see that you can depend on me to help you in other ways. Still, I felt uncomfortable and worried that he would not come around. It was obvious that my relationship with Moke Chee would result in heartbreak for us or for her father. I hadn't even told my parents that my friendship with Moke Chee had grown into a romance and that I wanted to spend the rest of my life with her. Never mind that Moke Chee wasn't white, wasn't Catholic, and lived on another continent. My mother had been after me to get a job and get married right after high school, like the rest of my family, so she would not take kindly to me marrying Moke Chee. That was a reality. I was willing to deal with her anger and rage but figured there was no reason for doing so before the fact. First, we'd wait for Moke Chee's father to change his mind, then I'd let my parents know of my intentions.

Meanwhile, Moke Chee presented me to her family. Each day, we visited one of her father's brothers and his sister. The two visits that remain vivid in my mind are the visits to Third Uncle and to Second Aunt. Maybe it was the contrast in their standard of living.

Visit to Third Uncle

Third Uncle was not as tall as Moke Chee's father but had the same handsome facial features. He was well dressed, and his house was a shophouse-style house like Moke Chee's father's, but his house was air-conditioned. It was furnished in classical and elaborately carved traditional Chinese furniture.

Auntie asked us what we wanted to drink. Their amah brought iced coffee out for me with an array of Malayan kaya and some Western cakes for tea.

Third Uncle asked me the usual questions about my family, my education, and my plans to achieve my career ambitions. He also asked questions about American society and racial bigotry, which made me feel defensive and uncomfortable. "Suppose a Chinese Malayan woman marries an American man, how will she be accepted, and how will their children, if they have children, be accepted?"

I felt so dumb. Neither Moke Chee nor I said anything about marriage to him, at least not in words, but if we didn't say it in words, we did say it with our visit and Moke Chee's presentation of me to him. All I could say was, "It depends. I don't really know, but there could be problems."

He said, "That's an honest answer. However, are you aware that a mixed-race family will likely encounter more problems than a same-race family?"

I responded, "I am. And that concerns me."

Third Uncle handed me a plate and said, "Good, you're aware then. Now, please, help yourself."

I liked Third Uncle. Beyond the same refined facial features of Moke Chee's father, he had the same refined manners and patterns of speech and gestures. They obviously were brothers. I think he liked me or at least accepted me. I thought the visit to Third Uncle was a success and hoped he would put in a good word for me with Moke Chee's father. The visit to Second Aunt was another matter.

Visit to Second Aunt

Second Aunt lived in a shophouse-style house that was sparsely furnished with four plain, wooden, cane back chairs positioned around a wooden tea table. There was a simple table against the wall, but the house contained no photographs or decorations.

Second Aunt was a small, thin woman with thin, white scraggly strands of hair hanging down over her shoulders. I could see blotches of scalp beneath her hair. Second Uncle-in-Law was also thin. He had a full head of salt-and-pepper-colored hair that he wore swept back. He stood straight with his shoulders back. He was almost as tall as me. He was wearing a white T-shirt and a white and blue-checkered sarong similar to the one I used for pajamas.

Second Aunt was quiet and held her right hand over her lips when she spoke. She and Moke Chee talked in quiet tones while Uncle and I talked. He had a kind face with thin lips and teeth so white and so perfect I wondered if he were wearing dentures. Uncle's eyes were penetrating but kind. His manner and his intelligence reminded me of Dr. Nickerson, my medical school mentor. He asked me questions like, "Tell me about yourself and what you're doing in Malaya. You're a Peace Corps biology teacher. Teaching is a fine career for a woman with family responsibilities, but will you be satisfied with a teaching career? Don't you have higher career aspirations? Are you satisfied with just a bachelor's degree? Don't you have higher educational aspirations?"

As a childless couple who viewed Moke Chee as the daughter they wished they had, I accepted Uncle's checking me out and also appreciated his mentorship. In answering his questions, I realized how shortsighted I was by only living in the present and not planning for the future. Now it hit me what my Peace Corps buddy John meant when he said that he was using the Peace Corps as a stepping stone to a future career. I was treating the Peace Corps as an isolated experience.

I told Uncle that I worked hard for my bachelor's degree and that I thought teaching biology was a noble profession—many men lived rich, rewarding comfortable lives and raised families while teaching biology. I also told him that I planned on earning a doctorate in genetics, becoming a professor, and conducting research at a university.

Uncle said, "If that's your intention, why aren't you pursuing it instead of dallying your time away out here?"

I said, "I don't think I'm wasting my time."

Uncle then asked me a question so direct that it threw me: "Why are you walking with Moke Chee? If you care for her, don't you know that walking with a European man will reduce Moke Chee's marketability? No self-respecting Chinese man will want as his wife a woman who walked with a European."

This might be an appropriate place to define the term "walking with" meant in Malaya back then. Teh Eng told me that "walking with someone" was similar to "going steady" in America but could also imply "sleeping with."

At first, I thought: My relationship with Moke Chee is none of your business. But then I told myself: Of course, we visited your house, and by doing so, we made our relationship your business.

I said, "Uncle, I promise my intentions with Moke Chee are honorable."

Moke Chee added: "Uncle, my father approves of my be-friending Jim. He is not concerned in the least with what old-fashioned, narrow-minded Chinese men might think about my friendship with Jim. He knows I would have nothing to do with a Chinese man holding that kind of outlook on life and marriage."

Uncle said, "If that is your father's stance, that's all I need to hear."

As we were leaving, I said, "Uncle, thank you for giving me many good questions to think about."

He smiled and replied, "It's not enough to just think about them. You must get some gumption and do something."

I said, "I promise I will. Thank you for your advice."

He said, "It was my pleasure. Come again."

On our way back to Moke Chee's house, I said, "I don't think I made much of a favorable impression with Second Aunt's husband. I hope he doesn't tell your father."

Moke Chee said, "Don't be too sure of that. He and Second Aunt are very protective of me. They don't have much money but have been very generous to me."

I said, "You're the daughter they didn't have, which makes me the son-in-law they didn't have."

Moke Chee said, "Something like that."

Rejected Again

After each visit to an uncle or aunt, Moke Chee told her father about them and how well each uncle and aunt accepted me. I hoped the reports that each uncle and aunt was favorably impressed by me might help change his mind.

I said, "Sir, I will be going back to Kuala Trengganu tomor-row morning, I want to thank you for your hospitality, and I want to ask if you would reconsider and give Moke Chee and me your blessing to marry."

He said, "I told you before that this is a topic not open for discussion."

I went upstairs and sat on the bedroom floor with Moke Chee. As we sat on the wooden floor of that little room, it was a joy to fantasize about our future together. We looked at the little treasures she collected as a child and talked about our childhoods and how we would raise our children. We talked about raising our children in a world where it was only her and me, unencumbered with responsibilities, and where it made no difference what color we were or where we were from. We remained committed to marrying each other and spending the rest of our lives together.

We committed to continue seeing each other on weekends during the upcoming school term.

When I got back to my house in Kuala Trengganu, I found Teh Eng and Boon talking on the front lawn. Boon was sharing the good news that he had been promoted to the Ministry of Education office in Kuala Lumpur and that he learned Teh Eng was up for promotion to a Headmaster position in January. Boon also had good news for me. The Ministry sent an Ustaz to Tengku Bariah, and I would be relieved of my Ugama classes.

Now that Tengku Bariah had an Ustaz, as if by magic, all those classes that were impossible to find for me to teach suddenly became available to teach. I was assigned one science, one math, and three English classes. In the last month of the year, I was also assigned to teach history.

Moke Chee's father had not given us his blessing to marry, but he had not forbidden us from seeing each other, so we did. Moke Chee continued to visit me in Kuala Trengganu each weekend and stayed with her cousin Tim Chee at the women teachers' hostel. My house became a stop for visitors, other Peace Corps Volunteers, other Americans, and Europeans in the flux of world travelers along with local friends. Our guests contributed to our Saturday parties. Moke Chee cooked dinner, and we ate, drank beer, and talked until a quarter to ten o'clock when Spa Er arrived to take Moke Chee to the women's hostel.

CHAPTER 24

One of the things I was all too aware of was that I was a temporary resident in Kuala Trengganu. Things I found novel for my two-year stint were, in too many cases, a reoccurring problem for permanent residents. The Northeast monsoon was the most obvious example of that. During the 1962-63 monsoon season, it started raining in November and didn't let up until February. In the early weeks of the monsoon, the river ferry was still operable, and Moke Chee could still visit me in Kuala Trengganu. We could get about town on my motorbike.

I purchased a plastic raincoat to wear when riding the motorbike. I blocked the rain from reaching Moke Chee as she tucked in close behind me. This kept us reasonably dry most of the time, but occasionally we got wonderfully soaked and had to shower when we got to my house and then change into dry clothes. Moke Chee didn't have dry clothes at my house, so she had to wear my clothes until it was time for her to go back to the women's quarters and then change back into her wet clothes for the ride back. Although she said she felt very uncomfortable wearing my clothes, she looked absolutely adorable draped in them.

We went to the movie theater more often in the rainy season, and Johnny Wu—my former Sultan Sulaiman student whose father owned the theater—would meet us in front of the theater with umbrellas, escort us in through the owner's entrance and seat us in the Royal Box.

As October progressed, the rain grew in intensity. Some days and some weeks were worse than others. By the first week of November, the rivers were too high and too swift-moving for the river ferry to operate.

The monsoon created a significant problem from the second week in November to the second week in December. The heavy dark gray sky seemed all the more gloomy because Moke Chee and I were stuck on opposite sides of the Trengganu River and couldn't visit each other. Moke Chee could not come to Kuala Trengganu, and I couldn't make it up to Kota Bharu, where we sometimes met. We continued writing to each other every day, and fortunately, the British engineers had constructed a cable line high above the river so that a rain-proof mail pouch could be pulled across the river on the cable.

I looked forward to receiving Moke Chee's letters every day and two on Monday. It was the one dependable indispensable ray of sunshine in my day. But by the second week, Moke Chee's letters became frantic because she wasn't receiving my letters. I, too, became frantic as she wrote: *Is it that you do not love me anymore and have grown tired of me? Hamza, you remember him, he's my Brinsford classmate, says you are a typical white man who amuses himself with a local woman, ruining her reputation, and then disposes of her when she is no longer of interest or use to him. Is it true what Hamza says? That since I am going back to Penang and will not be able to visit you in Kuala Trengganu on weekends, you no longer have use for me and have moved on to a woman of your own kind? I tell him you are not that kind of man. But what am I to believe when you do not write or answer my letters?*

I started writing two letters a day, hoping that if I sent more, there would be an increased chance one would get through. I stopped dropping the letters in the mail slot at the post office and handed the letters to the postal clerk. I made him cancel the postage stamps in front of me to make certain that the stamps on the letters weren't stolen by someone at the post office and that my letters were discarded. The postal clerk assured me that my letters were in the postal pouch and were being delivered safely to the other side of the river. I created such a ruckus that the clerk called the postmaster, who gave me an "undelivered mail" form to fill out and initiate an inquiry about my letters not being delivered.

I could feel Moke Chee's anxiety, and I was frustrated that I could not be with her to assure her and to show her that she was not just a plaything that I was abandoning. I felt hurt that she could even think that of me, but the reputation of white men in Asia was that they used local women as things for sexual pleasure. Indeed, the British expatriates and even Bankim in as much suggested I amuse myself with Moke Chee but not get seriously involved with her if I didn't want to ruin my career prospects. But that's not the kind of person I was. I thought that of all people, Moke Chee should have known that about me. I wanted to tell her that the stereotype her classmate was promoting didn't apply to me.

Moke Chee continued to write: *I went to the school office again today when I saw the postman arrive on his bicycle, but again the school clerk said I had no letter from you. It has been a month now since I have received a letter from you. At first, I thought it was the monsoon keeping your letters from me, but Hamza showed me mail that is getting through from Kuala Trengganu. Then I was worried that something terrible happened to you, and I was unable to reach you to help you. But if something bad had happened, Hamza said that you surely would have found a way to notify me. Hamza has been trying his best to comfort me. He reminds me every day that white men dump local women all the time and there is no reason to believe you are any different. I don't want to believe him, but what am I to think? He says you don't even care enough about my feelings to write and assure me that you still love me. Hamza said that he learned that my reputation is ruined because of you and that no man will ever marry me. Hamza has confessed his love for me and says he doesn't care what my reputation is. To show his love, he has asked me to go to the marriage registry with him in Kota Bharu and said he will ask my father for my hand in marriage when we get back to Penang. I'm so confused and hurt and feel so unloved and lost. Hamza has been such a comfort to me. He tells me every day that he loves me more than life itself, but I love you more than life. If, like Hamza says, you have tired of me, please give me the courtesy of telling me. Set me free. It will hurt but not as much as it hurts now. Do you care nothing for me?*

Another Unpleasant Storm

I continued receiving Moke Chee's letters pleading with me to write. The monsoon subsided, and I booked a seat on a taxi to Kuala Lumpur as soon as the school term ended. The Peace Corps again turned down my request to work with orphaned children living at St. Nicholas' Home. Instead, the Peace Corps assigned me to report to Dr. Hussein Mahathir in Alor Star on Wednesday of the following week. I was to work on a rural health project building water-sealed latrines in the State of Perlis along the Thai border. That gave me more than enough time to go to Penang and see Moke Chee and tell her I loved her and to tell her I wrote to her every day, and if she were still willing, to ask her father once more for his permission to marry her.

I heard the rumble of a taxi's diesel engine in front of my house and made one final check to make sure the window shutters were secured. I exited the front door and was not only surprised but overjoyed to see it was Moke Chee in the back seat of Spa Er's taxi. He had agreed to take her to my house and then down to Kuala Lumpur as a favor to her. Since her request for a transfer to Penang had been granted, this would be the last time that he drove her in his taxi. She and I were the only passengers. I wanted to kiss Moke Chee, but that would be inappropriate in front of Spa Er. I reached to hold her hand.

I took her hand in mine and held it, but she didn't hold my hand back. Her hand felt stiff. There was no sign of life in it. Before, when we held hands, I felt I was one with her. But now nothing was there. Nothing was flowing between us. Moke Chee was sitting next to me, and she stopped by to share Spa Er's taxi with me, but she seemed so distant. Her ready smile was gone, and her joyous, spontaneous disposition was missing. Her face was shallow and gaunt. She had lost weight. She looked like an empty shell of the Moke Chee I knew. I could tell something was troubling her. I said, "I wrote to you every day. I don't know why you didn't get the letters."

Moke Chee said, "I got them. A postal inspector came to the school and found that the school clerk was holding them back in a scheme hatched by Hamza. When I confronted Hamza, he said he did it for my own good. He said he loved me more than life and that it was better for me to experience a little pain now than bring a great deal of pain to my parents and Nanny and myself if I married you and followed you back to America. He said he knows that I love you, but that he loves me so much he can accept that and still wants to marry me, even if I love you. He says, even though he is Malay, he grew up playing sports with Chinese boys, and he speaks Hokkien. He eats pork, and though we have to be married as Muslims and I have to take a Malay name, I can keep my Chinese name and practice my own religion, but just not in public. As long as our children have Muslim names, they can follow Chinese traditions in our home."

She continued: "I'm so confused. He said if I marry him, I can give my parents my entire paycheck and Nanny can live with us and not have to work because we will have another servant to do the work. It sounds perfect. Except I love you.

He said if I marry you, I will be abandoning my parents and Nanny and that once I follow you back to America, I will be treated as a second-class person because I'm not white, and you will abandon me when you get back to your own kind. He says that after he and I have children, I will learn to love him."

I replied: "I can't tell you what to do. I love you and want to marry you. I don't know how I will exactly do it, but I promise I will take care of your parents and Nanny and you. You can trust me. But can you trust a man who deceived you by keeping letters that belonged to you and knowing that was causing you great distress? Can you trust a man who says he knows what is best for you? And it is Malay men who are able to abandon older wives for new younger wives when they lose interest in their current wives. For me, marriage is forever. There is no divorce, no abandoning a wife. It is forever."

Moke Chee replied, "He explained that he had my letters held back only because he loved me so much, and he wanted me to know how it would feel when you abandoned me. And then it would even be worse because he wouldn't be there to support me. He said he is a modern Malay man and only wants me for a wife, and even if he took a second wife later, I would always be his first and most important wife. And a Malay man who takes more than one wife must treat them equally. If one wife is given a house, the other wives must be given a house of equal value. And he said even if that happened, I would at least have my children and my parents and Nanny and a house. But with you, I would have nothing."

I said, "You will always have me."

Moke Chee said, "I want to believe you. I wish I could."

I didn't know what to say or what to do. Moke Chee was so independent, intelligent, and quick-witted. She could see through the facade of phonies, but that wasn't the Moke Chee sitting next to me in Spa Er's taxi. She was different. Her eyes had a distant look in them. Moke Chee was so strong and so independent and so intolerant of lies and injustice. I couldn't understand how she could accept what Hamza had done to her. She seemed brainwashed by him. It was as if she were in a drugged stupor, unable to think straight, and there was nothing that I could do to bring her out of it. She put all of her trust in the very person who deceived her. I couldn't get her to see that. There was no reasoning with her. I feared she was lost.

I thought what Hamza did to her was despicable and wondered why she couldn't see that he was capable of doing more. And if he determined what was in her own good now, what would he do if they were married. She would have no say. If Moke Chee wanted to end our relationship on her own or had decided she wanted to rekindle her relationship with her old boyfriend—or if she had met a new and honorable man—I would bow out quietly. But I wouldn't do so now, not with this man, not after what he did to her. I would stay and try to get Moke Chee to see what he did to her was fundamentally dishonest and manipulative.

I felt physically ill sitting next to Moke Chee talking as if Hamza had done her a favor rather than committing a great betrayal. I felt like running away, but I felt trapped in one of those maddening nightmares where there was no escape. Just four weeks ago, Moke Chee was dynamic, self-confident, loving, and caring. Now, the essence that made Moke Chee was missing. There was no light in her eyes and no smile on her face. It was as if she had lost her soul.

Moke Chee said in a flat, matter-of-fact way, "Gim Lan's husband has been transferred to Kuala Lumpur. She is living there now. I'm staying there overnight before going on to Penang. You are welcome to join me if you wish."

I said, "Yes, I would love that. Will it be alright with Gim Lan?"

Moke Chee said, "It will be alright with her."

I said, "Is it alright if I follow you to Penang, and are you still alright with me asking your father for permission to marry you?"

Moke Chee said, "Yes, of course you can follow me to Penang, but wait on asking for my father's blessing." Then Moke

Chee added, talking as if she were in a robotic or hypnotic voice, "Hamza waited until Spa Er picked me up and followed the taxi on his motor scooter. On the ferry crossing the Trengganu River, he made me promise to meet him and his family once we got to Penang. If I didn't agree, he said that he would hurl his motor scooter in front of Spa Er's taxi once we were off the ferry. He seemed so desperate that I believed he would do it. So, I promised Hamza that I would meet him and his family when I got back to Penang."

When Moke Chee told me that, I had to control myself to keep from puking. I thought: She is lost. The loving, caring, independent-thinking Moke Chee I loved is gone.

We sat in silence for the rest of the drive to Kuala Lumpur, and for the first time while I was with Moke Chee, time seemed to drag by. I was anxious to get to Gim Lan's house to see if Moke Chee's spirits lightened and to see if her strong and independent personality returned. It didn't.

More Sorrow

We arrived at Gim Lan's house at dinner time. We were invited to join the family for dinner, but I declined. I didn't feel like eating, and I guess neither did Moke Chee because she also declined dinner. Nanny asked—almost pleaded—that we eat something and seemed worried when we didn't. The children wanted to play with me, but my heart wasn't in it. Moke Chee talked to Nanny while I played with the children. Nanny's face had sadness written all over it. The children grew tired of me and went off to play on their own. I went to my room and didn't see Moke Chee again until the next morning.

Gim Lan's children did not, as they had when I stayed with the family before, come to my room and jump in bed with me. I was grateful for that. I waited in my room until I heard the taxi. Nanny had a worried look on her face and asked me to take something to eat on the way. I didn't want to hurt her feelings any more than I already had. I accepted the egg sandwich that she handed me. She forced a smile and said goodbye. I said thank you and goodbye. Her eyes followed Moke Chee getting to the taxi, so she didn't catch me looking long and hard at her. I thought that this would be the last I saw of Nanny. I wanted her image engraved in my memory. I had grown to love her. I was going to miss this gentle woman whose love was unconditional and boundless and, if need be, self-sacrificing. There was so much of her character in Moke Chee, the Moke Chee I loved, but I was afraid that I would never see that in Moke Chee again.

Intellectually, I told myself that what happened to Moke Chee was not my fault. I wasn't the one who betrayed her, but if I had not kissed her on Penang Hill, if I had not even gone to Penang, none of this would have happened to her, and Moke Chee would be exchanging letters with her boyfriend in Australia. And her parents and Nanny would never have had to worry about her going to America, and she would not have fallen victim to Hamza's treachery.

I should have kept my baggy pants until I went home to Chicago—or better yet—I should never have left Chicago. I should have stayed and married Lolly, gone to med school, and been groomed by Irma. I would have been miserable, but I'm far more miserable now, anyway. But at least I would be miserable by myself without dragging Moke Chee into my misery.

I was grateful there were two other passengers in the taxi to Penang. Moke Chee sat in the front seat while I sat in the back seat with the other passengers. Conversation, which had been so free-flowing and nonstop ever since the Teacher's Union picnic, was sparse and strained between us now. Sitting apart in the taxi enabled us to avoid the uncomfortable icy silence that had grown between us.

When the ferry left the dock in Butterworth, I asked Moke

Chee if she would join me at the bow of the ferry. She agreed. The sea breeze washing over us was so reminiscent of our boat ride back from Pulau Perhentian. I was tempted to tell her that this reminded me of falling in love with her riding back from Pulau Perhentian on the *Bintang Pagi*, but that's not why I invited her to be with me away from the other passengers.

I said, "It's early. I can get a taxi to Alor Star and report for my rural health assignment a day early. I feel my presence is making you uncomfortable. You can sort things out without me being in the way."

Moke Chee said: "There's no need for that. So much has happened these past weeks and months. As deceitful and awful as what Hamza did, he did me a favor by making me think about what I was doing to my parents and Nanny, and how selfish and awful I was being. It was so romantic being caught up in a romance with you—my 'stranger from abroad'—thinking that together we could overcome the very real obstacles in my life. But that was selfish on my part. I am an only child. I was told ever since I could remember that I had the sole responsibility of caring for my parents in their old age. And since being a little girl, the pact Nanny and I had was that she would live with me when I grew up, and I would care for her. For the sake of loving you, all that was thrown away. Hamza has shown me a way where I can keep my promise and faithfully fulfill my responsibility. Stay. It's only one more day. I'll be in Penang, and you'll be in Kuala Trengganu. This may be the last time we see each other."

I wrapped my arms around her even though we were in public. She laid her head against my chest, and for the briefest of moments, I felt her body melt into mine just as it had in the past, but she did not return my hug. Then her body stiffened. She pulled away from me, and she was gone again.

I felt like crying, but men didn't cry.

Alone with the Family

The taxi dropped us off at the taxi stand. I normally would have called a trishaw and loved sitting next to Moke Chee with her nuzzling against me, but I thought that would be too uncomfortable for us now, so I hailed a local taxi to take us to her house. We, as usual after a long taxi ride, took bucket baths. Then I followed Moke Chee to Annie's house, her friend on Irving Road. Moke Chee went back to the kitchen to visit with Annie. In times past, I would follow her, but this time I stayed out in front of her house and sat on the swing and watched some small boys pitch pennies. Gee Khor came to the front door and called, "Jim, come inside. Join us for makan."

I wasn't hungry. I hadn't even eaten Nanny's sandwich. I didn't feel like eating in the taxi. I slipped my shoes off and followed him to the kitchen. Annie had a bowl of hum choy tung ready for me and a tall glass of sweetened black ice coffee. Moke Chee was in an animated discussion with Annie's sister-in-law about the new school Moke Chee was assigned to and about Jenny Foo, who also taught there and was one of Moke Chee's classmates at Georgetown Girls' Secondary School and whose mother was Nanny's friend.

I felt good. Moke Chee was among longtime friends who loved and cared for her. She was where she belonged. I was accepted in that space for a while, but I feared that there was no room for me, not permanently, in that space. I saw Hamza fitting in that space even less so than me, but that was for Moke Chee and her family to decide. Annie and her brothers and Auntie made me feel at home with them, and this was the closest I felt that things were back to normal. At least the uncomfortable silence between Moke Chee and me had been vanquished.

As we walked the half block back to Moke Chee's house, I could feel the glee in Moke Chee slipping away, and there was nothing I could do to help her hold on to who she was. Maybe, I thought, if I weren't there and she was with—as her father said—"her own kind," the real Moke Chee who did not suffer scoundrels lightly would return, and she, her parents, and Nanny would be the better for it.

We arrived at her home. After cleaning up and shutting the house up for the night, Moke Chee went directly to Nanny's old room after bringing me the chamber pot instead of sitting with me on her bedroom floor and talking for hours more. I missed that but thought it probably best. I couldn't sleep and thought I heard whimpering coming from Moke Chee's room. I walked softly and listened first at my door and then at Moke Chee's door. I whispered, "Moke Chee, are you alright?"

There was no answer, so I knocked softly and whispered again. "Are you alright?"

Moke Chee said, "Go away."

I said, "Are you sure? Do you want to talk?"

She said, "Just go away. Leave me alone."

I did, but I didn't sleep. I heard Moke Chee's mother opening up the house before sunrise. I got up too. I had my things packed to leave. I felt that I had caused enough distress for Moke Chee and her family. Moke Chee's mother said. "There is trouble. Moke Chee crying. You not sleep. Clean up and eat first."

I went back to take a bucket bath. Usually, Moke Chee went first. The wash area out back was so familiar to me. Like home. I was sure I could find my way around it in the dark, but this morning it seemed foreign, like a place where I didn't belong. Mrs. Fong had Mr. Fong's little aluminum shaving bowl full of hot water ready for me to shave by the time I finished my bath. She also had her chocolate custard, a soft-boiled egg, and a piece of toast ready for me to eat. I wasn't hungry, but Mrs. Fong hovered over me. Her face was wrapped in worry. I couldn't add to this poor woman's distress or add another demon to her life. I forced myself to eat. I felt sick to my stomach but finished every bit and praised her with every mouthful I forced down. The room Moke Chee was sleeping in was immediately above the kitchen, and my conversation with Mrs. Fong woke her.

Moke Chee came downstairs. Her face, especially around the eyes, was puffy, and her hair was a mess. I loved her and wanted to take her in my arms and make all her problems go away, but I was her problem, and the sooner I got out of her life, the better. I said, "I'm sorry you couldn't sleep last night. I've brought enough pain into your life. Maybe it's better that I leave for Alor Star now."

Moke Chee said. "No. It's not you. Stay."

I could see Moke Chee was about to cry, and I was glad she left to take a bucket bath. I couldn't bear to see her cry. I was confused by her actions and by what she said. Mrs. Fong had a confused look on her face and called, "Ah Chee, eat."

Moke Chee came back from her bucket bath and was composed, but she still didn't talk to me. Not freely. She answered my questions or my observations of what I had read in the morning paper with one-word answers or simple sentences. I heard the church bells of Our Lady of Sorrows ring out and said, "I'm going to Mass. OK?"

Moke Chee said, "Go."

When I got back from church, Moke Chee was wearing pink lipstick and eyeliner and was wearing a white blouse and a flowing flowery skirt. Her face was expressionless but was no longer puffy. She was in the kitchen when I arrived, and when I went into the kitchen, she left for the sitting room. When I followed her into the sitting room, she left for the kitchen. She had told me not to leave for Alor Star but was still avoiding me.

Then I heard the sound of a motor scooter out in front of the house, followed by two beeps from a motor scooter horn. Moke Chee seemed to come alive. There was a smile on her face, and as she started running out the door, she told her father, "I'll be back." But nothing to me. She didn't even look at me as she ran past. I went to the window to watch her rush down the stairs from the stoop to the street and swing her leg over the back seat of the motor scooter as she had done with my motorbike and ride off with a little Malay man not any bigger than her. This is the first time, except for the brief visit to Annie's house yesterday, that she had any life to her since she picked me up in Spa Er's taxi on Friday in Kuala Trengganu. My heart sank.

I watched Moke Chee ride off with another man while she left me at her house waiting with her parents. Her father, who was consumed in working the *Sunday Times* crossword puzzle as if nothing in the world was happening, probably wasn't aware that Moke Chee had gone off with who knows who to who knows where. Moke Chee's mother looked at me with a face full of confusion, pity, and hurt. Her mouth was moving, and her cheeks pulsed in and out as she opened and closed her mouth. It was as if she were chewing on something or trying to speak, but she had nothing in her mouth and didn't speak. She went to the back of the kitchen and started scolding who knows who for who knows what. I wish there was something I could say, something I could do to silence the demons that haunted her, but I was afraid that I would only stir them up even more.

I went to the kitchen and sat at the kitchen table. Mrs. Fong stopped her angry scolding and brought me a cup and filled it with tea. Then she brought a plate of biscuits and said, "Eat." She hovered over me, smiling like an adoring contented mother, and put her hand on my shoulder. I was surprised and pleased, and comforted. That had been the first time she touched me, or for that matter, it was the first time a Malaysian touched me with affection other than Moke Chee. And now, not even Moke Chee touches me. Moke Chee was gone with another man, but I felt like this elderly couple's son-in-law and told myself: This will be the last I see of them, and this is how I will remember them. Mr. Fong in his intellectual pursuits and Mrs.

Fong hovering over me and mothering me the best she could. I think she liked me the first time she met me. She saw me as a person and a possible suitor of her daughter, and she seemed pleased with me from the start.

Still, I couldn't figure out why Moke Chee wanted me to stay another day in Penang if she was going to leave me with her parents and go off with Hamza. I didn't know Moke Chee to be mean. Why was she doing this to me? Was she intentionally humiliating me for the pain I brought into her life and the life of her parents and Nanny? The Moke Chee I knew and loved wasn't vengeful or mean. She was kind and caring. I didn't know this person she had become, and I didn't like her like this. How could she have changed so much in four weeks? Maybe I misjudged her from the start. No, that couldn't be. This behavior was an anomaly. Or was it? I couldn't think straight.

I was angry at Moke Chee for abandoning me and leaving me alone with her parents, but surprisingly I felt more comfortable being alone with her parents now that she was out of the house. And equally surprising, her parents also seemed to be very comfortable with me. It was as if my being there alone in the house with them was completely normal. I felt like I was their son-in-law. It was weird.

In a little over an hour but less than two, I heard the sound of a motor scooter in front of the house. I ran to look out of the window expecting to see that Moke Chee had returned, but it was Hamza alone on his motor scooter. His eyes looked red, like he was crying. I didn't wait for Mrs. or Mr. Fong to unbolt the door. I rushed to open it myself and ran out, worried that something had happened to Moke Chee. The rage that I had so far been able to contain was about to burst out. If she was hurt in any way, I was ready to kill him with my bare hands right there on Irving Road. But he said, "Moke Chee has something to tell you. Get on."

I went back inside to tell Moke Chee's father that I was going to meet Moke Chee. He momentarily looked up and said,

"Ah," and went back to his crossword puzzle. Mrs. Fong closed the door behind me and watched from the window as I rode away on Hamza's motor scooter.

I said, "What's this about?"

He said, "Moke Chee wants to tell you herself."

I said, "Where is she? Why didn't she come home to tell me."

Hamza said, "She's at my uncle's house at the Malaysia Teachers College. My uncle is inviting you to his house. He wants to meet you."

Here it comes. The big dump. After what we've been through, she could have spared me the embarrassment by telling me in private that it was over between us. Why was she doing it before Hamza and his family? Maybe it was a concession he was extracting from her, some weird requirement that she prove she is honorable and worthy of his marriage. She wouldn't do it otherwise and must know I loved her enough to go along with one more of Hamza's schemes. Will she ask me to attest to our relationship being honorable? I'm tempted to say it wasn't, to blow up Hamza's scheme, but I can't, not even to him. I'm not him. I'll tell the truth and attest to our relationship being honorable and to her being an honorable woman. It disgusted me, but I'll do that for her.

When we arrived at Hamza's uncle's house, I was surprised to find Nancy Ottinger there. Nancy was a Peace Corps librarian and a colleague of Hamza's uncle. She was selecting some of his paintings for an upcoming exhibit at the college library. While Moke Chee and Nancy were chatting, Hamza's uncle showed me his paintings. He was an art teacher at the Malayan Teachers College and painted in what he described as a post-Cubist style. He said, "Hamza here and Moke Chee don't think my paintings are art. They say they are lifeless and unrealistic and just decorative patterns of paint. What do you think?

I said, "I'm a biologist. I know nothing about art, but I could tell your paintings are of the buildings on campus, and the colors are pleasing. I like the way you paint the shadows of the buildings. I wish I could paint like that."

In the meantime, Moke Chee and Nancy came over to where Hamza's uncle was about to explain his painting to me.

Hamza's uncle said, "There you see. I have an unbiased affirmation of my work."

Then Hamza said, "Jim, tell me, if America is so great, why do they produce such inferior products?"

I was taken aback by his comment that seemed to come out of nowhere.

Hamza stepped over to where he was facing Moke Chee, and he rose up on his toes so that he was an inch taller and wearing a smile as he said: "Take my uncle's car, for example. He paid a huge price for his 1960 American Plymouth. It looks big and attractive, but the passenger front window crank keeps falling off no matter how often he brings it to the repair shop."

Hamza was bouncing up and down now and playing with his fingers while staring into Moke Chee's face as if he was making a statement to her rather than asking me a question. I had no idea how or why he brought this up when we were discussing his uncle's paintings, but I figured he wanted Moke Chee to equate me with the American-made Plymouth that was big and attractive but nonetheless defective and worthless. Minimally, he obviously was trying to humiliate me in front of Moke Chee. I was certain he was attacking me and trying to draw me into a confrontation.

I decided not to fall victim to his attack, but I wouldn't let it go unanswered. I had mastered the art of the put-down as a child. I replied: "That's because Malayans don't know how to properly maintain an American automobile, and they lack the skills to make the simplest of repairs."

Moke Chee and Hamza's uncle burst out laughing right in Hamza's face. Nancy tried to stifle her laugh. Moke Chee laughed so hard she could hardly speak, but she managed to say while laughing, "You had that coming. You tried to embarrass Jim and put him down in front of all of us—and Jim turned the table on you. The laugh is on you."

Moke Chee was still smiling when she whispered in my ear, "I'm following Nancy home. I told her you and I are getting married. Let me talk to my father tonight."

Then Moke Chee said, "With that, it's time to go. Thank you for your hospitality, Uncle. I'm following Nancy home. Hamza, I'm counting on you to fetch Jim safely back home."

That was totally unexpected and weirder than anything I had ever experienced. I was stunned but delighted. I couldn't stomach Hamza and wanted nothing to do with him. I wanted to take the bus back to Moke Chee's house but felt obliged to accept a ride on Hamza's motor scooter.

Hamza drove me home, and I was prepared to hop off his motor scooter in case he decided to commit murder-suicide with me on back. He said, "Jim, I congratulate you. The better man won. I tried every trick to win Moke Chee over, and you played it straight. It turns out you won the prize."

I said, "I don't see Moke Chee as a prize to be won. If she loves me, I want her to love me for who I am, not because I beat out some other man."

He said, "You may think I played dirty, but I believe all is fair in love and war, you know."

I said, "Not when it hurts other people."

He said, "That's just it. If Moke Chee goes to America, she will leave her parents and servant behind. Will she be happy?"

I knew he was playing mind games with me and trying to make me feel guilty now. I thought to myself: You jackass, you think that hasn't been weighing on my mind since I first resisted the urge to kiss her while dancing at The Green Parrot, and you think that is still not on my mind. It irritated me that he called Nanny a servant. She is a person with a name, just as Moke Chee is a person, not a prize. I'm not going to give you the satisfaction of seeing my disgust for you. You're not worth it.

I said, "Moke Chee will be happy as long as she is with me."

Hamza's body seemed to slump, and after a pause, he said, "You're right. I only wish she loved me as deeply as she loves you."

I knew he felt vanquished, and that made me feel good. I hated what he did to Moke Chee, but I didn't let on. Instead, I said to Hamza: "I know how hurt you feel. In that sense, I feel we are kindred spirits, like brothers."

Hamza said, "I wish you hadn't said that. Now I feel worse about what I did to you."

If he were too ignorant or uncaring to realize it himself, I decided that I would let him know the real harm he did and laid it on him: "It wasn't to me. It was to Moke Chee. You withheld her letters. I could feel her anguish in the letters she wrote to me. Surely, you must have seen it in her. She lost so much weight worrying about what had happened while you added to her anguish by telling her lies. That's not what someone does to the person they supposedly love."

We arrived safely at Moke Chee's house. I couldn't get off that motor scooter fast enough and was relieved to rid myself of that manipulative, self-centered, slimy scumbag. Moke Chee's mother opened the door for me. She had a puzzled and worried look on her face and asked where Moke Chee was. I reassured her that Moke Chee was fine and visiting some American friends and would be home shortly. Hamza drove off. Moke Chee's mother spat in the gutter toward his direction and called upon a spirit to curse him.

I went back in to take a bucket bath. I felt filthy after my encounter with Hamza. I washed myself a second time, but the filth seemed to cling to me. I couldn't rid myself of the filthy feeling and washed myself a third time. Shortly after I came out of the bath, I heard another motor scooter outside the house and went to the window, worried it was Hamza back for more. I was relieved that it was Don Ottinger bringing Moke Chee home. She seemed to be the old Moke Chee that I knew back before the monsoon. She went in the back to take a bucket bath. I stood outside the bath door, and we talked nonstop while she poured buckets of water over herself. After her bath, we asked her father if he wanted to go to the padang to eat.

CHAPTER 25

It was like old times. Mr. Fong reserved a table. I followed Moke Chee from hawker stall to hawker stall, ordering all sorts of small plates of food. Mr. Fong told all his stories of growing up in Penang. I had heard the stories enough times to tell them myself, but I enjoyed being with him as he relived his childhood, youth, and adulthood. But this evening was different. His voice and manner took on a sense of reverence as, for the first time, he spoke of his internment by the Japanese occupying forces. His eyes fixed on mine. He always looked into my eyes when talking to me, except when he told me stories of times past about his childhood or the family, when his eyes would fix on the horizon. But now, he looked deep into my eyes. Yes, he wanted me to know about the atrocities his captors inflicted on him, but he also wanted me to know what he endured and his will to endure.

He said: "I was held in a cell with two others. They dragged each of us out of the cell every day for interrogation. They thought I was hiding Englishmen. I wasn't. The Japanese didn't believe me and beat me with the buckle end of a leather belt. They said that if I gave up the name of any Malayan who helped them, they would set me free. I could have gained my freedom by giving them any random name, but I told them I can't tell you what I don't know. They wouldn't believe me. On the first night, my granny came to me in my sleep and said, 'You will be released by your captors in three days. Don't eat the food they give you and don't drink the water. Have faith. I will see to it that you will be freed in three days' time.'

"I told my cellmates about Granny appearing and telling me not to eat the rice or drink the water the guards gave us. My cellmates ate my share of the rice and drank my share of the water. The rice had sand and insects in it, and the water smelled of petrol.

"When the first cellmate died, the second cellmate, an Indian man, pleaded with me to ask my granny to rescue him. He, too, died in captivity.

"On the third day, the guards dragged me out of my cell. I was unable to walk on my own. They brought me to an interrogation room. They said this is your last chance. Tell us where the English are, or we will slit your throat. Again, I told them I cannot tell you what I do not know.

"They sat me on a chair. A soldier pulled his long sword out of its sheath and told me to close my eyes and hold my head back. He grabbed a fistful of hair and jerked my head back. I felt the cold steel blade of his sword traverse my throat. I felt no pain and thought they had killed me, and I was thankful my death was not painful. But the rest of my body still ached, and I could hear laughter. I thought, how can I still hear if I'm dead? I opened my eyes, and the captain in charge was standing over me and said: 'You're no use to us. You can go.'

"But I couldn't walk, so two burly guards dragged me to the front gate and threw me out on the street. Each kicked me for good measure. Fortunately, Mother and Nanny came to the prison every day to pray and to plead for my release and to wait for any news of my condition. If not for them, I would be among the hundreds of nameless people left on the side of the road to die. They carried me home and nursed me back to health. But I was still too weak to work, and we were penniless."

He paused for a moment to collect his thoughts, clear his

throat, and take a long drink of hot tea. Then, he continued, "The Japanese occupying forces stole all of my money and mother's jewelry. Penniless and too frail to work. I swallowed my pride and relied on Nanny to make cakes to sell in the market to keep the family alive. Before that, we were well-off. Not wealthy, but well-off. We had three servants, but only Nanny stayed. She loved Moke Chee as her own and wouldn't abandon her. In that sense, we were fortunate. Now, old and penniless and unable to work, I'm dependent on Moke Chee to support me."

What Next?

Walking back home across the padang, Mr. Fong again held my arm to steady himself. That made me feel good, but I knew already that this wasn't a walk I would make with him as his son-in-law. Initially, I felt good about him telling me about his unjust captivity during the war and sharing with me the reversal of his fortune, as well as the humiliation of his servant supporting his family. I thought that showed he trusted me, and perhaps he trusted me enough to grant me permission to marry Moke Chee. But he also relayed to me how dependent he was on Moke Chee to care for him. Suddenly, it dawned on me that his sharing of his refusal to relent under torture—to the brink of death—was his way of showing me that he would never relent. He would never give his blessing for me and his daughter to marry.

Mr. Fong hadn't kicked me out of his house, and he didn't forbid Moke Chee and me from seeing each other. We weren't planning to marry right away. Time was on our side, and I hoped he would relent and give us his blessing.

When we got back to the house and cleaned up to prepare to go to sleep, Moke Chee and I again sat on the floor of her room and talked about our future. We decided I should wait to ask for permission to marry Moke Chee until after I completed my rural health assignment and returned to Penang. I was taking an early morning taxi to Ipoh, so it was time to sleep.

Moke Chee left to go to Nanny's old room to sleep. I tried but couldn't sleep. A thought kept buzzing in my mind, and I feared that Moke Chee's father would not give us his blessing, and without it, our relationship was at a dead end. I worried about what Moke Chee would do. Despair blanketed me. Moke Chee couldn't sleep either. I heard her tossing.

Hope Dies

I heard Moke Chee knock at her father's door and ask if he were asleep. He was, but when she said she needed to talk to him, he said, "Enter."

She told her father that she couldn't sleep because she was confused. She asked him to tell her what to do. She loved me more than she could love any other man. And if he did not grant her permission to marry, no other man, except Hamza, would want to marry her, knowing that she loved another man. She said: "Hamza said he would marry me even if I loved Jim, and that he would allow me to turn my entire paycheck over to you and have Nanny live with us." She also told her father that while she would have to convert to Islam on paper, she could keep her Chinese name and customs. She said: "If you will not give me permission to marry Jim, will you give me permission to marry Hamza?"

I felt sick to my stomach again.

Moke Chee's father roared like a lion, "No. You do not have permission to marry Jim, and you do not have permission to marry Hamza. Oil and water do not mix. You must marry your own kind or not marry at all."

Moke Chee came to my door sobbing, and I said it was open. I sat up in bed, and she sat beside me. I held her in my arms, and she buried her face in my chest, sobbing. She said, "I know him. He will never relent. He will never give us his blessing. I can't marry without his blessing, and he will never grant it."

Moke Chee didn't have to tell me that he wouldn't relent. He as much told me at the padang when he said that he withstood three days of torture to the brink of death on principle. If the Japanese occupying forces could not get him to relent, there was nothing that I, nor anyone, could do to get him to change his mind. I wish I could be angry at him, but I couldn't. I didn't agree with his resolute stance, but I understood and respected him. He was protecting his only daughter.

Moke Chee continued: "I want you to know that I will always love you no matter who I marry. Hamza said that he knew I would always love you, but that doesn't matter to him because he has enough love for both of us."

Oh no, I thought. We're back to that again. I wanted to reason with her. To tell her Hamza was not an honorable man and deceived her once and could be lying to her again and will change his tone once she marries him.

I said, "Your father said he wouldn't grant permission to marry him either."

She said, "Hamza said that he and I could just go to the registry and get married and then ask for my father's permission."

I said, "Isn't that just one more act of deception? Can you be happy with a man so steeped in deception? He deceives; he lies. Under no circumstance can you trust him."

She said, "He said that he only does it because he loves me so much." Then she added, "Without you, I'm so empty; I need someone who will love me."

I said, "I will always love you, and you will forever be in my heart."

"Don't say that," Moke Chee said. "You must find someone who will love and cherish you as much as I do, and you will. You won't be here for me, and I need someone who will fill the void in my heart and accept that I will always love you. Hamza said he will."

I didn't reply. What more could I say? Hamza was not a good man, but who she married was her choice, not mine. It seemed as if she wanted to marry him to punish herself. I couldn't save her from herself. There was no reasoning with her. She continued sobbing. By now, her body had melded into mine. She said, "I feel so safe in your arms," and I held her until she fell asleep. I wanted to hold on to her like that forever, but I let her slide down on her own bed to sleep while I slipped away to Nanny's room and tried to sleep.

Morning came, and I heard Moke Chee's mother opening up the house before the sun rose. I packed my things. The door to Moke Chee's room was unlocked. I didn't want to wake her but wanted one last look at her, so I opened the door just a crack. She was still sleeping, on her side, with her knees drawn up toward her chest in a fetal position. Looking at her, I realized that I would never see her again. It hurt so much that I couldn't stay any longer, so I tried to make as little noise as possible going down the stairs. I went to the kitchen to thank Moke Chee's mother and say goodbye to her. She had an anxious, hurt look on her face and asked me to stay and eat and wake Moke Chee, but I said no to all of that. I had to go. The sooner I departed, the better. I left the house, 70c Irving Road, that contained so many wonderful moments for me, and I didn't look back this time. I knew the old woman was standing on the stoop, watching me walk away. I could feel her eyes follow me down Irving Road for the last time. I forced myself not to turn and wave this time. I didn't want her to see me crying.

I continued on my way, walking the two miles to the taxi stand rather than taking a trishaw. It would hurt too much to sit in a Penang trishaw alone.

CHAPTER 26

I had planned to go back to Penang after my rural health assignment, where Moke Chee and I were going to work with the orphan children who remained in residence at St. Nicholas' Home over the school holiday, but that all changed now. Instead, I would go to Kuala Lumpur to resign from the Peace Corps and return home.

January was the start of a new school year. It was an ideal time to separate before the new school year began. Boon had been promoted to the Ministry in Kuala Lumpur, and I didn't like my new Headmaster. Teh Eng was transferred to another town to become a Headmaster, and I would be left in our house all alone. But most of all, with the prospect that Moke Chee had already married Hamza, being in that big house on weekends would be too painful. There was nothing for me in Malaya except more pain and loneliness and the likelihood of still another waste-of-time and humiliating assignment. The time to put the Peace Corps and Malaya behind me had long passed.

I had a two-week health assignment with Dr. Mahathir in a remote village, and I wrote Moke Chee a letter telling her I had left before she awoke because I couldn't bring myself to say goodbye and that she would forever remain in my heart. I told her to forget me and find an honorable man who would give her the love she deserved. I also wrote to Mr. Fong to thank him for his hospitality.

After the two-week-long assignment on the road, I arrived back in Alor Star with Dr. Mahathir and the other Volunteer, Art. Dr. Mahathir's wife greeted us and said, "Jim, while you were away, you received a letter from Mrs. Wolter."

I thought: How did my mother know I was here? I was worried something bad had happened at home. But I saw the thin envelope had a Malayan stamp, and the return address said Mrs. Moke Chee Wolter, 70c Irving Rd., Penang. I didn't know what to make of that.

I didn't expect to ever hear from Moke Chee again. I thought she must have written Mrs. Moke Chee Wolter as the return address out of habit. I couldn't read the letter during lunch with the Mahathirs. I decided to wait until I was alone to read it. After dinner, Art and I shared a taxi to Ipoh. Art intended to stay overnight in Ipoh and then get a train north to Thailand. My plan was to go on to Kuala Lumpur and exit the Peace Corps. Art fell asleep on the way to Ipoh, so I read Moke Chee's letter.

That changed everything.

I opened the envelope. Moke Chee's letter was addressed to *My Dearest Darling Husband Jim*. I was stunned. She wrote: *Today I received your letter and am so happy. When I awoke to find you had left, my life felt so empty. I knew I could marry no other man but you. I was miserable until receiving your letter. I love you so. Please come back to me. My father said he also received a letter from you and wanted me to read it, but I told him I had my own letter and did not need to read his. You are the only one I love and the only one I want to spend the rest of my life with, regardless of whether my father gives us his blessing or not. Hurry back to me. I long to be with you and in the safety of your arms.*

Moke Chee signed her letter *Your loving Wife Forever*, and wrote: *P.S. By the way, you left a shirt behind. I can smell your presence on it and wear it as my pajama top.*

Fortunately, the taxi Art and I took made a stop in Butterworth. I told the taxi driver that I was exiting there. I boarded the ferry and hailed a taxi to take me to Moke Chee's house.

As the taxi approached 70c Irving Road, I saw Moke Chee's mother on the front stoop tossing kernels of rice onto the street for a flock of sparrows and then ducking back inside the house and closing the door. The taxi came to a stop in front of the house, and Moke Chee's mother appeared at the window with a scowl on her face and then disappeared. I sat still in the back seat. I had been so excited that I hadn't paused to think. Moke Chee's letter was ten days old. Perhaps things had changed with her again. I wasn't sure if my reappearance would be welcomed. I looked at the house that had been so familiar, a place I felt welcomed. Now, looking at the house, I felt like an outsider. I wasn't sure that I was doing the right thing in returning. I thought maybe I should ask the taxi driver to take me back to the taxi stand or to wait in case Moke Chee didn't want to receive me and I wasn't allowed in the house.

The taxi driver put his left arm over the front seat and turned his face toward mine, and said, "70c Irving Road. This is it. This is where you wanted to go, isn't it?"

I looked up and down Irving Road to see if Hamza's motor scooter was parked nearby. It wasn't, so I said, "Yes, thank you," and pulled an additional dollar out of my pocket for making him wait. I got out of the taxi. In a few minutes, Moke Chee and I would be reunited. I wanted it to be forever. I was sure of that. I wondered if it would be.

Is There Hope This Time?

My stomach was in knots climbing up the three steps to the front door at 70c Irving Road—even more so than the very first time I went calling on Miss Fong. I wasn't sure whether to knock on the door or call for Moke Chee through the window. I was plagued with indecision. I was overthinking this simple act, but I feared whatever I did would be wrong. Fortunately, Moke Chee's mother looked out of the window again. And again, she had a scowl on her face, but then recognizing me, she smiled and shouted, "Ah Chee, it's Jim. He's returned."

She opened the door. I slipped off my shoes. Moke Chee came running into my arms. I swore to myself in that instant that I would never let her go, no matter what. I had a sample of life without her, and I couldn't tolerate it. Moke Chee's mother smiled broadly and insisted I have something to eat while Moke Chee's father kept reading his newspaper. I said, "Hello, Mr. Fong."

He put down his newspaper, looked at me, and said, "Good afternoon," and then went back to reading the afternoon paper. Everything was back to normal.

Moke Chee's mother served me tea and biscuits. I asked Moke Chee if she were willing to go to St. Nicholas' Home with me as we had originally planned and see if I could still work there during the rest of the school holiday. She agreed.

The next morning, Moke Chee and I walked to the Macalister Road bus terminal and rode the bus to St. Nicholas' Home, where we visited with the home's director. The director told us there were eight girls who had no families and suggested we take two girls at a time on a day outing. Moke Chee and I intended to provide the girls with a family-type experience and to demonstrate to the Peace Corps that working with the girls at St. Nicholas' Home was a worthy school holiday assignment.

Moke Chee and I took the girls, one older and one younger, to the places and did the things we would have done with sighted children in the ten- to twelve-year-old age range.

Things were back to normal between Moke Chee and me, and with her mother and even her father. Moke Chee's father said, "When you left two weeks ago, I thought that was the last of you, but then you returned."

I didn't know how to take that. He offered the observation so matter of fact with no display of emotion—either sadness or joy. And he offered no further comment. I was just relieved and happy that he didn't throw me out of his house.

I said, "I love Moke Chee, and she loves me, and I still would like your blessing to marry her."

He didn't respond to my request but said, "I told Moke Chee I received your letter and offered it to her to read, but she told me she had her own letter from you and didn't need to read mine."

I didn't know what to make of what he said. He didn't say we had his blessing, but he also didn't say we didn't. My relationship with him was back to being a friendly guest, and for now, that was the best I could hope for. I suppose he thought with Moke Chee in Penang and me in Kuala Trengganu that our relationship would wither. But our relationship continued to grow.

Back to Kuala Trengganu

This time when I departed Penang, Moke Chee saw me off. We kissed farewell upstairs in her bedroom. We held hands in public but didn't kiss in public. I looked out of the taxi window at Moke Chee standing on the front stoop of her house with her mother standing beside her. Tears were in Moke Chee's eyes. Her mother wore a warm smile. I wanted to hold the vision of Moke Chee in sight as long as possible and longed for the day I would see her again. When the ferry crossed over to the mainland, I got out to admire the green hills of Penang Island—Moke Chee's "island in the sun"—set against the baby-blue sky. I missed Moke Chee, so I wrote her a letter telling her how much I loved her and that I missed her already. I wanted to post it as soon as I got to Kuala Trengganu.

Usually, when I returned to Kuala Trengganu, Teh Eng was already back and welcomed me with a smile. But the house was empty. Teh Eng was promoted to Headmaster of his own school in another town. If I couldn't be with Moke Chee, I wished he could have taken me with him to his new school.

Thankfully, Boon's wife and son were still next door to me in Kuala Trengganu. Boon had been promoted to the Ministry in Kuala Lumpur, but Nina remained at Sultan Sulaiman Secondary School, and Boon returned to Kuala Trengganu on weekends. Most importantly, by Tuesday of the new school term, I started receiving daily letters from Moke Chee, and each evening I wrote to her before turning in for the night. Our letter-writing routine was back to normal and not interrupted. In addition to writing to each other every day, my good friend Bong allowed me to use his shop telephone to call Moke Chee at Grandmother's house at ten o'clock every Sunday morning after attending Mass at St. Mary's. After speaking to Moke Chee, sometimes I stayed with Bong and had lunch with him and his family. Other times I met other teachers at "The Green Door Restaurant" for lunch.

I started the new school year at Tengku Bariah with no idea of what I would be teaching. Before leaving for the December holiday, I had informed Ratnam that I would leave Malaya after the second trimester in August 1963 and that he should make out my teaching schedule accordingly. He assigned me to be the Form III Form Master. I was assigned to teach English, math, and science.

One day in March 1963, I received a notice from the Peace Corps office in Kuala Lumpur that Peace Corps Volunteers were no longer to have motor scooters, housekeepers, laundry service, or refrigerators. I was told that a truck would arrive the next day to pick up my motorbike and refrigerator. I didn't mind losing the housekeeping and laundry service since I had been cleaning my house and washing my own clothes since

January. I didn't even mind losing the refrigerator, but I did mind losing the motorbike.

The bicycle ride from Sultan Sulaiman to Tengku Bariah was a sweaty forty-minute bicycle ride each way to school and back. All the extra hours of cycling forced me to cut back on my activities in Kuala Trengganu. The biggest loss was having to drop out of my Mandarin classes at the Chinese night school and dropping my tennis club membership.

So from March to August of 1963, I rode my bicycle until Luke drove the Peace Corps pickup truck up the east coast while visiting volunteers. He stopped at Tengku Bariah to have an exit interview with Low Tim Fook and me. Low gave Luke an earful of positive but bland platitudes about me that could pretty much have applied to any teacher.

Luke told me he had to fly back to Kuala Lumpur and that Donna and Eva, two of the Peace Corps nurses, were going there at the same time as I was. He asked if he could leave the truck with me so I could drive the truck and the nurses to Kuala Lumpur at the end of the school term. I agreed, and he told me I could use the truck in Kuala Trengganu while I had it. So, I got to use the truck for two weeks.

Post-Peace Corps Plans

When I requested a two-year leave of absence from medical school in August 1961 to join the Peace Corps, I intended to return in 1963. But medical school in Chicago was out of the question now. I revised my plan. I would study tropical medicine at the University of Singapore Medical School. Moke Chee agreed to teach school in Singapore or Johor Bahru. After finishing medical school, I would practice medicine in Malaya. But my application to the University of Singapore wasn't even considered because only applicants from Malaya or Singapore were admitted to the school. That plan was dead.

Our fallback plan had multiple moving parts, but Moke Chee and I were sure we could get them all in order. I had completed half of the graduate hours required for a master's degree at Northern Illinois University, so our plan was that I would complete a master's degree at NIU while applying for a doctoral research fellowship in genetics at other American universities. Moke Chee would follow me to the United States at a later date.

I wrote to the chairman of the biology department at NIU, and he wrote back, saying that he would assist me with that plan. I wrote Penn Winter and asked if he had a part-time position in the next Peace Corps training programs at NIU. Penn wrote back, saying that he had a full-time position for me and suggested that I go to school part-time. I accepted Penn's offer, which settled the matter of my schooling. That was the easy part.

When Moke Chee accepted her scholarship to study in England, she had to sign a contract to teach for five full years in Malaya after she returned. She had just completed two of the five years, so our intent was to purchase back the remaining years of her contract and for her to get a teaching position in America. Here's where our plan began to fall apart. The cost of buying back Moke Chee's contract—$25,000 in American currency—made it impossible.

Our next option was for Moke Chee to remain in Malaya while I completed a doctorate degree and for us to visit each other on long holidays. We still had not obtained the blessing to marry from Moke Chee's father. We hoped to gain it before I left for America, and if not, then perhaps he would after seeing our dedication to each other over three more years. It seemed a perfectly reasonable and feasible plan to two twenty-three-year-olds.

Red Tape

Moke Chee and I approached her father for his blessing to marry during the May holiday. Again he refused. Now the August holiday was upon us. My exit from the Peace Corps was at hand. This was the time Moke Chee and I had planned to marry. I went to Penang to be with Moke Chee and asked her father for his blessing one more time. It had been a year since I had begun asking him for permission to marry Moke Chee, and for a year, he refused to give us his blessing. He remained true to form. He was resolute and again refused. Our future was in limbo. September arrived. It was time for me to make my way back to Kuala Lumpur and depart for Chicago. So, Moke Chee and I put our marriage plans on hold. We would wait.

Moke Chee accompanied me to Kuala Lumpur so I could help her obtain a visa before seeing me off. We were directed from one office to another at the U.S. Embassy before getting to an American official in charge of granting visas. He was a patient listener. I told him that Moke Chee and I were engaged and explained that she needed a visa because we planned to meet each other during our respective holidays. He told us being engaged was an insufficient reason for issuing a visa, but marriage was.

That was it. Moke Chee's father's blessing aside, we went directly to the Malayan Marriage Registry.

We found the Marriage Registry in a maze of offices located in the government building known as Jam Besar (Big Clock). We found an inefficacious clerk who explained to us in elaborate detail that we had to pay fifteen dollars each for an application fee and another fifty dollars each for the marriage certificates. He told us it would take at least three weeks and possibly eight for all of the documents to make their way through the appropriate channels. We realized we needed help in moving our application through the channels at a quicker pace. I knew Kashim, the Peace Corps' Office Manager, who was a minor but important member of the Malayan Ruling Party. I went to Luke and asked for his help.

Luke held the position of Director of the Peace Corps in Malaya and was also a romantic at heart. He was aware of my plans with Moke Chee and was sympathetic to our plight. He relieved Kashim of all his other Peace Corps responsibilities and assigned him to help Moke Chee and me get married. Kashim immediately took our application in hand and drove us in his car back to Jam Besar. We followed him from office to office, gathering signatures and official stamps. We needed one more signature, that of Mentri Besat, who was the chief minister of the district, but he had already left his office. Kashim said that he was meeting with him at a political rally that evening and would obtain his signature then. He told us to come to the Peace Corps office first thing the next morning.

We were at the Peace Corps office at eight o'clock on September 10, 1963, and true to his word, Kashim had our marriage license application ready. He also made an appointment with a magistrate to marry us at two in the afternoon and told us we had to round up two witnesses.

My buddy John was assigned to the Peace Corps office during the August school holiday as a Peace Corps Volunteer Assistant to the Director. He confided in me that he was being considered for the position on a permanent basis. He then confided in me that if he got it, he and Regina would marry. He asked me to keep all that to myself, which I did. He agreed to be a witness at my wedding. Moke Chee's neighbor, Lay Leng, was a student at the University of Malaya and agreed to be Moke Chee's witness. Luke allowed me to use the Peace Corps truck for our wedding and honeymoon vehicle.

Moke Chee and I drove to the university to pick up Lay Leng. She had just finished lunch and was dressed in a white cheongsam for the wedding. About twenty college girls accompanied her to the Peace Corps truck to see her off and showered her with flower petals. They surrounded the truck to catch a glimpse of that American man she was marrying. She and Moke Chee laughed, knowing that the girls thought it was Lay Leng getting married.

There was little traffic between the university and Jam Besar. We didn't want to arrive too early, so the three of us went to a nearby florist. Moke Chee picked out orchids for the bride and bridesmaid bouquets and boutonnieres for John and me.

I started getting anxious that we would be late, but we arrived at Jam Besar ten minutes early, and I was pleased to find that Kashim was already there with a group of Peace Corps Volunteers. John was with Ray Sparrow, who was teaching architecture at the university, and my old roommate Mike Frazer and Bob Reed were waiting for us. I was overwhelmed by the support that my fellow Volunteers, Luke, and Kashim gave me. It was something they didn't have to do, and I never expected it. Ray was our self-appointed wedding photographer. Without him, we would never have had wedding photos, and without Luke, we could never have gotten married. Luke came through for us when we needed him most.

Kashim led our party through a maze of hallways in Jam Besar until we reached the wedding magistrate's office. The magistrate was a short, serious-looking man seated at his desk in shirt sleeves and with his suit jacket draped over the back of his chair when we arrived. He stood up and greeted Kashim while putting his suit jacket on. Kashim introduced each of us to the magistrate. I was glad that staring at someone was not impolite because I couldn't take my eyes off the magistrate's face. When he spoke, his upper lip didn't move. In fact, his entire face was immobile while speaking. Only his lower jaw and lower lip moved. It was as if he were a marionette.

He spoke in a monotone voice. After checking our photo identification cards to make sure we were who we said we were and legally old enough to marry, he asked Moke Chee and me if we were there to be married of our own volition. He then read the statute from a book that legally marries a woman and a man. After reading the statute, he read the marriage vows while Moke Chee and I repeated them. Then, he told us that before officially pronouncing us husband and wife, he had to read the statute about dissolving our marriage if we ever desired.

Moke Chee and Lay Leng were holding hands during the ceremony, and when the magistrate started reading the statute to dissolve our marriage before we were even pronounced husband and wife, they started giggling. They stifled their giggles, but I could see their shoulders quivering. It was all I could do to keep from laughing. To begin with, I had imagined that if I ever married, I would be waiting at a Catholic church altar for my bride to walk up the aisle with her father. Here in Jam Besar, it was unreal from the start. Now, it bordered on the absurd and hysterical, but it was what we had to do to get Moke Chee a visa to the United States.

We were officially married.

After the ceremony, John said: "I thought it was touching that Moke Chee and her bridesmaid were crying during the ceremony."

I didn't have the heart to tell him that they were giggling, and I didn't feel like engaging in guy talk with him. For the first time, I felt a sudden weight of responsibility—for Moke Chee and for sharing her responsibility to care for her parents and Nanny. I could no longer act as an individual. Everything I did from now on affected the lives of four other people. It was a heavy responsibility but not a burdensome one. I had often thought about how Moke Chee described the responsibility she felt toward her parents and Nanny. I recalled her saying that was part of who she was, but I didn't understand. Now, I understood how she felt about her responsibility to them and how that was a part of who she was. And I welcomed it as part of who I was. I had, by the simple act of saying "I do," become substantial as a person. I liked the feeling.

We invited the magistrate, Luke, Kashim, Lay Leng, and

the Volunteers to join us for a marriage banquet. The magistrate and Kashim declined, but Ray and Mike brought their girlfriends, and Luke joined us. Luke provided the Champagne for the banquet and, aside from Ray's photos, gave us our only wedding gift: a Malaysian salad service made of buffalo horn with silver handles. Luke told us that Sheridan picked it out for us. Receiving wedding gifts had never entered my mind, so I treasured the gift Sheridan and Luke presented to Moke Chee and me, as well as the photos Ray presented to us. Our wedding was impromptu and thrown together in less than twenty-four hours. It was nothing like I ever imagined. Except for not having Moke Chee's father's blessing, it was more beautiful than I could have wished for. I was married to the woman who, for the first time in my life, made me feel loved and who was committed to spending the rest of her life with me.

Now, we had to tell my father-in-law and the family.

Married to Moke Chee

Moke Chee was staying at Gim Lan's house in Kuala Lumpur, so Nanny knew we were getting married. Immediately after our wedding, we went to Gim Lan's house and performed the tea ceremony. The tea ceremony was performed first by Moke Chee and then by me. I didn't anticipate participating in the tea ceremony. When Moke Chee got up from kneeling, she handed me the teacup. I had been taught by the nuns that Catholics only bow to God. Here, I was expected to kneel in front of Nanny. I now was Moke Chee's husband, so I knelt in front of Nanny out of respect for who she was and the respected position she occupies in our lives. I hoped the nuns would approve. I served Nanny her cup of tea while pledging my fidelity to her. She smiled at me and said, "I know. Don't worry about me. You promise to take good care of my daughter."

Nanny spoke to me in a commanding voice. It was the first and only time she spoke to me like that. I understood her concern. That's all I wanted to do in my life, but I lacked the Chinese vocabulary to appropriately pledge my fidelity to Moke Chee, Nanny, and Moke Chee's parents. I said, "I will. I promise."

Nanny took my arm to lift me up. She and Moke Chee hugged. Then I put my arms around both of them. Nanny accepted my hug.

The following morning we drove back to Penang. We told Moke Chee's parents. Moke Chee's mother, my mother-in-law, smiled and blessed us. She asked Moke Chee, "Did you wear a beautiful white wedding dress when you got married?"

Moke Chee wore her red cheongsam to the wedding, but she told her mother, "Yes."

Her mother said, "You must have been beautiful."

Moke Chee rose, and I knelt before my mother-in-law and said, "Mother, I pledge my fidelity to you. I promise to take good care of Moke Chee and you. And Moke Chee was a very beautiful bride."

Moke Chee's father stood by and watched in silence. He looked crestfallen. Moke Chee stood before him with a cup of tea in her hand. She said, "Please, Father, may I serve you a cup of tea?"

He said, "You are my only child. I would disown you if I could. But I can't. I'm too dependent on you. You have been disobedient and have broken my heart, but I have no option but to accept it."

Tears welled up in Moke Chee's eyes. He sat down. She said, "Father, I promise I will always be your daughter. I will take care of you."

Pain and sorrow painted this good, strongly principled man's face as he accepted the cup of tea from his only child. He blessed her and reached down with his right arm and helped her rise. I was happy for Moke Chee, but guilt and sorrow gripped me.

He remained seated. I knelt before my father-in-law and

presented him with a cup of tea with both hands, and said, "Father, I promise my total fidelity to you, and I promise to always love and care for your daughter. I promise to raise your grandchildren to respect you and your culture. Please, may I have your blessing?"

He accepted the tea and said, "You have my blessing." Then he added, "A daughter marries and enters her husband's family. A son brings his wife into the family. A daughter leaves her family. That is the way it has always been. I trust you and your family to welcome and care for my daughter."

It seemed to me that he was saying out loud something that he had been thinking and worrying about since Moke Chee's birth. I could tell he was worried about Moke Chee being accepted into my family, especially if she were in America, away from her own family and friends. I had pushed to the back of my mind how Moke Chee would be received by my family. A deep sense of sorrow came over me, and I wanted to tell him that my family's custom was for the married couple and their children to be closer to the woman's family than the man's. I hoped my family would accept, support, nurture, and love Moke Chee and our children, but if they didn't, I vowed to myself that I would protect them from the toxicity of my family.

I said to my father-in-law: "Father, I promise you that I will always love, cherish, protect, and care for Moke Chee and care for you."

He didn't want me as his son-in-law and did all in his power to prevent Moke Chee from marrying me. He had every reason to throw me out of the house or at least refuse to accept a cup of tea from me. But the Chinese tradition and custom were so strongly ingrained into his being that he accepted my humble gesture of filial piety. After accepting the offer of tea, he reached down with both arms and helped me rise. Next, we went to Grandmother.

Grandmother showed no emotion when we went to tell

her we were married and to pledge our fidelity to her. When it was my turn to serve her tea, she spoke to me in Hokkien: "You are a European. This is not your custom. You are not obliged to serve me tea. If you desire, you need not do so."

I knelt before Grandmother and held the cup of tea out to her with both hands, and said, "Grandmother, I pledge my fidelity to you and promise to always love and care for your granddaughter and her parents. May I have the honor of your blessing?"

Grandmother accepted the tea and said, "I accept your pledge and your promise. You must take good care of Moke Chee. We will be too far away to help her. She will have only you, so you must care for her. You have my blessing." She touched my arm, signaling me to rise.

As I rose, I thought of my father-in-law serving Grandmother tea many decades ago when he was young and strong and had a bright future of aspirations and dreams that he didn't get to realize. What sustained him were his customs and traditions.

Moke Chee and I then went to the various aunties and uncles to perform the tea ceremony and receive their blessings. That night we had a wedding party for twenty relatives and my father-in-law's best friends. I sat at a table next to my father-in-law, along with seven of his brothers and friends, while Moke Chee sat at another table with nine aunties. We had the wedding dinner party out of respect for my father-in-law. It was an opportunity where Moke Chee and I could each publicly show our fidelity to him.

They Lived Happily Ever After—Almost

I couldn't believe this was happening to me. I had been attracted to Moke Chee because of her physical beauty, and then I was intrigued by her open, trusting, and outgoing personality and her intellect. But it was her value system and the depth of her love and dedication to her father, mother, and Nanny that enticed me to want to spend the rest of my life with her, sharing in that love. I loved Moke Chee and observed her culture with intense interest and intense curiosity. I wanted to marry her, but it never occurred to me that in doing so, I would be immersed in her culture, and now here, I was fully immersed and participating in it. I knew I wasn't the son-in-law that my father-in-law desired, but I also knew he appreciated my showing my fidelity to him publicly. Given the circumstances, his allowing me to publicly demonstrate my filial piety to him was far more than I deserved.

That night, for the first time, I got to spend a night with Moke Chee in her room, the room she grew up in, the room where she assembled all her little treasures. I held her in my arms, our bodies melding one into the other and breathing together as one. She breathing out, I in, synchronized, I in, her out. She nuzzled her face against my neck just under my chin, and we talked in whispers. Whispered dreams for the future, our future, filled the air until we fell asleep. In the morning, we woke together and went downstairs and then out back to take our bucket baths. This time together. I shaved with the little aluminum bowl of hot water that my new mother-in-law set out for me. Afterward, Moke Chee and I had breakfast together. It was so normal. It was what we should have been doing for the past year.

My father-in-law had not yet come downstairs for breakfast. It was unusual for him to sleep in, and I was worried but said nothing to Moke Chee or my mother-in-law. Finally, I heard the staircase squeaking, which signaled he was coming downstairs for breakfast.

When he entered the room, he handed me a thick leather-bound book from his library. I rubbed a layer of caked-on dust from its leather binding with my hand and read the title: *Kama Sutra*. My father-in-law said, "This will help you keep your wife and yourself happy."

I said, "Thank you." I didn't know what I was thanking him for because I had never heard of *Kama Sutra*. I opened the cover and read the subtitle: *A thousand and one illustrated positions for coitus with detailed descriptions and accompanying instructions.* I turned to a random page and saw drawings that, as a youngster, would have earned me much favor with my buddies, but a rap across the knuckles from my father and ten "Our Father" and five "Hail Mary" penances. I had no intention of ever looking at the book but was happy he gave it to me because I took it as a sign of acceptance at long last. Now, Moke Chee and I only had one day left before I had to be at the Kuala Lumpur airport. Before packing my things, I showed Moke Chee how to operate the tape recorder, so we could exchange tapes and hear each other's voices. Then, while alone before departing for Kuala Lumpur, I recorded a message for her.

Moke Chee accompanied me to Kuala Lumpur. We went to the American Embassy to obtain a visa for her, only to learn that even though we were married, Moke Chee couldn't obtain a visa until she was released from her contract with the Malayan government. That meant Moke Chee couldn't get a visa for three more years. We had to revise our plans yet again, but that was a minor item we would deal with later. We were married, and that was all that mattered.

The following morning was very difficult. I didn't want to leave Moke Chee. Worse, I knew she didn't want me to leave, and I wanted to dedicate my life to caring for and pleasing her. But we had decided to make a sacrifice now for the prospects of a better future—for us and for the family we would someday have.

CHAPTER 27

What I was doing was not uncommon for a husband in Malaysia in 1963. Husbands went to other countries—usually Australia or England and sometimes Canada or America—for further studies in pursuit of better career prospects. The sacrifice of family separation for a year or two as an investment in the future was consistent with Chinese-Malaysian family values. I told myself, and Moke Chee and I told each other, that my going to America to complete a master's degree and apply for a doctoral research fellowship was not atypical by Chinese-Malaysian customs. But inside, I felt selfish.

The airplane's cabin door shut. It seemed a lifetime ago that I had arrived in Malaya, leaving life in Chicago behind and setting out, if not to change the world, at least to make a constructive difference in a distant land. Now, I didn't think I had.

The plane rolled down the runway, gained speed, and then we were airborne. It was too late now, but I knew I made a mistake. Make that two mistakes. I shouldn't have left Moke Chee. I missed her. She was the only reason I didn't exit the Peace Corps earlier. I married her because I wanted to be with her for my entire life, and now I was leaving her behind. Also, I shouldn't have signed up for employment to train the next group of Peace Corps Trainees. I didn't leave Malaya with a positive attitude toward the Peace Corps. What could I share with the Trainees? Lower your expectations. Stifle your idealism. Don't expect to change the world. That won't go over very well.

We landed in Da Nang, Vietnam, for a few minutes, where two young men dressed in military uniforms boarded the flight. They slid past me to take the window and middle seats. They looked young enough to be my students. I noticed puffs of smoke adjacent to the runway and asked, "What's that?"

The one by the window replied, "Artillery, Sir."

I said, "Don't you think it's too close to the runway? They should be practicing somewhere else."

Again the one by the window said, "Sir, that's not our fire. That's Viet Cong. They're just letting us know that they're there. They're not trying to hit us."

I had another glass of wine and wondered if my two young Americans were just trying to frighten me. I appreciated them taking my mind off of leaving Moke Chee behind while we flew to Hong Kong. I learned that my seatmates were both nineteen-year-old riflemen and the only two in their company of two hundred and fifty men to complete their deployment in Vietnam without being wounded or killed. I told them that I had read that only American advisors who were at least twenty-one years old were sent to Vietnam. They quickly dissuaded me from that notion and said that American soldiers had to fight because the South Vietnamese didn't want to fight for the American-installed, corrupt South Vietnamese dictator. What they told me was so different from what I had been reading in the *Manchester Guardian* newspaper and *Time* magazine. That worried me.

We changed flights in Hong Kong, and again they were my seatmates.My young companions and I parted company in Los Angeles, where I caught a flight to Chicago. I spent the time writing Moke Chee a letter and trying to figure out how I would let my parents know that I was married. I rehearsed multiple scenarios and settled on none.

Telling My Parents I'm Married

I arrived home Friday morning. The sun had not yet risen. The kitchen light was shining out the window over the kitchen sink and reflecting off of my father's car. My parents were preparing to go to work. They heard my taxi pull into the driveway. My mother looked out the window. I paid the driver. I still had my house key and took it out of my pocket, but my father had the door open before I reached the top of the stairs. They seemed stunned and delighted to see me.

My mother put both her hands on my cheeks and said, "We were just saying that you would be home this weekend because you have to report to work on Sunday." She stepped back and said, "Let me look at you. You are so skinny. You have to eat."

My mother looked me over. I held out my left hand with my wedding ring on my finger. My mother kept looking at me, smiling, but seemed not to take notice of my ring. That was odd because there wasn't a detail in her house or about her children that missed her eye. With my mother doing the talking, my father was quiet. I noticed him looking at the gold ring on my finger. He knew and remained smiling. I decided this was the best time to tell my parents that Moke Chee and I were married.

I lifted my left hand and said, "You haven't asked me about my wedding ring."

My father said, "We noticed it but thought you would tell us when you wanted to tell us."

I said, "Do you remember the photos I sent home with the Malayan art teacher in them? Her name is Moke Chee. She and I were very good friends, best friends, and then we started dating and fell in love. We got married just before I left for home."

My mother interrupted, "You have so many girlfriends. Why her?"

I said, "Ma, they were just girls I went with, but Moke Chee is different. I want to spend the rest of my life with her. I love her. She feels the same way about me. We tried to break off our relationship but couldn't, so we decided to marry before I came back home."

My mother looked past me, over my shoulder, as if expecting to see someone, and said, "Then where is she? I hope you didn't leave her behind."

I said, "There's a bunch of red tape. It's a long story. I'll explain later."

My father said, "Carrie, we have to start heading to work."

My mother said, "If she can't come here, you better go back there to be with her. It's not natural. A husband and wife should be together."

I said, "We'll talk about that later. What do you want me to make for dinner?"

My mother said, "There are leftovers in the icebox. Put it on the burner at about five-thirty. We'll be home as usual."

I'll have to get used to American English again.

My parents left for work. I was relieved. I thought my mother would throw a fit and figured she still would, but that would be later, and I would just let her rant. I unpacked my things. My room was just as I had left it. It looked familiar but seemed strange. I felt I no longer belonged there. I was a stranger.

My brother Bill had been using my Volkswagen while I was in the Peace Corps, so I walked to Addison Street and took the bus to the post office to purchase a stamp and mail Moke Chee's letter. I also bought forty airmail envelopes. I planned to write Moke Chee every day and to make tape recordings to send to her. I called Penn Winter to let him know that I was back and to learn when he wanted me to report to work. He wanted to see me first thing Monday morning. He said that Peace Corps Malaysia V was already staying at the Rice Hotel and I would stay there with them during training. I told Penn I preferred to stay alone in an apartment, and he said that a key part of my assignment was to be embedded with the group. I agreed to join the group on Sunday. I should note that six days after Moke Chee and I married, Malaya united with the island of Singapore and the colonies of Sarawak and Sabah in northern Borneo to become Malaysia.

Training Malaysia V and VI

Arriving at the Rice Hotel brought back memories of staying there with my group. I felt I was once again going back to a place where I didn't want to be. The Peace Corps Malaysia V Trainees were already on campus bonding with each other and eager to learn and to prove their competence and worthiness. I wasn't much older than them and younger than some, but I felt like an old man. It was my job to be with them twenty-four hours a day, seven days a week. I had my own room at the hotel but shared the bathroom down the hall and ate breakfast, lunch, and dinner with them. I attended some lectures and was on call to answer any and all questions. I was with them, but not one of them. I felt out of place.

Naturally, the Trainees asked, "How was it?" I tried hard to explain by way of humorous anecdotes. They enjoyed the stories, but I felt it was a disservice to only present humorous stories. I tried to focus my comments on my positive experiences with the Trainees and Malaysian townsfolk.

The university received requests for speakers, and Penn assigned me to one speaking engagement per week with local civic groups and church groups. I had dozens of slides of Malaysia and arranged them to show a day in my life as a Volunteer in Kuala Trengganu. I showed slides of the people who filled my daily life—from my students and colleagues to townsfolk, fishermen, and friends. I didn't share slides of Moke Chee, her parents, or Nanny, or any of her family and friends. Those were too personal and made me feel lonely. They were too painful to share. I included scenes of my school, places of worship, types of housing, street scenes, market scenes, flooded streets, and palm trees at Christmas time. I didn't have a set script, but I reflected on what I was doing and thinking and feeling at the time I snapped the photo. The presentation took about twenty-five minutes, followed by ten to fifteen minutes of questions. The standard questions included: "What did you miss when you were there? What do you miss from Malaysia?"

I talked about missing my family and how I would get homesick. I was less specific in answering questions about what I missed from Malaysia. I would say that what I missed most from Malaysia were the people, my students, and my Malaysian friends. But I added that I was glad to be back home. My audience loved to hear that. Of course, I missed Moke Chee, but I didn't want to talk about her to a group of strangers. I wasn't ready to share our story.

An Unforgettable Day

Luke visited NIU in late November 1963 on his way from D.C. back to Malaysia. It was a short visit to meet the Malaysia V Trainees. I was glad to see him and even happier to learn he would join me as one of the keynote speakers on November 22 at the luncheon sponsored by NIU's School of Journalism for newspaper publishers and editors of newspapers who were from mostly small rural towns in the northwest quadrant of Illinois.

I had been dreading speaking to this group ever since Penn gave me the assignment a few weeks earlier because I recalled reading editorials from some of the papers calling the Malaya I Trainees "Naive hippy long-haired Kennedy kids who had nothing to offer and were guaranteed to fail in another Democrat boondoggle." I had to admit the naïve part accurately described me at the time, and that made me uncomfortable because I wasn't sure I was much less naïve now. I didn't want to admit that my skill as a biologist was not appropriately used, so how would I convince this audience that I provided a useful service that a Malayan couldn't have provided?

I told Penn about my negative feelings and begged off the assignment, but Penn said, "This is your chance to set the record straight and prove them wrong, as only you can."

While driving together to the luncheon in my 1954 VW, Luke said I should speak first to give a firsthand account of my experience, and then he would wrap up with an overview of Peace Corps Malaysia and the Peace Corps' global objective. I thought it would be better if he spoke first, but he insisted that I go first. I decided that since I only had one opportunity to speak to such an influential and important group of newspapermen—yes, they were all men—I would not waste their time talking about myself.

I knew I would be giving Luke a curveball, but I figured my comments would be so controversial and that the questions that followed would eat up so much time that Luke wouldn't have to speak. He gave me the impression that he didn't want to speak at the luncheon any more than I did. I decided to tell the group what the teenage soldiers told me about being foot soldiers in Vietnam and having to fight the Viet Cong because the South Vietnamese soldiers wouldn't fight for the corrupt dictator installed by the United States. My teenage companions' statements had been bothering me, and who better to share them with than newspaper editors and publishers? After all, my flight home was part of my Peace Corps experience, wasn't it?

Luke and I were seated at a table in front of the podium, which was on a raised platform. We were seated with the Dean of the School of Journalism and various officers of the newspaper association. After lunch, the Dean gave some welcoming remarks and introduced the Master of Ceremonies, who was to introduce me. The format was that I would speak for four to six minutes, then Luke would join me, and we would take questions from the floor. I figured I would open with: "I want to share a conversation I had recently with some American teenagers I met when my plane landed in Da Nang on the way home ..." But that all went out the window.

The Master of Ceremonies introduced me, but as I stepped on the platform to go to the podium, a young woman, a student, I thought, rushed past me from backstage and handed the Master of Ceremonies a slip of paper. I stood next to him, and he said, "Just a minute," to me. He leaned into the microphone. I could see the thin slip of paper in his right hand wiggling. He read: "This just in. The President has been shot. President Kennedy has been shot while riding in his motorcade in Dallas. There is no word on the seriousness of his condition. He has been rushed to the hospital emergency room. Now, I'll turn it over to you, Jim."

At first, I thought this was some kind of sick joke on a Kennedy kid, but there was absolute silence in a room of around sixty news people—all literally sitting on the edge of their chairs—so it couldn't be a joke. I said, "I know you want to get to telephones, but please join me in a moment of silence for President Kennedy and our country."

After a pause, I said: "I have one story that I want to share with you because you are very powerful. You speak to hundreds of thousands of people who are motivated to read about our country and the world. I want to give you a news tip. On the way home, I met two teenage combat riflemen who got on the plane in Da Nang. They told me they were foot soldiers, not military advisors, because the South Vietnamese refused to fight for the corrupt dictators we installed in South Vietnam. Those two nineteen-year-old riflemen were the only two in their company of two hundred and fifty men to complete their deployment in Vietnam and return home without being wounded or killed. Our government is not giving us an accurate account of what we are doing in Vietnam. Thank you for being polite. I'm sure you want to get to a telephone and call your offices." With that, the assembly rushed out the doors.

Luke said, "I thought they were playing some sort of sick trick on us and knew you would handle it. What made you think of telling them about teenage soldiers fighting in Vietnam?"

I said, "It's a true story far more important than one Peace Corps Volunteer's odyssey."

Luke shook his head in agreement. "How bad do you think it is?"

I said, "Very bad. If it weren't, they'd say right away. I think."

Luke said, "Agreed."

We drove back in silence to the Center for Southeast Asian Studies, where the Peace Corps Office was located. Formal activities for the Trainees were called off for the day. Most gathered around TVs, holding out hope for a miracle. It didn't arrive.

Hearing Moke Chee's Voice

Saturday morning, I drove Luke back to O'Hare airport to start his trip back to Malaysia.

After dropping Luke off, I decided not to return to campus, and I spent Saturday night with my parents. I contacted the overseas telephone operator and managed to schedule a three-minute telephone call to Moke Chee at Grandmother's house that night. It was Sunday morning in Malaysia, and the transmission was full of static, but at least I got to hear Moke Chee's voice, and she could hear mine. I could hear the fear in her voice. She was worried about what would happen to America after President Kennedy's assassination and wanted to know if I was safe. I assured her that I was, and I could hear the relief in her voice. But then I heard sadness slip into her voice when the operator cut in to tell us our three minutes were up.

The first time I talked to Moke Chee via telephone was from the Rice Hotel in DeKalb after I got my first paycheck. We talked for forty-eight minutes, and it cost $144. I was broke, so after that, I told the operator to cut in and end our calls after three minutes. That way, I could afford to call Moke Chee every week. The three minutes went by so fast. I had tape recordings from Moke Chee that I played over several times, and I sent her tape recordings. I could listen to Moke Chee's voice at the end of each day.

Altering Graduate School Plans

I was taking two graduate classes. My Peace Corps responsibilities prevented me from attending classes on a regular basis. It was very difficult for me to keep up. I was concerned that my goal of obtaining a doctoral fellowship in genetics was disappearing. Although my professors and graduate advisor encouraged me to keep on track, I felt burned out. I met with Penn to see if I could alter my Peace Corps responsibilities. He said that I couldn't.

By the end of the first semester in 1963, I had been accepted into a doctoral program at the University of Wisconsin in Madison and was waiting to find out if a research fellowship would be offered. Penn was making plans for training Peace Corps Malaysia VI and invited me to be part of the training. He said Eddie, the surveyor from Malaya I, would join the training program periodically. All that was left for a master's degree at NIU was to complete a genetics project and submit my findings—the methodology of my research and the results of my effort to implant chromosomes into a chicken embryo—to the graduate faculty for review and possible publication. That was straightforward enough, and with Eddie helping out periodically on my Peace Corps responsibilities, I accepted Penn's offer to join the Malaysia VI training program.

There was only one problem, I could tell from Moke Chee's voice on the telephone and from her letters that our separation over another three years was not sustainable. One thing I was grateful for was that Irene, the wife of my old Peace Corps roommate Mike Frazer, would visit Moke Chee. In fact, it was Mike's letter to me stating that my separation from Moke Chee was very difficult for her and that I had to return to Malaysia immediately. That convinced me to end my studies and return to Malaysia.

Can I Go Back to Malaysia?

I had never discussed my personal relationships with my parents before, but they had noticed the toll that the separation was taking on me. My mother and father approached me and said my plan to get a graduate degree in America while Moke Chee was in Malaysia was wrong. I told them I was working on returning to Malaysia with the Peace Corps and waiting to hear from them.

My father said, "Forget about waiting for the Peace Corps. Go now. A husband and a wife should be together."

My mother added, "We have money set aside for you. You can buy a ticket and look for something to do to support yourself, or we will support you, but you must go back. That poor woman is waiting for you to pursue your dream. That's not fair to her, and it's not natural."

Penn grew to know me as well as anyone, and he must have seen how the separation was wearing on me. He took me aside and asked if I wanted him to nominate me to escort Malaysia VI to Malaysia.

I said, "I can't tell you how much that would mean to me."

A week later, he said, "Bad news. My nomination was rejected. But have you considered reentering Peace Corps Malaysia as a Volunteer with Malaysia VI?"

I said, "Is that possible?"

He replied, "You'll never know unless you ask. Why not write Sarge a letter? You have my backing."

Penn let me use his secretary to dictate a letter to Sarge Shriver. I introduced myself and asked if it were possible for me to follow Malaysia VI to Malaysia. I thought that was a simple request, but it was met with resistance in Washington, D.C., and in Kuala Lumpur. Penn had told me that unnamed administrative types in both cities were opposed to letting me rejoin the Peace Corps because they reasoned I was doing it to be with Moke Chee. Of course, if anybody had asked me, I would have admitted that was the reason I wanted to reenter the Peace Corps. Penn told me that others also supported my return to Malaysia regardless of the reason. There was a stalemate, so it was up to Sarge to break the stalemate.

I learned from Penn that Sarge asked Norb, who was the first Peace Corps Malaysia Director, and Luke, who was the outgoing Peace Corps Malaysia Director: "Was Jim a good Volunteer?" When both answered, "Yes," he telephoned me.

I answered the telephone in my room at the Rice Hotel late one evening, and Sarge was on the other end. He said, "Is this Jim Wolter the Peace Corps Volunteer from Malaysia?"

I said, "Yes."

He said, "This is Sarge Shriver. We met in Kuala Trengganu. Do you remember me?"

I recognized his voice and the way he spoke. There was no mistaking it. I said, "Yes."

He said, "Jim, I have your request to return to Malaysia here in front of me. I understand you were an excellent Volunteer, and you're married to a Malaysian art teacher and want to go back to Malaysia to be with her. Is that correct?"

I said, "Yes."

He said, "You know what it takes to be a Peace Corps Volunteer, and you're willing to give it your best effort."

I said, "I am."

He said, "That's all I need to hear. Pack your bags. A travel voucher will be sent to your home address right away."

I said, "Sarge, I can't thank you enough."

He said, "Tell your mother I send my regards."

I wondered if he remembered calling my mother or had a note of it in my Peace Corps file, but whatever it was, I was grateful. I told my mother that Sarge sent his regards. That made her day.

I left for Malaysia as soon as training and selection finished.

My graduate advisor thought I was making a mistake in not completing my research and getting a master's degree and then going on for a doctorate. I told him that it would have to wait. The biology department chairman granted me a two-year extension to complete my degree. I wrote to the University of Wisconsin and told them I was reentering the Peace Corps and would contact them when I returned to the United States. All that was left for me to do was wait.

I could hardly wait to have the travel voucher in hand, but I had mixed emotions. I wanted to be with Moke Chee, but I was going back into the Peace Corps, and my life for the next two years would be governed by decisions made by the Peace Corps staff in Kuala Lumpur. I had no confidence in their decision-making. I didn't trust that I wouldn't again be placed in an assignment that met the expedient political needs of the Peace Corps staff in Kuala Lumpur. If their decisions only affected how I would live my life for the next two years, I could handle that, but their decisions now affected how Moke Chee would live her life and even the lives of her parents and Nanny. But at least we would be together.

The Headmaster of Westlands Secondary School, where Moke Chee taught, wrote to the Peace Corps stating that his school needed a biology and math teacher and requested that I be assigned there. I knew there was a new Peace Corps Director in Kuala Lumpur, and I learned that John, my best Peace Corps buddy, had achieved his goal and was appointed an Assistant to the Peace Corps Director in Kuala Lumpur. I trusted John's judgment and trusted he would see the benefits of assigning me to Westlands Secondary School.

I was wrong.

CHAPTER 28

My journey back to Moke Chee took me from Chicago to Los Angeles to Hong Kong, and then to Kuala Lumpur. I thought about how settled my life would be once I reunited with Moke Chee, lived with her parents, and began teaching biology at Westlands Secondary School. I could also work with the girls at St. Nicholas' Home on weekends and introduce them to my new extended family. If I weren't the luckiest man alive, I didn't know who was.

When I arrived in Kuala Lumpur, I saw Moke Chee and John waiting to greet me. Suddenly, it hit me that I had gained fifteen pounds while I was in the United States, and I worried Moke Chee wouldn't recognize me, but she did and ran to greet me while John stood back. I presumed my best Peace Corps buddy was giving us a moment to ourselves, but he was standing rigid and not smiling as Moke Chee and I embraced. There was an officious air about John. While I was grateful that John provided Moke Chee with transportation to the airport, and while at any other time, I would have cherished spending time with him, I was anxious for him to move on. Moke Chee and I needed time alone. We were married but needed time to be reacquainted after seven months of separation.

I reached out my hand and said, "John, thanks for bringing Moke Chee to meet me. Before you dash off, I understand congratulations are in order on your marriage to Regina and on being appointed a full-fledged Peace Corps administrator."

John shook my hand and said, "I'll give you a lift back to the city."

I said, "How about dropping us at the Kowloon Hotel?"

Once we got to the hotel, John said, "Jim, there are a few things I have to let you know. We received a request from Moke Chee's Headmaster requesting you to be assigned to Westlands Secondary School, but we determined an assignment there would not be good for you because it would entail you living with Moke Chee's parents and being encompassed in her world of family and friends."

John's condescending attitude irked me. I didn't expect this of him. I didn't know this waddling duckling who was trying to pass as a swan. I said, "What's wrong with that?"

John said, "We decided it would be better for you to strike out on your own and make your own friends."

I said, "What makes you think I won't make my own friends in Penang?"

John ignored my question again. Back when we were Trainees and Volunteers talking about the things guys talk about—girls—he advised me that he found the best way to end a relationship was to have a preplanned script, which explained that breaking up was in the best interest of the girl. He had to stick to the script, acting rational, collected, and cool, and ignore the pleadings of the soon-to-be ex-girlfriend. Now, he was doing that to me.

John said, "We've placed both of you at the Chinese Boys' Secondary School in Kampar. We think Kampar is an ideal place. It is close enough for Moke Chee to occasionally go back to Penang to visit her parents, but not so close that you will be running back there every weekend. We haven't found you a place to live yet, so initially, you'll have to stay at a hotel in Ipoh and take a taxi to Kampar."

I was pissed. Who was he, or they, to determine how often Moke Chee would visit her parents? This was the very thing I was worried about when thinking about reentering the Peace Corps. Not only would I be stuck living with decisions made by the Peace Corps personnel in Kuala Lumpur, but the control freaks would try to control Moke Chee's life, too. I asked, "By the way, John, did you or anyone in Kuala Lumpur ask Moke Chee, or even think about asking her, if she wanted to transfer from her school in Penang?"

John hesitated for a moment. I could tell he was thinking of ignoring my question, but he must have thought he had to respond. He said, "Naturally, since you traveled halfway around the world to be with her, we assumed she wouldn't mind living a few hours from Penang to be with you."

It made me angry that John didn't refer to Moke Chee by name. I said, "You assumed on Moke Chee's behalf without consulting her. How American, how Peace Corps, of you."

John said, "Jim, we took the extraordinary step of bringing you back to Malaysia to be with her. You should be grateful."

I was grateful but also angry. I said: "Who said I'm not grateful? I am. I'm just saying Moke Chee should have been extended the courtesy of being consulted about being transferred. Also, it won't be necessary to find housing for me. I'll live with Moke Chee's cousin at the family rubber estate in Kampar, and if Moke Chee agrees to be transferred, so will she."

John hesitated, not knowing what to say. His neck turned red, and I could see the pulse of his bulging carotid artery pick up. He said, "Jim, you know that will defeat the purpose. You'll have to have other lodgings. One of the reasons we didn't want you staying in Penang was to prevent you from living with and spending time with Moke Chee's family."

I said, "OK, John, I'll stay at the rubber estate until you obtain permanent housing. That will be better than staying at a hotel in Ipoh and running up an unnecessary expense for the Peace Corps."

John said, "I'm inclined to say staying with family even temporarily is a difference, without a distinction, but Otis Pitts has the final say. I'll run your suggestion by him and get back to you."

I said, "You do that. While you're checking with Pitts, I'm heading to Penang with Moke Chee for a few days. I need to pay my respects to my father-in-law and mother-in-law and family elders. We'll be at the Kampar Rubber Estate by next Saturday. You can reach me there."

John said, "One more thing before you go, Jim. You know that since I am now a Peace Corps Administrator and you are a Peace Corps Volunteer, our relationship can no longer be what it once was. We can't be like we were."

That was obvious to me by the way John carried himself, with his chest all puffed up like a chickadee trying to be a peacock with self-importance, and by the way he spoke at me rather than talked with me. But him stating it the way he did, and in front of Moke Chee, hurt me. I lost my most trusted Peace Corps friend, my main buddy, but so did he, and it didn't seem to bother him a bit.

John had been my closest Peace Corps friend. I had thought we understood each other. He should have known I was pleased for him to get the job as an Assistant to the Peace Corps Director. Back when we both served on the Volunteer Advisory Council, I shared my ideas with him, and he passed off my ideas as his. I let him take credit for my ideas because I knew he was angling for a Peace Corps job, and I wanted to help him. I was mistaken in thinking John was a true and trusted friend as loyal to me as I was to him; finding out he wasn't—hurt. He and I had shared so much. He shared his dream of using the Peace Corps as a stepping stone to career advancement. During training, he viewed April as a woman who could be a helpmate in achieving his career goals. I stood back and didn't compete with him for her affection even though I found her attractive. I was that kind of friend.

John was even a witness at my wedding to Moke Chee. Now, he went from being my best Peace Corps buddy to Otis' errand boy. The person in front of me looked like John and sounded like John, but I didn't know this person. As his friend, I should have been sympathetic and supportive, but I felt jilted and hurt. I struck back.

I said, "That's fine with me, John. Just so you know, in my view, the best administrator is the least-seen administrator. Understood?"

John's face seemed to turn ashen. He hesitated. I stared him in the eyes and forced him to reply.

"Understood," he answered.

John left without shaking my hand or wishing Moke Chee and me well. I figured Otis would have John make finding permanent lodging for Moke Chee and me his number one priority. That was fine with me. I would use whatever housing John assigned me as my official residence, but if Gim Kooi and Ah Chai wanted us to reside with them on the rubber estate and if Moke Chee wanted to stay there, that's where we would stay. What would John and Otis do if we lived on the rubber estate? Kick me out of the Peace Corps for residing with my Malaysian family?

I never saw John alone in person again after our encounter in the lobby of the Kowloon Hotel. The feeling of the old Peace Corps camaraderie that existed between John and me was gone, shattered.

Reuniting with the Family

After settling in our room at the Kowloon, Moke Chee and I called Gim Lan and arranged to see her and Nanny. Gim Lan called her sister Gim Kooi in Kampar to tell her to expect us the following morning. Gim Kooi was elated to hear that Moke Chee and I were assigned to the Chinese Boys' School in Kampar, and she immediately invited us to live with her on the estate.

Moke Chee and I took a taxi back to the Kampar Rubber Estate early the next morning. I looked forward to seeing Ah Chai, my new cousin-in-law who was the estate manager and was married to Moke Chee's cousin-sister Gim Kooi. He also was one of the two family members who were most accepting of me. As a senior family member, he approached Moke Chee's father on my behalf in an attempt to persuade him to grant Moke Chee and me permission to marry. He even spoke to Grandmother and told her to give me a chance because I was a good man.

Ah Chai and Gim Kooi and their three children were standing at the front door of the estate house wearing broad smiles as our taxi pulled into the estate's long elliptical driveway of crushed seashells. Orchids the size of four-foot-tall shrubs were planted on both sides of the driveway, which was as long as a football field. Gim Kooi and Ah Chai were pleased to see us because life on a rubber estate was akin to living on an island isolated from civilization. With few visitors, Moke Chee and I were a welcome addition to estate life.

When I elected to give up completing a master's degree in biology and to pass on pursuing a doctoral degree in genetics so I could return to Moke Chee in Malaysia, I knew becoming a research geneticist was no longer going to be possible. I began thinking about other post-Peace Corps career options. After driving around the Kampar Rubber Estate with Ah Chai while he explained all the duties required in producing, harvesting, and processing latex—and a host of other responsibilities of an estate manager—working as a Planter was high on my list if I couldn't gain admission to medical school in Singapore.

Ah Chai stopped the Land Rover and inspected a swath of trees with declining latex production and calculated the number of trees that had to be replaced. He also inspected a pathway, a bridge that was being constructed, and the road we were traveling on. He told me that he enjoyed all the different tasks he had to do to keep the estate profitable. The responsibilities of a Planter appealed to me. I looked forward to discussing the idea of a Planter's life with Moke Chee after dinner. Moke Chee and I hadn't talked about what we would do post-Peace Corps now that I had given up on pursuing a research professorship in genetics. I thought tonight would be a good time to start. As Moke Chee and I got ready to settle in for the night, Ah Chai invited me to join him for a drink at the Planters Club in Kampar.

It was only my second night back with Moke Chee, and I wanted to spend it with her, but as a new family member, I had to graciously accept my older cousin's invitation. Moke Chee nodded to me, indicating it was alright with her to accept Ah Chai's invitation. After entering the club, Ah Chai introduced me to his friends and ordered drinks. Then he said, "Jim, I know you would rather be with Moke Chee—and we will be back to the estate in short order—but I wanted to talk to you alone. I don't want to alarm you or frighten Moke Chee, but she can't be assigned to the Chinese Boys' School. I'm not worried about you there, but for Moke Chee it will be hell. What bloody fools would assign a Chinese woman married to a European man to a Chinese Boys' School, especially in Kampar? The Chinese, especially the boys, are very proud and chauvinistic. I'm telling you this so you know what I'm going to do. First thing tomorrow, I'm putting a call in to the CEO, and I'll have Moke Chee transferred to the Methodist Girls' School in Ipoh. My driver will take her there. Now let's take our leave and get you back to your bride."

Back Home at 70c Irving Road

The following morning, Ah Chai had Su Blee, his driver, fetch Gim Kooi, Moke Chee, and me to Penang. Entering the house at 70c Irving Road felt like coming home, and it felt so natural being with Moke Chee's father and mother again. My mother-in-law made me her chocolate custard, and my father-in-law shared stories of his childhood and joined us at the padang for rubbish in the evening. It was as if I had never left.

Moke Chee and I made the rounds to see uncles, aunties, cousins and friends, and we took the little Barbarians to the creameries and visited Grandmother. I was stunned by the reception I received from Grandmother. She was sleeping in her favorite lounge chair on the veranda when we arrived. We tiptoed past her because heaven help anyone who woke Grandmother up from her nap. We sat in the sitting room discussing something with Sui Lay, waiting for Grandmother to wake.

When Grandmother did wake, she rose from her favorite lounge chair and walked into the sitting room. There was an immediate hush. Grandmother walked straight toward me without saying a word. She was less than five feet tall, yet projected a physically imposing figure. She stopped immediately in front of me and hovered there, larger than life, with the folded afternoon newspaper in her hand. I held my breath wondering—as did Moke Chee, her cousins, nieces, and nephews—what Grandmother was going to do. Grandmother being Grandmother, I gripped the arms of the terribly uncomfortable wooden antique Chinese armchair and prepared myself to be swatted in the ear with the newspaper like an irritating fly. But instead of swatting me, Grandmother unfolded the newspaper and presented it to me with both hands, and said, "Here, you might be interested in reading this."

Never had Grandmother brought the newspaper to anyone. It was others who brought the newspaper to Grandmother. I was relieved and elated and honored. I loosened my grip on the arms of the chair and received the newspaper with both hands. I was momentarily speechless and could barely say thank you in Mandarin. Grandmother nodded her head in acknowledgment and went back to the veranda to continue her nap. I looked to Moke Chee. She was beaming. Grandmother had given us a gift.

That was my baptismal. I was accepted as a member of the family. I couldn't wait to get back to Kampar to tell Ah Chai about my good fortune and to thank him for interceding with Grandmother on my behalf. Of course, Malaysia being Malaysia, Ah Chai heard all about Grandmother and the newspaper before we got back to Kampar.

The following Saturday, Ah Chai sent Su Blee to drive us back to Kampar. After arriving, Ah Chai said, "You have an urgent message to call Mr. Johnstone in Kuala Lumpur. But before you do, I want you to know that I spoke to the CEO, and he's assigned you to schools in Batu Gajah. So act surprised when you're informed of that. Batu Gajah is a nice little town. Of course, you are still welcome to stay with us. We'll have to get you your own car to commute to Batu Gajah. Here's Mr. Johnstone's telephone number."

Transferred Again

When I reached John, he said, "I told Otis about you living with family on the family rubber estate, and we think that would defeat the purpose of your not being posted to Penang. So you're being posted to Batu Gajah instead."

I said, "John, you know how Chinese families are. Moke Chee has family in Batu Gajah too."

There was an awkward moment of silence on his end. Then he replied, "We were concerned that might be the case."

I knew John well enough to tell by his voice he was bluffing. I was sure he hadn't thought about Moke Chee having family in Batu Gajah. But that didn't matter. Ah Chai said Batu Gajah was a nice little town, and Moke Chee and I were together. The small details were of no matter.

John went on, "But at least you won't be living with Moke Chee's family members. We've arranged for you to stay in one of the Resthouse cottages. As for your assignments, you are posted to Sultan Yussuf Secondary School, and Moke Chee is posted to St. Bernadette's Convent School. For your information, the CEO sounded annoyed with us and told us he thought posting both of you at the Chinese Boys' School in Kampar was inappropriate. Otis didn't take kindly to the CEO's remarks and wants you to know we are more than a little peeved that the CEO's comments indicated there was outside interference with our placement process."

The CEO was Bankim Daarum, my old Headmaster. He hated it in Kuala Trengganu and was constantly bemoaning his post and calculating his next promotion by the Ministry of Education instead of fully enjoying his current position. I could imagine his stony face dressing down John and Otis and then watching their reactions with amusement as he usually did, without a hint of emotion. I was delighted by that image. I said, "Maybe it's just that he knows more about the culture of Chinese schools than you and Otis."

John had regained his composure enough to say, "The Resthouse Manager is expecting you."

I said, "We'll check in tomorrow."

John and I never spoke again after that. I wish we had.

CHAPTER 29

Ah Chai drove Moke Chee and me to Batu Gajah, which was twenty minutes from the Kampar estate. Ah Chai said, "Batu Gajah has a hawker stall famous for its clam chow-fun."

While we enjoyed our lunch, Ah Chai obtained useful information about Batu Gajah and our new schools from other customers. I marveled at his ease in starting conversations with total strangers. He got directions to my school and to Moke Chee's school and learned that her school started a half hour earlier and ended a half hour later than mine. He said that was a good thing because he was told there was a shortcut from the Resthouse to Moke Chee's school that required following a path through a forested area. It would be best for me to walk Moke Chee to school and then double back to my school in the morning, then meet at her school in the afternoon so as not to invite trouble for her along the secluded path.

Ah Chai and Gim Kooi drove us up Jalan Chankat, past the golf course, and past the entrance to a military base. We found the Resthouse at the end of the road at the very top of the hill. The Resthouse was quiet, with no one in sight. Ah Chai and I wandered around to the back, where the staff's living quarters were, and found a portly Chinese man who introduced himself as Cheong, the Resthouse Manager. With him were two barefoot preschool-aged children—a girl in a yellow sleeveless dress and a younger boy wearing only a white singlet. Cheong was also barefoot and dressed simply in blue shorts and a white singlet. It turned out that Cheong was more caretaker than Manager since guests seldom frequented this Resthouse.

Cheong pointed to two cottages on the compound. He said both were unoccupied, but the cottage had to be cleaned before we moved in. To do that, we had to go to the Public Works Department (PWD) to have the water turned on. Cheong told us the cottage nearest the road would be ours because the other one was already reserved for the PWD's electrical engineer, who was completing his studies in Germany.

Cheong escorted us to his best room, the honeymoon suite, and said it was ours until our cottage was ready for occupancy. The room was large, similar to the bedroom that I stayed in atop Penang Hill, and had a large king-sized bed, a sitting area, a writing desk, a bathroom with a Western-style toilet, and a shower with hot running water. There was one drawback to staying at the Resthouse, which Ah Chai pointed out.

Ah Chai told us about a military checkpoint manned by sentries that could be a problem on our way to the Resthouse. He said: "Jim, you will notice the sentries eyeing Moke Chee in a very vulgar way. It is best to pay no mind to them. They are likely rural folks, ruffians, who don't know any better. If they make vulgar comments, ignore those also. Don't give them any reason to say you provoked a confrontation. As a man with a beautiful young wife, you may find that difficult, but you must exercise discipline. You might consider purchasing an automobile."

I thought Ah Chai was being too wary of the sentries, who were likely like my school boys, and told him that Peace Corps Volunteers weren't allowed to have cars.

Ah Chai and I shook hands. Moke Chee and I watched Ah Chai and Gim Kooi drive off. We were on our own.

Another First Day at Another New School

Moke Chee and I checked into the Resthouse on Sunday afternoon. The Manager informed me that since the Europeans left Malaysia, there were no guests—or, at best, only an occasional one—so there was no dining service. We would have to take our meals in town. Moke Chee and I walked to town for dinner that evening. It was an easy downhill walk. We had curry at an Indian restaurant. The walk back uphill to the Resthouse was more challenging but nonetheless pleasant in the cool evening air. I noticed the sentries were considerably older than my former schoolboys. Ah Chai was correct. They did eye Moke Chee as we walked past. We took to walking on the far side of the road, with me walking between Moke Chee and the sentries.

It was a few degrees cooler at the top of the hill at night, which made for good sleeping as we were cocooned under our mosquito net. Getting under the mosquito netting was necessary after sunset because the Resthouse area was infested with swarms of mosquitoes in the early evening and again at the break of dawn. I never experienced so many mosquitoes. A tribe of macaque monkeys inhabited the forest surrounding three sides of the Resthouse and provided the mosquitoes with a regular food source. Moke Chee and I sat indoors with the overhead fan turned to full speed to keep the mosquitoes at bay before retreating for cover under the mosquito net.

We were eager to get to our new schools. We had to get breakfast at our schools' Tuck Shops because the Resthouse didn't serve breakfast. We rose early, showered, and started walking to school. The sentries guarding the military base entrance again ogled Moke Chee when we walked by. I took Ah Chai's advice and acted as if they weren't there. Ah Chai's warning about how isolated and potentially dangerous the shortcut path to the Convent School was also correct. It wasn't a place for Moke Chee to walk alone.

We arrived at St. Bernadette's Convent School and found Sister Coleman standing at the gate, welcoming students and staff with a smile and a blessing. Sister Coleman was a tall woman dressed in a white habit. Seeing a Sister always made me feel like a small schoolboy, and today was no different. I said, "Good morning, Sister."

Sister Coleman had a tuft of gray hair peeking from under her habit. She was, I would learn, thirty years older than me but had a youthful face and blue eyes.

"Good morning. You must be Mr. and Mrs. Wolter. I'm Sister Saint Coleman. This is Sister Agnes. Mrs. Wolter, if you follow me, we'll get you started."

I watched Moke Chee follow Sister Coleman into a building, and I went to my school.

When I arrived at Sultan Yussuf Secondary School, I went to the Headmaster's office and found both Mr. Khoo Teck Keong, the Headmaster, and Mr. Lee Sim Chin, the Senior Assistant, waiting for me. Mr. Khoo was a man about fifty years of age with a soft, kind-sounding voice. He said, "Welcome, Mr. Wolter."

Mr. Lee then said, "We need someone to teach Form V Physics and Form V Math and a Form V Advanced Math class. If that is agreeable to you, we would like you to teach those classes."

I said, "I've never taught advanced math, but I'll do my best."

Mr. Khoo shook my hand and said, "Thank you. If you need anything, my door is always open."

Mr. Lee handed me the syllabi for my classes. I followed him to the faculty room, and he introduced me to the teachers and asked them to let me know which desks were available, and then he left. I selected a desk and then was invited to join the faculty members seated in the lounge area. I was recruited by Mr. Khor to be an Assistant Scout Master and by Mr. Serjet Sing to play goalie on the faculty field hockey team. I excused myself to go to the physics lab. Entering the lab, I felt like a kid in a toy store. Not only did I have a physics lab filled with equipment, I had a complete photo lab at my disposal. I could hardly contain myself.

Our First Home

When Moke Chee and I got back to the Resthouse after our first day of school, Cheong was waiting for us. He said, "Your cottage is ready, but first, you have to go to the PWD to have the water turned on."

Moke Chee stayed at the Resthouse while I walked back to town and went to the PWD office, where I was informed by a clerk that before they would turn the water on at our cottage, I had to pay forty-eight ringgits for water used at my house in Kuala Trengganu. I told the clerk that I paid my water bill at the time I vacated that house. He informed me that water was still being used at the house after I left, and I had to pay for it. Apparently, the two young British Voluntary Service Overseas women who moved into my old house left the country without paying for the water that they used. My choice was to pay or go without water while fighting the PWD bureaucracy. A year ago, I would have relished fighting with the bureaucracy, but that was then. I paid the bill and said, "Thank you."

Two days later, Moke Chee and I moved into our first home. To say we moved is an exaggeration. All we had to move were two suitcases of clothes. We had nothing, just each other, but that was enough to make that little one-story creamy-colored stucco cottage, with its weathered red tile roof and baby blue-painted walls inside our home. The cottage was furnished with cane chairs in the sitting room. In the bedroom, there was one twin-sized bed, a dresser, and a chair. The kitchen had one small table and four chairs. Next to the kitchen was a servant's room with a plank bed. The bathroom had a Western-style, four-legged cast-iron bathtub, a Western shower, a bathroom sink, a mirrored medicine cabinet, and a Western-style toilet. It had cold running water. The kitchen had a sink and a place for a stove, but no stove and no refrigerator.

We walked the one-mile-plus to town and ate dinner at the hawker's stand. It was dark by the time we walked back. Every time we walked past the sentries guarding the entrance to the military base, Moke Chee walked on the side of me away from the guards. I was glad it was dark out so the guards couldn't ogle her, or if they did, neither of us saw them do it. We were about to spend our first night in our own home. The bed was half the size of the Resthouse bed, and Cheong told me he would order a larger bed for us, but Moke Chee and I found the twin-sized bed adequate.

The cottage backed up to a bamboo forest. There were two thick-trunked mango trees between the house and the forest. I strung a copper wire between the trees to hang our clothes out to dry. As a bachelor, my old routine was to soak the clothes I wore for the day in soapy water overnight and hang them out to dry before leaving for school. Then I only needed a bathroom sink. Now I had a bathtub, so I included Moke Chee's clothes with mine and then rinsed the clothes and hung them between the mango trees.

When we got back from school that first day, I noticed our clothes were missing from the clothesline. I went to see Cheong, and he gave me our clothes, all ironed and folded in a neat pile. He said, "I took the liberty of taking your laundry in. If you leave clothes on a line unattended like that, the monkeys will abscond with them. I can do your clothes for a small sum."

I said, "The Peace Corps won't allow me to have laundry service."

He said, "Mrs. Wolter isn't in the Peace Corps. The monkeys will steal your clothes. What if I do her clothes for ten ringgits a month and do yours for free?"

I shook his hand and said, "We have a deal."

The Peace Corps reimbursed Volunteers for the cost of renting a stove and a refrigerator but not for their purchase. I went to Cheng Wat, the husband of one of Moke Chee's cousins in Ipoh on her father's side. He told me it would cost less to purchase the stove and refrigerator than rent, so he worked out a rent-to-purchase agreement for me. Cheng Wat had the stove and refrigerator delivered to our house, along with basic kitchen utensils and an electric tea kettle, pots, china, and cleaning supplies as a gift from the family.

That first month set the pattern for the succeeding months. During weekdays, we were in school, and two nights a week, I played field hockey. The other weeknights, we socialized as a couple with family in Ipoh and faculty in the area. There were two brothers, Peter and Paul Salvaratnam, teaching at my school. Peter introduced us to the local parish priest at St. Joseph's Church and invited us to their house in Batu Gajah. Soon, we assimilated into their families. We became the godparents to Peter's children and attended Paul's wedding ceremony, which lasted six hours. Paul took joy in taking me to visit his neighbors in Batu Gajah's Little India.

Every second weekend we tried to go to Penang to check in on Moke Chee's parents. On one of the alternate weekends, we stayed at the rubber estate, and on the other, we stayed in Batu Gajah for school activities. On those evenings, we visited family in Ipoh or socialized over dinner with teacher couples from our schools.

The faculty dinners were always held at Chinese restaurants in Ipoh. There were usually at least ten to twelve people and at least ten courses of food that were served one course at a time. It was customary to eat family style with the course set in the center of the table.

At dinner parties, the preferred drink of men was brandy. They boasted about the number of bottles, not glasses, that they finished. One of the favorite activities was trying to get someone drunk. It was always me. The way it worked was they would have a general toast to start the night, and then all the men downed their drinks. The men would fill their glasses and propose another toast. After a few toasts, one man would call the name of another and say, "Yum sing," which meant "bottoms up." The men took turns calling my name. I wasn't prepared for that at the first dinner party and got blind drunk, much to the delight of the other men. After that, Moke Chee and I arranged to sit next to a planter, and Moke Chee kept her glass filled with Chinese tea while mine was filled with brandy. When my name was called to yum sing, I took Moke Chee's tea glass, downed the contents, and slammed the glass back on the table while she emptied my brandy in the planter and filled the glass with tea. I was surprised at how easily we pulled that off. I hated to waste brandy and hated poisoning the plant, but I hated getting drunk and being sick even more.

CHAPTER 30

Moke Chee and I lived at the top of the Batu Gajah hill in our little cottage all alone for three months. I literally and figuratively was on top of the world, living atop the hill and walking with Moke Chee to and from school, holding hands with a bundle of our student exercise books tucked under my right arm. The morning walk to school was a lovely downhill stroll. There was no better way to start a day.

Climbing back up the hill in the blistering hot afternoon sun with humid air thick as soup after a day of standing at the chalkboard and walking desk to desk monitoring students' work was more of a challenge. Halfway up the hill, an oasis awaited us. Providing a cool respite was a stand of flame-of-the-forest trees with broad branches ablaze with red flowers casting an umbrella of shade across the edge of the village padang. We stopped there in the cool shade and treated ourselves to a glass of freshly squeezed ice-cold sugarcane water each and shared a bowl of ice kacang from hawker stands nestled among the trees. Sharing a bowl of shaved ice over red beans, sweet corn, attap seeds, and seaweed jelly all topped with palm sugar and coconut milk was the perfect setting for telling each other the highlights of our school day and to rest. That leisurely respite fueled our walk the rest of the way up the hill. The day couldn't have been better scripted except for having to walk past the two sentries guarding the military checkpoint on the way to and from our little cottage on the hill.

Soon after we moved into the cottage—and now two years after we married—Moke Chee was pregnant. Our new neighbor, the PWD engineer, moved into the other cottage fresh from Germany in April 1964 with his blonde-haired, blue-eyed German bride. He was a Malaysian Chinese who looked much younger than his bride. We never mixed socially with our new neighbors. We had our own social circle by the time our neighbors moved in, and they seemed cold and indifferent to our initial efforts to be hospitable. We invited them to join us for dinner at our favorite hawker stall, but they declined, so we never invited them again.

They had their cottage patio screened in and kept a captured baby macaque monkey in the enclosure. They may have thought me a busybody when I warned them that a baby wild animal may look cute, but they grow up to be strong wild adults that can't be managed, and it was better to set the baby free where it could live with its natural family in the wild. They told me that they were capable of making their own decisions. That evening a troop of monkeys destroyed their enclosure, and at daybreak, adult macaques perched overhead on branches of two huge mango trees in our back compound and screamed at our neighbors and at us. They threw mango pits at us whenever we were outside, and one day a gang of macaques came down the trees to the ground and threatened to charge us. It was frightening. I worried that it was only a matter of time before they followed through on their charge and grabbed one of us. I was relieved that Moke Chee and I would be leaving for the May school holiday, but before we departed for Penang, I again told our neighbors that they better give the baby macaque back to the troop before someone got injured.

I also told our neighbors that I was doubly worried because Moke Chee and I were going to be parents soon, and we feared a gang of macaques might try to kidnap our baby. I didn't want Moke Chee to experience the additional anxiety of having to worry about that because she was already experiencing severe morning sickness and her pregnancy was starting to show. Walking back up the hill, after spending a full day on her feet at school, became a more difficult chore for her, even with the stop for ice kacang and sugarcane water. Worse, I thought I caught a portion of the sentries' crude comments that were something to the effect of: "The white man's pleasure is showing."

Moke Chee remained a good sport and carried on without complaint.

Moke Chee and I closed up our cottage before walking to school on the final Friday of the first school term. Mr. Khor agreed to give us a ride to the Ipoh taxi stand, where we began our travel to Penang.

Soon-to-be Grandparents

When we arrived at Moke Chee's house, my mother-in-law, in addition to making me chocolate custard for strength, made Moke Chee a bowl of "or chai," which is a big hunk of fatty, gelatinous pig's knuckle steamed in soy sauce with chunks of ginger, sugar, and other Chinese herbs that was intended to nourish the expectant mother and baby during pregnancy. Auntie Gan, Choo Choo's mother, also sent Moke Chee a bowl of pig's knuckle along with a bottle of Benedictine DOM liqueur, which was also thought to be good for the mother. I consumed as much, or maybe even more of the DOM than Moke Chee and can attest to its medicinal properties. At no time did I experience morning sickness.

Moke Chee relished the "or chai," but I thought it was so greasy that it added to her morning sickness. I kept my thoughts to myself because consuming the dish during pregnancy and after giving birth was part of Moke Chee's heritage. She earned the right to be fed "or chai" by her mother and aunties. One of the Chinese remedies that Moke Chee found soothing was having me rub Ipoh Yeow, an oil with a eucalyptus aroma, on her neck and chest.

My father-in-law gave no outward expression that would indicate he was about to become a grandfather. He had learned through experience and through lessons passed down from his elders that it was best not to anticipate the birth of a baby. He did tell me that there were two inheritances I should know about because Moke Chee showed little interest in her inheritances. One inheritance was passed on from his father to Moke Chee's generation, and the other inheritance was from Granny, his grandmother.

The first inheritance, as stipulated in Moke Chee's grandfather's will, was sixty hectares of land on Penang Hill. The land was to be divided evenly among the children of his children. Since Moke Chee was an only child, she was to get a full share, not be divided among any siblings. A portion of the land was planted with rumbuntan trees across from St. Nicholas' Home. At one time, the land included the grounds of St. Nicholas' Home, but Moke Chee's grandfather donated that land to the missionaries. The other portion of the land faced the sea and was populated by squatter farms and an unauthorized Chinese cemetery. He told me that the will was on file in the government office, waiting for Moke Chee and her cousins to have it executed.

Also, one female member of Moke Chee's generation was to inherit the power to be a medium from their great-great-grandmother. The power passed from great-grandmother to great-granddaughter. Since neither Moke Chee nor any of her female cousins received the gift, my father-in-law said it seemed to have bypassed her generation and would be vested in a great-great-granddaughter. He said, "Be vigilant. Stay alert. The gift may manifest itself in one of your daughters."

Being a medium and communicating with supernatural

powers struck me as more of a curse than an inheritance, but to appease my father-in-law, I said: "I will, I promise."

He replied, "Ah, ah," and nodded his head in the affirmative. He seemed pleased by my promise.

I didn't believe in such things, but I admit while he told me of Granny's inheritance, I felt my spine crinkle and said a silent prayer: Please, God, protect my daughters and any and all future generations of daughters from becoming mediums.

The two weeks of holiday in Penang seemed to fly by. Moke Chee was getting bigger, and our excitement about becoming parents was growing. Now, I wished even more that we could have stayed in Penang, where Moke Chee would have had the comfort of being close to her parents, and they could have enjoyed participating in the expectancy of their grandchild.

When Moke Chee and I returned to Batu Gajah, our neighbors had finally set the baby monkey free. They rebuilt the screen cage on the patio, and this time they filled it with birds. Then one day, the patio cage at our neighbor's cottage and all the birds were gone. The blonde-haired, blue-eyed German woman, who seemed so ill at ease and out of place in Batu Gajah, was gone. Now, the engineer was living next door all alone. We seldom saw him. When he did show up, it usually was with a lady, but never the same lady twice.

By June, it not only became more difficult for Moke Chee to walk up the hill, but the sentries also started snickering and making comments to each other when we walked past. When they spoke loud enough for Moke Chee and me to hear, I could tell their comments were obscene from the color of her face. She refused to fill me in, saying, "They're ignorant. Ignore them. They're not worth the bother."

That Friday afternoon, Ah Chai sent Su Blee to fetch us to Kampar for the weekend. I told Ah Chai the sentries were starting to make obscene comments about Moke Chee when we passed them. Ah Chai suggested getting a car.

"I like the idea of a car, but I'm afraid that's not an option."

Ah Chai said, "If it's finances, I will help you out."

I said, "It's not that. Peace Corps Volunteers can't even have motorbikes, much less cars."

Ah Chai said, "That's ridiculous. Malaysian teachers have automobiles. Look at the number of teachers' cars parked at your school. Besides, Moke Chee isn't a Peace Corps Volunteer, and the automobile is for her. What is there to prevent her from having one? Good Lord, she's expecting. Forget about the sentries' lurid comments. You can't expect Moke Chee to climb that hill after teaching all day."

I said, "I'll have to ask Kuala Lumpur."

Ah Chai said, "Are you sure you trust your wife's well-being to the judgment of that lot? It is better to purchase the automobile and then let them explain to Moke Chee's father why his expectant daughter can't have it. As long as you don't flaunt it, they will elect not to know you have one."

I said, "I don't know how to go about buying a car in Malaysia."

Ah Chai said, "First, you have to decide what kind of automobile you want."

I said, "A small used car that's in good mechanical condition but not too expensive, maybe up to $2,000RM, and not flashy or too costly to operate."

Ah Chai said, "It's best we see Cheng Wat. Are you up for a drive to Ipoh in the morning?"

Ah Chai telephoned Cheng Wat to let him know what I was looking for in a car and made an appointment for us to see him. Moke Chee, Ah Chai, and I drove to Cheng Wat's office in Ipoh on Saturday morning.

Cheng Wat said, "One of my business associates has a 1962 Austin Mini. He is asking $2,200RM for it but agreed to accept $1,800RM. That's a very good offer. My friend has other cars, but I think this is the one that best meets your needs. Look it over, test drive it, and if you like it, we'll make the deal."

The Austin Mini arrived. It was light blue and cute without

being flashy. Moke Chee loved it, and I thought it was perfect. We agreed to purchase the car.

With that, Moke Chee and I became car owners, and Moke Chee didn't have to struggle walking up the hill after standing and climbing stairs at school all day. Best of all, we were able to whiz past the sentries. We continued to stop off for our freshly squeezed sugarcane water and ice kacang in the afternoon and share the hilarious surprises our students treated us to each day.

Owning a car was not a big deal to my Malaysian colleagues. I worried about what to say when the Peace Corps learned I had a car and figured I would simply tell them it was Moke Chee's car and that I purchased it for her. What would they do? Try to make Moke Chee sell the car? Not having to hide driving a car from the Peace Corps gave me a sense of freedom.

The drive to Penang for the August holiday was easier now that we had our own car. It was a relief to be back in Penang for two full weeks rather than just a weekend. Moke Chee enjoyed her mother's cooking and the "or chai." She was over the morning sickness, but I continued to rub Ipoh Yeow on her neck and chest and now on her tummy as our growing baby stretched it. Rubbing Moke Chee's tummy with Ipoh Yeow was supposed to reduce the stretch marks. When I did that, our baby moved inside her. We were both excited to feel the life inside her respond to my stroking her belly, and we sang lullabies to the baby and held conversations with the baby. We told Sean—Moke Chee was positive the baby was a boy and picked the name out of respect for Sister Coleman and her Irish heritage—multiple times a day how much we loved him.

We decided that we would have Sean attend local primary and secondary schools as Gim Kooi and Ah Chai did with their children rather than have them attend boarding schools as other European Planters did. We thought they could then go to the United States or England for college, preferably Harvard or Oxford. We planned to visit my family in the United

States for Christmas every two to three years, so Sean and our other children would get to experience snow and an American Christmas, as well as get to know their American family. At some point, when Sean and our other children were old enough to visit their American family on their own and when it was time to go to college and make their own way in the world, the United States and Western culture wouldn't be completely foreign to them.

Shaggy

There was a hawker stall in Batu Gajah that had a beautiful dog with fluffy shaggy hair that was all white with the exception of a black ring of fur around one eye. Moke Chee loved to feed noodles and clams to the dog, so as soon as we sat at a table, the dog came to her, wagging its tail. I complimented the cook on the beauty of his dog, and he told me she was going to have pups and that I could have one if I wanted. I thanked him and thought nothing about it until one day, Mr. Khor and I went there to share a bottle of beer after a scout meeting.

The cook approached me and said his shaggy dog had given birth to four pups, three males and one female, and that he still had the female if I wanted it. No one else wanted the female pup, so if I didn't take it, he was going to drown it in the river. The pup was all dirty, and its coat was caked in mud. I thanked the cook but told him, "No, thank you."

I don't know. Was it the beer, or was it the biologist in me? As I sipped my beer talking to Mr. Khor, and watching the pup in the mud, the thought of that little life being extinguished in the Klang River troubled me. I then violated two personal tenants. I was adopting a pet when I had always advocated against Peace Corps Volunteers adopting pets because, after two years, what would become of their animals? I had witnessed Volunteers adopt pets and then struggle to find homes for them when it was time for them to leave Malaysia. Additionally, I was making a major decision without consulting Moke Chee.

The first was easy for me to ignore because I was planning on staying in Malaysia after my Peace Corps tour was completed. With the second, I rationalized that having a puppy would be good practice for having a baby. Moke Chee did not accept my rationalization. She correctly pointed out that we were in no position to take care of a dog and a baby. I offered to take the puppy back to the hawker stall. But she said, "It's so filthy. Let's clean it first."

Then Moke Chee said, "You can't take a puppy into your home and then just give it away."

Shaggy became our first baby. She went everywhere with us, including the cinema and restaurants, where she sat on Moke Chee's lap. She went back to Penang with us. Our girls from St. Nicholas' Home loved to play with Shaggy, and she was so gentle with them. She went to the Kampar rubber estate with us, where she drank beer with Ah Chai and me.

Final School Term 1964

Moke Chee and I returned to Batu Gajah in September 1964. We added one more wrinkle to our set routine. I wanted to be married in a Catholic church before our baby was born. Moke Chee and I were attending St. Joseph's Church in Batu Gajah on the weekends when we did not return to Penang. The pastor, Father Nabaise, assigned a young French priest, Father John Morea, to prepare Moke Chee and me for marriage.

Some of the faith, including Sister Coleman, considered him "not right in the head." I found him friendly and not at all like the priests I had known in my parish back home. First, he insisted we call him John. Then he asked if I believed that

I was making my vows to Moke Chee in the presence of God when we were married by the magistrate. I answered yes. He said: "You're married in the eyes of God. What's your worry? A church ceremony and the official paperwork are just to satisfy the bureaucracy of the Church."

John Morea asked Moke Chee why she wanted to be baptized as a Catholic. When she replied that I was Catholic and we were going to raise our children Catholic and she wanted to go to Catholic heaven with us, his response was that being baptized Catholic was not a necessary precondition or necessarily a guarantee of going to Catholic heaven, if there is one. He came to our house once a week for dinner, and we had far-ranging conversations for several months. He became part of our extended family.

Moke Chee and I started our hospital plans for the birth of our baby. Initially, we considered going to the General Hospital in Batu Gajah because it was just down the hill from our cottage, and Moke Chee's cousin, Lin Chee, was the Head Midwife there. However, several people suggested that, if we could afford the price, St. Mary's Maternity Hospital in Ipoh was better because it was run by Catholic nuns, and they specialized in only delivering babies. We met with the nuns, and they assured us a doctor would be called should Moke Chee require one, but in almost all cases, like the government hospitals, a doctor was not required to deliver a baby. We wanted the best for our baby, and I wanted the best for Moke Chee, so we elected to have our baby delivered at St. Mary's.

Our teaching of Form V classes took on an urgency as the Cambridge Examination approached. There were more intense reviews of the subject matter and of possible questions on the exam and after-school tutorials. My students were more than ready, and my primary job at this juncture was to instill in them the same level of confidence that I had in them.

December Holiday

As with every December since turning eighteen, I celebrated turning twenty-six years old by letting my draft board in Chicago know where I was and what I was doing. With that done, Moke Chee and I drove to Penang. When we arrived, we had two surprises. The first was a box containing a Christmas present from my mother and father. It wasn't yet Christmas, but we opened the box. The box contained a folded-up aluminum Christmas tree that was colored a light sparkly purple. It stood about four feet tall and was about three feet wide. Moke Chee's father gave us permission to put the tree up on a table in the sitting room. There was a separate box of a dozen balls, which were also purple but a pinker shade than the tree, and were about two inches in diameter wrapped in string. I didn't like gaudy aluminum Christmas trees when I was living in Chicago. I preferred the green color and pine aroma of a real tree in the dead of winter. But here in Malaysia, with greenery everywhere, the contrast of light sparkling off shards of purple aluminum strands sprinkled the air with a festive feeling. It was four feet by three feet of purple gaudiness, yes, but it was beautiful.

The second surprise was when my mother-in-law brought Moke Chee's baby crib out of storage. It was wrapped in multiple layers of fabric. First, she untied the rope—which was the length of a cotton clothesline—that bound the outer red-and-white checkered oil-cloth covering, which revealed a second covering—a pretty white cotton baby crib sheet with images of tan teddy bears with red bow ties—that covered a still-intact mosquito net. And all the coverings removed revealed the cutest little wicker crib in pristine condition, just as it must have been when it was put away more than twenty years ago.

I could imagine baby Moke Chee sleeping in the crib. She had to be adorable. By the smile on my mother-in-law's face,

I thought she, too, imagined herself a young mother admiring the life she brought into the world. My father-in-law, who made no secret of having wanted a son and not a daughter, initially acted indifferent to the unwrapping, but stepped forward to direct the uniting of the clothesline. In wanting a son, my father-in-law raised his only child as he would a son. Encouraging her to be independent and to think for herself, and not be bound by the societal definition of a subordinate woman. This definitely defined Moke Chee's strong character of not being intimidated by gender or the societal rank of others.

I was filled with nostalgic joy and pride of what was to come as I carried the crib while thinking that my father-in-law must have carried the crib when he was a young expectant first-time father. The crib was well-constructed of beautiful handwoven wicker, more like the ones I saw in Chicago's Marshall Field's department store than in the local shops in Ipoh or Penang. I didn't ask, but I imagined my father-in-law purchased the crib from his own import-export company.

Moke Chee told me how she used to play dolls with Nanny, and they used the crib to put the baby doll down for a nap. She added that she had been too young to think about having her own real baby, but Nanny told her that one day the crib would hold her baby and that Nanny would be there to help her care for the baby.

After Moke Chee and her mother finished preparing and hanging the mattress pad, pillow, cylindrical mini Dutch wife, and mosquito net on the clothesline to air out, Moke Chee and I took time to visit the private hospital in Penang just in case Sean decided to make his debut early. The midwife at St. Mary's Hospital in Ipoh told us the baby would come sometime in January.

Malaysia, a country with a predominantly Muslim population, still celebrated Christmas, but the Christmas celebration was a quiet affair and much less commercialized than in the United States. Moke Chee and I attended Christmas Day

Mass, but we didn't exchange gifts ourselves. New Year's Eve, by comparison, was celebrated by all of Malaysia. I found out that the E&O Hotel had a traditional New Year's Eve Dance. I wanted to plan something special for Moke Chee, so I made a reservation at the E&O for New Year's Eve.

I was disappointed by the room. I had expected something more elegant. The room reminded me of the rooms I stayed in at discount hotels. There was a bed and a writing table, and the bathroom had carpeting and wallpaper that seemed old and tired. Since we were only staying for one night, it was fine. We were there to dance in the new year.

The concierge directed us to the ballroom, and then the maître d' escorted us to a table one row back from the edge of the dance floor and about thirty feet from the bandstand. A waiter took our drink order, and when he returned, I wrote our room number on the tab and signed it. I couldn't help but think about the contrast from my first visit to the E&O, when I was escorted out.

The ballroom was about a forty-foot square with a low ceiling and a huge crystal chandelier. All the tables were full, and the dance floor was packed when the band played. The room had poor acoustics, and the band consisted of only six musicians, so the band sounded tinny even when Moke Chee and I danced immediately in front of them.

We danced just about every dance, including the fast and Latin numbers, even though Moke Chee's delivery date was only a few weeks away. We left shortly after midnight when the ballroom began to empty, and Moke Chee and I retired to our room. The mattress was thin, the pillows lumpy, and, worse, the walls were thin. We could hear motorcycles racing up and down Lemur Farguher, and it seemed as if we were in the middle of the street. I called the front desk and asked for a different room or for the hotel to lodge a complaint with the police and ask them to put a stop to the racing outside so we could sleep.

CHAPTER 31

We anticipated our baby might be born while we were on holiday in Penang, and I hoped for it so Moke Chee would have the support of her family and friends, but it didn't happen that way. We prepared to head back to Batu Gajah. It was a challenge, but we put the crib in the back of our small car and took it back to Batu Gajah. It was just a matter of weeks before baby Sean would join us. All of us were so happy and so excited, and I promised to call Grandmother's house as soon as the baby was born.

Once settled back in Batu Gajah, we set up the wicker basket next to our bed. We re-established the routine of driving to see the midwife at St. Mary's Maternity Hospital every week. She continued to reassure us that everything was progressing as it should. I memorized every turn in the road and every possible roadblock in preparation for the time we would have to dash to the hospital. Occasionally, a long freight train crossed the road. That stood out in my mind like a bookmark because the freight train was the only thing that could possibly delay our getting to the hospital on time. I also made sure the Austin Mini had a full tank of gas, and each night I checked the tires. We had everything that was in our power under control. Now we waited for nature to bring us our baby.

The baby was late, but the midwife said everything was proceeding well and that both Moke Chee and the baby were healthy and well. All we needed was patience. Nature would take its course. After each visit, we left the maternity hospital feeling happy and reassured and tried our best to be patient, but we longed to see and to hold our baby, to love this child of our love.

The month of January 1965 passed, and Chinese New Year was approaching. We were looking forward to returning to Penang for the weekend to celebrate Chinese New Year with Moke Chee's parents and all the family at Granny's house. But that Wednesday, February 1, shortly after midnight Moke Chee was awakened with abdominal and back pains. She said, "I think the baby is coming. We had better let Sister Coleman know I won't be in school."

I said, "Should we head to the hospital?"

Moke Chee said, "No, it was just one pain. Let's see if there are more."

The pains continued and started coming at regular intervals as the sun rose. I said, "We can let Sister Coleman know on the way to the hospital."

We got in the car, and sure enough, Sister Coleman was standing out by the front gate of the school. I pulled to the side of the entry where Sister Coleman was greeting everyone. She bent forward to look in the window at Moke Chee and me with a smile on her face and in her eyes and said: "It's time, isn't it?"

Moke Chee said, "I'm sorry I won't be in school today. We're on our way to the maternity hospital." Sister Coleman told Moke Chee not to worry about her students and also assured me that she would let Mr. Khoo know why I wouldn't be in school today.

With Sister Coleman's blessing, we were on our way. Moke Chee was experiencing pains at frequent intervals. Fortunately, there was little traffic in the morning, and there was no freight train. We were happily anticipating the arrival of little Sean. A room, the room Moke Chee had been shown on previous visits, was waiting for her. I could stay with Moke Chee until the midwife came in to examine her.

The midwife came to the waiting room and told me Moke Chee was indeed experiencing labor pains, but it would be a while before the baby was born and that I should go about my normal day because they had everything under control and there was nothing I could do. I told the midwife that I wanted to stay with Moke Chee. I sat next to her and held her hand. I felt so helpless. Periodically, the midwife came by to examine Moke Chee, and I was sent to the waiting room. I went to see the Matron and asked that a doctor be called. She discouraged that and said it would be an extra expense. I told her it didn't matter. I was worried about Moke Chee and the baby. I used the Matron's telephone to call Ah Chai and asked him to let Moke Chee's parents know she was in labor and that I would call when the baby was born.

Moke Chee was in labor all morning and afternoon. The darkness of the night arrived, and still no baby. I prayed the rosary over Moke Chee, and she asked me to teach her how to pray the rosary. We prayed the rosary together well into the night. It was pitch black outside and equally dark in Moke Chee's room when suddenly, from the wall facing Moke Chee's bed, the wall where a crucifix hung, a soft golden-rose glow appeared. It grew larger and expanded quietly—soon filling the entire room until a sense of calm enveloped the room. It was, I felt, a divine presence. The presence didn't speak words that I heard with my ears, but I felt the words inside my body and heard the words inside my mind: "Don't worry, everything will be alright." Being sleep-deprived, I figured it was my imagination, as I was in a dream-like state.

I didn't mention the vision to Moke Chee until we were talking about her experience at the maternity hospital some days later, and she asked, "Did I fall asleep? Was I dreaming? Or was there a golden-rose glow that filled the whole room while I was in labor? It made me feel safe, and a voice came to me, not through my ears but inside my head, that said, 'Everything will be alright.' "

Moke Chee went on, "It was the most beautiful glow and feeling I ever felt. It gave me the most wonderful feeling, and I wished it would never leave. Was I dreaming?"

I said, "You were awake. Your eyes were open, and you were saying the rosary with me when it happened. I experienced it, too, and I thought I was dreaming because I was tired. We couldn't both have the same dream at the same time."

The vision occurred at about midnight, and shortly after that, the midwife on duty came to tell me to go home and rest because Moke Chee would need me to be at full strength to help her with the baby after it was born. Moke Chee agreed that I should go home to get some rest. Before I left, I made the midwife promise me she would call the doctor in to help with the delivery and told her I would not leave until she put a call in to him. After she assured me she had, I went home to take care of Shaggy.

Early the next morning, I drove to the maternity hospital. Our baby was born at 1:15 a.m. while I was home with Shaggy. Moke Chee was being checked by the doctor, so a nurse brought our baby out for me to see. She said, "Congratulations. You have a healthy baby boy. Both baby and mother are doing fine. Would you like to hold him?"

He was the most beautiful little miracle that I had ever seen. His little red face was sticking out of the yellow cotton blanket that had the word "naughty" printed on it as a design. I said, "Absolutely."

I held many nieces and nephews, but holding this little miracle was different. He seemed to mold into my body as if we were one. I asked the nurse: "Is it alright if I kiss him?"

She said, "Of course. He will love a kiss from his father."

She said the word "father," and I was so proud. I kissed him on the forehead where there was a little red mark and indentation, and I said, "I love you, little Naughty."

When my lips touched his forehead, I realized for the first time the depth of my love. Yes, I loved Moke Chee, but she was able to care for herself, and she was independent and able to love me in return. But this little helpless innocent was completely dependent. He could do nothing for himself. His very life, sustenance, and even his character, the kind of person he would grow to be, and the kind of life that he would lead depended on us. I wanted to be the kind of father to him that I wished my father had been to me.

The nurse said, "Don't call him Naughty. Call him by his name, James Junior."

I said, "Don't you mean Sean?"

She said, "No. Mrs. Wolter was very explicit. She said he had to be named James Allen after his father."

Pointing to the marks on little James' head, I asked, "What are these marks from?"

The nurse explained: "When you left last night, we called the doctor as you instructed. The doctor had to use forceps to turn James. He was in the wrong position, and that is the reason he was unable to come out on his own. They are just superficial marks and will disappear in a few days."

The doctor came out of Moke Chee's room and said, "Both mother and baby are fine. I was called in the nick of time. He was in a breach position and would never have been delivered without having to make an incision and use forceps."

I said, "Thank you. May I see my wife now?"

He said, "Of course. Go right in."

I went into Moke Chee's room. Moke Chee was now more than my wife. She was a mother who gave me a child for us to cherish, nurture, and love. Her face lit up when she saw us. She was always beautiful, but never more beautiful than that moment. I wanted to hold her and kiss her and handed our baby to the nurse and did. My mind was full of visions of our happy little family, but then another nurse came into the room. I recognized her as the short midwife who was on duty when I left last night and who promised to call the doctor before I left the maternity hospital.

Moke Chee's face turned red, and she screamed: "A devil! Get her out of my room! She's a devil!"

Sister Evelyn, a short, square-built Chinese midwife who was dressed in her white nun's habit, approached Moke Chee's bed and said without empathy: "Now, now. You had a difficult delivery, but all is well now. You have a beautiful, healthy baby boy, and your husband is here."

Moke Chee screamed, "Get her away from me! Her head is covered, but I can see horns coming out of her head. She's here to steal my soul and my baby. Get her out! She's evil!"

Sister Evelyn tried to continue toward Moke Chee, but the Matron, who was also the Reverend Mother, stepped in front of her to block her approach to Moke Chee's bed and said, "Sister Evelyn, perhaps it's best you leave for now."

Sister Evelyn's face turned red. She seemed embarrassed. I was also embarrassed. I could think of nothing worse than calling a nun the devil with visible horns growing out of her head. A mood of disquiet gripped me. I grew up with the utmost respect for nuns. I respected them even more than priests. I felt sorry for Sister Evelyn and wanted to apologize. I was worried about Moke Chee. I had never seen her like this and worried about what happened. My dreams of a happy little family were awash now with fear. I never saw anyone react like that and never expected Moke Chee to react like that. Yes, she was outspoken but never would she call another person names. She was grounded in reality and would never intentionally hurt someone. Her believing she saw horns growing out of Sister Evelyn's head frightened me.

I held Moke Chee and said, "It's alright now. I'm here. I won't let anything happen to you."

I felt like a liar saying that because something obviously did happen to Moke Chee and I hadn't been there to protect her.

Matron said, "She became very agitated when Dr. Mendez showed her the forceps that he was going to use and told her that he was going to make an incision. We had to give her ether, and she became more agitated when we placed the ether cup over her nose and mouth. She fought us, and Sister Evelyn pinned her arms and held her down. It was the only way we could deliver the baby safely. She is still under the effects of the ether. It will wear off, and she will calm down and be much better after she gets some rest."

Matron's words calmed me, but Moke Chee did not calm down. She asked for a telephone and called Grandmother's house and had one of The Barbarians run to get her father. She told her father that he had a grandson and then told me her father was absolutely delighted to have a grandson born on the first day of the Chinese New Year. He said that was a good omen and now was more accepting of, if not outright approving, our marriage and finally giving our marriage his blessing.

Word of little James' birth traveled through the family, and Ah Chai called the maternity hospital to congratulate us and to invite me to celebrate James' birth at the Kampar Planters Club with him that night. I stayed with Moke Chee and the baby until it turned dark at seven o'clock and then went back to our cottage to pick up Shaggy. I wrote to my parents that James was born and wrote my draft board in Chicago that I was now a father. I took Shaggy with me and dropped the letters off at the Batu Gajah post office before continuing to the rubber estate.

Ah Chai was all smiles, congratulating me and slapping me on the back when I arrived at the estate. He exclaimed: "Do you know what this means for the old man? Having his first grandson born on the first day of Chinese New Year? It is a great omen, a great honor. It means face-saving for him to family, friends, and neighbors. His only daughter married a European, but the European gave him a grandson on the first day of Chinese New Year. Let's celebrate."

I didn't want to break the news to Ah Chai that my part was very minimal. It was all Moke Chee and her long and painful labor that brought Jimmy into the world on the first day of the Chinese New Year. Taking credit for births was a manly thing in Malaya, and this was not a night to contradict tradition. It was a night to celebrate and take one more step toward the family's acceptance of me.

Ah Chai drove us to the Planters Club in Kampar. It was packed with European and Malaysian Planters celebrating Chinese New Year. Ah Chai bought the club a round of drinks in honor of James' birth and passed a box of Cuban cigars around.

Moke Chee was confined to the hospital for seven days. She continued to scold Sister Evelyn and called her a devil anytime she saw her. Moke Chee told me that when the ether mask was put over her mouth and nose, she recalled rabbits being euthanized in science class at St. George's with ether and was afraid that she was being put to death. She also thought that Dr. Mendez was going to pull her insides out with the forceps.

On top of that, while holding her down, Sister Evelyn told Moke Chee: "This is what you deserve. You were sinful having sex, and now you have to suffer pain for your sins. How much are you enjoying sex now?"

A New Life for Us

At the end of seven days, I picked up Moke Chee and Jimmy—we now called our baby Jimmy—from the maternity hospital. It was obvious driving back to our cottage that Moke Chee had changed. She wasn't the same happy, confident, trusting person I brought to the hospital. She held Jimmy in her arms and continued to retell her ordeal in giving birth, interspersed with warnings to be careful of approaching cars and bicycles.

She repeated her ordeal over and over again like a broken record. I said, "It's over; forget it. We have a healthy baby and a bright future. Think about all the good things."

"What good things?" Moke Chee replied. "You didn't have

them cut you and try to kill you. I'm sorry. I didn't mean that. I love you. But that woman wasn't a woman. She was the devil posing as a nun. I saw her horns under her habit when she was holding me down. The worst of it is that nobody believes me."

I told her: "They gave you anesthesia, and Matron said that the side effects sometimes cause people to imagine things."

I sensed that Moke Chee was angry with me. She remained quiet for a while. "My beautiful baby has marks on his forehead. Do you think they hurt him?"

I was frightened and confused. I didn't know what to do or say. I answered: "Matron said the marks were from the forceps. The doctor used them to turn Jimmy so he could come out."

Moke Chee said, "He cut me down there, too. You don't mind? Will you still love me?"

I wanted to pull to the side of the road but didn't. Maybe I should have. Instead, I told her while driving, "I'll always love you forever and whatever lies beyond forever."

Our journey to the hospital was full of hope and happiness, and our ride back was full of fear and sadness. I didn't know what to do and never felt so inadequate and helpless. I reached over and put my hand over Moke Chee's. I thought a private hospital operated by Catholic nuns would provide the best care, but I was wrong and felt guilty. There was nothing I could do to undo what Moke Chee had been put through.

Moke Chee had no experience with babies and became frustrated when Jimmy didn't take his bottle and then burped a good portion of it up. She was worried that he wasn't getting enough nourishment. Since my siblings had kids, I had more experience with babies, so I took over feeding him and stayed up most of the night with Jimmy because he didn't sleep. Shaggy stayed on the floor next to Jimmy's cot. She had sniffed him head to foot when he first came into the house and must have decided he was hers. I took Jimmy back to stay at the hospital the next day while I drove to Kuala Lumpur to pick up Nanny.

Once Nanny arrived, she took care of Jimmy and Moke

Chee and ran the household. Jimmy and Moke Chee and I all settled down. If there were such creatures as angels on Earth, Nanny certainly was one. With Nanny taking care of us, Moke Chee could rest during the day, but continued to have nightmares about the birthing ordeal every night.

We returned to Penang the second week after Jimmy's birth to visit his grandparents and Granny. I was surprised to see my father-in-law growing a white beard. He told me, "It's tradition. I'm a grandfather now. I have the privilege of growing a beard."

He continued, "This lets everybody know that I'm a grandfather. And of a grandson born on the first day of Chinese New Year. His sign is the serpent. The head of the serpent means he will be very clever. That is a good omen."

We walked with Jimmy across the back lane to present him to Granny. She lifted his blanket to get a full view of her newest great-grandchild. She said, "Jimmy. A boy born on the first day of Chinese New Year. That is a good omen."

Granny looked at Jimmy's feet and pointed to the star-shaped markings on the soles of his feet, and said, "This is a good sign. He will travel far in life." She smiled and tapped me on the arm twice, each time saying, "Good, good," and then went to lie down for her nap.

Nanny made friends with Cheong and learned from him as the Resthouse Manager what was in season at the market. She gave me instructions on what to purchase on my way home from school. Moke Chee was starting to sleep through the night and could help Nanny with cooking and caring for Jimmy. Nanny brought calm and stability to our household and lives and was in full control of the house and of Jimmy. I thought it would be good for Moke Chee and me to spend Moke Chee's last weekend of maternity leave at the Cameron Highlands before she returned to teaching full-time. We made a reservation at the Old Smokehouse Inn and told Cheong at the Resthouse where we were staying in case he or Nanny had to reach us.

Moke Chee and I spent time walking the beautiful, land-scaped grounds in the cool highland air and lingered in the English garden. We discussed when I would complete my Peace Corps obligation and become a Planter and of using my bonus money as a Planter to purchase a cottage in the Highlands, where we would spend alternate holidays. In the evening, we sat by the huge stone fireplace in the Old Smokehouse lobby listening to music and planning for Jimmy's future. Moke Chee was sure he would be a neurosurgeon. While Moke Chee ordered a Pimm's No. 1, I sipped a Gibson cocktail paired with a locally grown pickled scallion. At night, we slept in a huge soft bed. The thick down comforter kept us toasty warm and seemed to shelter Moke Chee from her awful nightmares. In the morning, a soft knock at our door announced the arrival of a pot of hot tea and toast with butter and marmalade awaiting us just outside our room, along with the morning newspaper. After morning tea, we took a warm water shower and then went to the restaurant for breakfast. It was magical.

We arrived back at our cottage in Batu Gajah feeling relaxed and refreshed. A month passed, and as we were on our way down the hill to St. Bernadette's, Moke Chee was unusually quiet, as if deep in thought before saying, "I think I'm pregnant again."

I pulled the car over to the side of the road and took Moke Chee's hand, and asked, "Is that possible? Jimmy was just born."

She replied, "That's what I thought, but I'm sure of it."

I asked, "If you are, where do you want to have this baby?"

"In Penang. At the American Mission Hospital. She is due in January. I'll tell Sister Coleman today, and I'll ask to extend my December holiday. Or, if not there, the General Hospital here. But I really want to give birth in the American Mission Hospital in Penang."

I said, "I wish we had gone there with Jimmy. I think you'll get better care at that hospital."

Moke Chee told Sister Coleman that we were going to have

another child, and Sister Coleman—besides granting Moke Chee maternity leave again following the December school holiday— was delighted that our family was growing.

We settled into our old routine. Moke Chee had, it seemed, only recently ended her morning sickness and now was experiencing it again. Fortunately, her nightmares of giving birth to Jimmy had stopped. During the day, she expressed both fear of having another bad experience and hope that it would be different at the American Mission Hospital.

Mr. Lee approached me one day and told me our school was taking delivery of locking metal storage cabinets and that he needed help removing the wooden wall shelves in the lab preparation room to make space for the cabinets. I agreed to help him on a Saturday, and he offered the wood shelving to me. I gratefully accepted.

Jimmy was outgrowing the baby crib. Moke Chee and I looked to purchase a baby bed, but it cost more than one month's allowance. We were short on funds because of the cost of the maternity hospital and the projected cost of the American Mission Hospital, so I planned on purchasing lumber bit by bit to build a bed for Jimmy myself.

I scrubbed and sanded the shelving down to bare wood before painting it white. Moke Chee painted decorations of flowers and bunny rabbits and ducklings and wrote a nighttime prayer on the headboard. There was enough lumber left over to also make a playpen that would be up off the floor away from insects. We were ready for the arrival of our new baby.

December 1965 Holiday

It was amazing how we could pack into our Austin Mini and drive to Penang on weekends and holidays. Moke Chee, Nanny, Jimmy, Shaggy, and I, along with the wicker baby crib, all fit in that little car. We dropped Nanny off at her association house before heading to Moke Chee's parents' house.

Before departing for our holiday, I wrote my draft board a letter letting them know that my twenty-seventh birthday in December was approaching and that I was in Malaysia as a Peace Corps Volunteer teacher. I also reminded them that I was married and a father and that I had no confirmation of their receipt of my prior notification of becoming a father.

I also wrote to the Peace Corps office in Kuala Lumpur, notifying them that I planned to provide the orphan girls at St. Nicholas' Home with day outings during the December school holiday. I received no response from the Peace Corps office, so I assumed they had no alternative plans for me. The girls—Abby, Olivia, May, and August—had become a part of Moke Chee's and my extended family, so rather than plan special outings for them, we had them join in with whatever we planned for the day. They enjoyed holding Jimmy and feeding him and tickling him and, of course, were fascinated to feel the new baby move in Moke Chee's tummy. We were a family. I had hoped that someday I would have a large family with many children, and now I had one. Come the new year, we would even have one more.

We didn't have to wait for the new year for our new baby. Moke Chee's mother wanted to clean and move some crockery that she had stored away. Moke Chee wanted to help her while I went to play badminton with Eng Lay, one of our cousins, and his friends. When I returned later, Moke Chee told me her water had broken and the baby was coming. I rushed Moke Chee to the American Mission Hospital. We were excited to have and hold our newest baby but also apprehensive, given Moke Chee's first experience. I feigned calmness and said to just tell the doctor that you are afraid of the pain and want the shot. Moke Chee agreed to do that.

Both of us told the nurse that Moke Chee had a difficult delivery with our first baby, and she wanted the epidural to control the pain. The nurse assured Moke Chee that she would tell the doctor. When Dr. Fleming came by to introduce himself, we also told him that Moke Chee was scared from her first delivery and wanted an epidural. He nodded his head and calmly said he had delivered hundreds of babies and would deliver ours without complications. I wasn't allowed in the delivery room but felt assured all would go well until I heard Moke Chee tell the doctor once more that she was frightened and wanted the shot. I heard him shout at her: "If you don't shut up, I'm going to walk out of here and leave you alone."

I shot up from my chair in the waiting room and opened the door to the delivery room, but as soon as I did, a short, muscular nurse blocked my way. She put her hand on my chest and said, "Now you go sit down and leave us to our work. You'll only be in the way here."

She made it clear that she was there to physically restrain any intruders. I didn't want to get in a wrestling match and distract the doctor from attending to Moke Chee, so I meekly turned around and sat quietly like a reprimanded schoolboy.

It was less than an hour later when a young, slender nurse came out with a baby wrapped in a blanket. She said, "Congratulations, you have a baby girl. Both the baby and mother are fine." She pulled the blanket back to expose the baby's face. I expected to see a beautiful, tiny red face like Jimmy's, but I was shocked.

The baby's face was distorted with one eye up and the other down, and its face was covered with hair. I said, "Are you sure the baby is alright? Its face is all distorted and covered with fur. It's a shame it's a girl. Other children will make fun of her. Are there special homes for babies like this?"

The nurse replied, "That's because she's just been born and came through the birthing canal. In a few minutes, her face will transform to normal, and the birthing hair will fall away. You have a beautiful, healthy baby daughter. Do you want to hold her and then see your wife?"

When I held my daughter for the first time, I again felt the depth of love when I held baby Jimmy. But this time, I also felt something more primitive, more animalistic, which I feared was in me but tried to deny. I was opposed to violence, but as I held my baby daughter to my chest, I knew that I was capable of murder. If anybody ever hurt my baby girl, I knew I was capable of killing them without hesitation. That feeling frightened me, yet at the same time, I found it reassuring.

When I walked into her hospital room, Moke Chee greeted me with a big smile. I put our baby down next to her and held the two of them. Moke Chee said, "Will you go home and bring Jimmy here? I want to see him, and I want him to see his beautiful baby sister."

Moke Chee turned to our baby daughter and said, "Sheana, Daddy is going home to bring your big brother Jimmy to see you."

I left very happy. There was a difficult moment in the delivery room, and while I was still pissed that Dr. Fleming had threatened Moke Chee, I was relieved that she wasn't seeing anyone sprout horns.

I brought Jimmy, along with Moke Chee's father, to see his Mommy and baby sister. The five of us couldn't be happier.

That night, I wrote my draft board another letter telling them that Sheana was born and asked them to update my draft status. Again, I didn't receive a response from the draft board but figured that they decided not to bother with me since I was married and the father of two and would be turning twenty-eight years old in less than a year.

Post-Peace Corps Planning

After my first stint with the Peace Corps, I realized how fast Peace Corps service goes by. Once I returned to Moke Chee and saw her parents, it was clear to me that I had to stay in Malaysia after my Peace Corps term was over. I applied once more to Singapore University Medical School. Once more, my application was rejected, even with a letter of recommendation from Dr. Alister Wilson, my father-in-law's physician. There was no getting around the fact that I wasn't a natural-born citizen of Singapore or Malaysia.

I knew it was possible to work for the Ministry of Education as a consultant on a series of two-year contracts. That had no certainty and no stability. Besides, if I worked for the Ministry, I would rather teach students than be a consultant. Working for the Ministry as a consultant was my job of last resort.

I told Ah Chai that I was interested in becoming a Planter after my tour with the Peace Corps, and he offered to teach me. He told me that it could be a difficult and lonely life at times, but also financially and personally rewarding. Being a Planter and living on a rubber estate was the lifestyle that most appealed to me and to Moke Chee. So my post-Peace Corps goal was to become the Assistant Manager of the Kampar Rubber Estate under Ah Chai and then become Manager when he moved to a larger estate. Everything was in place.

On the weekends that Moke Chee and I stayed at the rubber estate, Ah Chai introduced me to the various aspects of managing the estate. I realized I had a lot to learn. I knew nothing about rubber production, but neither had Ah Chai, and now he was one of Malaysia's top Planters. I was a quick study and confident that I would quickly learn all about rubber production from Ah Chai. I felt positive that my post-Peace Corps career had taken shape as my family was growing. I was anxious to move on to the next step in my life.

CHAPTER 32

Ours was a romance encumbered with external obstacles and resistance that we, young and in love, braved and overcame undaunted. We forged ahead, putting in place a plan to achieve our dreams. Moke Chee had fulfilled her obligation to teach five years in a government school, and by year's end, I would have fulfilled my obligation to the Peace Corps. My life as a Planter was set. Or so I thought.

Way back, it seemed decades ago, when I first entered Peace Corps training in DeKalb, myself and the other male trainees were instructed to inform our local selective service draft board of our status as Peace Corps Trainees. And again, once we were inducted as Volunteers and sent to our overseas assignment, we were to inform the draft board of our status as Peace Corps Volunteers and our location in Malaysia. I followed that directive, and each December, I wrote my draft board in Chicago to notify them of my status as a Volunteer and where I was located in Malaysia. Usually, within a couple of weeks, sometime in January, I received a notice back from the draft board stating that my draft deferment was continuing.

I also notified the draft board when I got married in September 1963 and of Jimmy's birth in February 1965, and then again of Sheana's birth in December 1965. I received an acknowledgment of my notifications of my marriage in September 1963, but not of Jimmy's birth, Sheana's birth, or my December 1965 notification of my status as a Peace Corps Volunteer teaching in Malaysia. Since I was twenty-seven years old and married with two children, I figured that the draft board considered me ineligible for the draft and simply didn't bother notifying me. I couldn't be more wrong.

A Surprise Telegram

It was February 1966, a few days after Moke Chee and I celebrated Jimmy's first birthday with Sister Coleman and a few friends at our house. I was in the physics lab, supervising my students conducting experiments calculating resistance in copper versus aluminum wire. Alvin came running into the physics lab, gasping for breath as he said, "Sir, excuse me, the Headmaster wants you to report to his office immediately."

I said, "My students are near the end of an experiment. I'll be there as soon as my lab is over in about twenty minutes."

He said, "Excuse me, Sir, you have to go right now. You have a telegram. It is very important."

I was very concerned. "Did something happen to my parents back home?"

He said, "No, Sir. It is worse than that. You have been drafted. You have to report back to Chicago in forty-eight hours, or you will be arrested. The Headmaster wants to see you right away. I will monitor your lab."

By now, my students sat silently, listening intently to what Alvin was telling me. I turned to my students and said: "Everything will be alright. You carry on just as if I were here. I'll be back. If the lab ends before I return, you know how to clean up and put the equipment away properly. Can you do that for me?"

My students replied, "Yes, Sir. Thank you, Sir."

I walked quickly, half running, to Mr. Khoo's office. He was sitting at his desk. Miss Kew, the new Senior Assistant, was sitting in one of the two chairs in front of Mr. Khoo's desk. Mr. Khoo said, "Please, Mr. Wolter, have a seat. You have a telegram."

He handed me the telegram. This was Malaysia, so I wasn't surprised that it had already been opened. I read it. Alvin had been accurate in reporting its content. I said, "I don't understand this. There must be some mistake. Family men aren't supposed to be drafted."

Mr. Khoo said, "Perhaps there is a mistake."

He pushed the telephone toward me and said, "Perhaps you should call the Peace Corps Office in Kuala Lumpur."

I picked up the receiver, and the operator said, "Number, please." I said, "Please connect me to the Peace Corps Office in Kuala Lumpur."

I spoke to Josh Gould in the Peace Corps Malaysia Office. It was his position there was nothing the Peace Corps would do or even try to do with regard to my being drafted because some members of Congress were accusing the Peace Corps of being a haven for men avoiding military service. He suggested that I call the Embassy but said not to mention he suggested I call.

I called the Embassy and spoke to Mr. A. Lloyd Ferris, an Administrative Assistant to the Ambassador. He spoke a lot of legalese, which boiled down to there was nothing the Embassy could do. I kept repeating, "There must be some mistake. I'm married with two children. My marriage and my two children are registered with the Embassy. Can't you, at a minimum, tell the draft board that?"

Mr. Khoo saw my frustration and said, "Jim, please hand me the telephone."

I handed Mr. Khoo the telephone. After the formalities of introducing himself and asking who he was speaking to, he said in a firmer voice than I had ever heard him use: "Now, Mr. Ferris, if you please, tell me the name of your immediate superior. I see; Mr. Brown. Now, please put me through to Mr. Brown."

Mr. Khoo held the phone for a while and then said, "Yes, Mr. Brown. I am Mr. Khoo Teck Keong, the Headmaster of Sultan Yussuf Secondary School, which happens to be our King's alma mater. We have a situation that I'm informed only you can resolve. Mr. Jim Wolter is a Peace Corps teacher assigned to our school to teach Form V physics, mathematics, and advanced mathematics. All of his students are preparing for the Cambridge Examination. I don't have to tell you what an important position Mr. Wolter occupies in our school and that his students' futures, whether they have a future, is absolutely dependent upon him. Now, just this morning, he received a telegram ordering him to report to Chicago within forty-eight hours for a physical examination and possible induction in the armed services or face being arrested by government marshals. There is absolutely no one here who can teach Mr. Wolter's classes. I'm begging you to intercede on my school's behalf, on our students' behalf, and have the order for him to return to the United States within forty-eight hours vacated until the Peace Corps can send an adequate replacement for him. Needless to say, our King will appreciate your efforts."

Mr. Khoo listened for a few minutes and then said, "This school term ends in May." He was quiet and then said, "Thank you, Mr. Brown. I will convey that to Mr. Wolter. He should disregard today's telegram. You will confirm that by letter. Thank you, and good day."

Mr. Khoo hung up the phone and said, "Mr. Brown said you can disregard this telegram. The Ambassador will request you receive a deferment. You will have to go to the Embassy to sign some papers. Instructions will be sent in the mail."

A letter followed instructing me to meet with Mr. A. Lloyd Ferris in the Embassy first thing the following Monday. Mr. Khoo gave me permission to take Monday off, and I drove to Kuala Lumpur alone Sunday afternoon. Moke Chee, Nanny, and the babies stayed in Batu Gajah. I stayed at Bill Gan's house. Bill is Choo Choo's older married brother. Choo Choo and her younger sister Mai Mai lived with him. I had to go to the Embassy on several occasions, and each time my visits gave the Gan sisters an avenue for a night on the town. But with the reality of being drafted into the military and the prospect of being sent to fight in Vietnam hanging over my head, I felt Choo Choo and Mai Mai were treating me to my last supper.

Another Telegram

Within two weeks, I received another telegram directing me to report to my draft board in Chicago no later than noon on Tuesday, May 31, 1966, for a physical examination. I had hoped the draft board would reclassify me because I had a wife and two children. It didn't. But at least Moke Chee and I had three more months in Malaysia. All the plans we set in motion were shattered.

Initially, we thought about Moke Chee moving back to her parents' house with the children and Nanny until I found out where the military would send me. I was certain it would be Vietnam, and Penang had recently been designated a rest and recreation station (R&R) for American troops fighting in Vietnam. I would visit Moke Chee and the children in Penang during my R&R periods. But then it sank in that I could be incapacitated or killed, so we decided it was better to stay together as a family, so the children could experience having a father as long as possible. I prayed I would be stationed somewhere other than Vietnam where Moke Chee and the children could follow and we could continue living together as a family unit. It was a time dripping with anxiety and worry. I tried to flush the thought of going to Vietnam from my mind by concentrating on teaching my students, but reminders were everywhere.

Since I was being drafted, there was no point in spending weekends in Kampar learning to be a Planter. We visited Penang every weekend so Moke Chee's parents could enjoy their grandchildren. I felt as if my life in Batu Gajah was slipping away and I couldn't hold on to it. This period of time seemed so unreal to me. It was as if I were observing someone else going through it. I was doing an admirable job keeping up a strong front amid the reality and the seriousness of being drafted.

Leaving Our First Home

Our final week in Batu Gajah was a blur. There were two separate faculty going-away parties. I hated going-away parties. I found them too much like wakes. But I attended the parties out of consideration for my colleagues and Moke Chee's colleagues. With the farewell parties finished—and with cousin Cheng Wat having found people to purchase the Austin Mini and our appliances—all we had left to do was find a suitable home for Shaggy.

Moke Chee and I had dinner one more time with Ah Chai and Second Cousin-Sister at the Kampar rubber estate on the last Friday night before departing for Penang, but we didn't stay overnight. The first thing Saturday morning, before we locked our cottage doors and returned our keys to Cheong, cousin Cheng Wat sent a lorry to pick up our appliances and household goods. The appliances were unloaded at one of his shops, and he had the baby furniture delivered to Nanny's relatives in Penang.

We chartered a taxi for our last trip from Ipoh to Penang. Moke Chee, Nanny, our two children, Shaggy, and I piled into the taxi. I still hadn't figured out what to do with Shaggy. Ah Chai said he'd keep her on the estate, but not as a house dog. She would be a guard dog and would be caged during the day and turned loose at night with his other two dogs. Moke Chee and I couldn't live with the thought of her having to fend for herself after such a pampered life. True, she was a dog, but she was like our first baby. As it turned out, we couldn't find a home that we thought was suitable for her, so we decided to take her to America with us.

What Could Be Worse than Getting Drafted?

We arrived at Moke Chee's parents' house at the end of the first week of May. We kept the wicker baby crib for Sheana to sleep in, and we placed mats on the floor of Moke Chee's bedroom for us to sleep on while Jimmy slept in the bed. Our first week was packed with making preparations to return to Chicago in time for me to report to the draft board on May 31 while staying with Moke Chee's parents as long as possible. Then there was Shaggy.

We had to get the appropriate vaccinations and health clearance from a veterinarian for her, as well as have the appropriate metal shipping cage built to travel. We did all this while making the farewell rounds to family and friends. It was an exhausting time, but everything was going well until one day, we had a scare that shook us to the core.

One afternoon, the Friday before we were to leave Malaysia, we went to wake Jimmy from his morning nap for lunch. We found him sitting on the wood floor, playing with the plastic toys Auntie Gan had given him. He was smiling, but his singlet was wet with vomit, and his diaper was soiled with diarrhea. We picked him up to clean him, and he felt like he was burning up, and his body seemed to lack his typical muscle tone. After cleaning him, we tried to give him a bottle, and what he didn't throw up then passed through him as diarrhea. He had always been an active and very alert baby and was rapidly becoming lethargic. We went to Grandmother's house to call Dr. Wilson, but he was home ill, so Grandmother had her driver take us to the American Hospital.

Jimmy was immediately admitted to the emergency room. He was so dehydrated that the pediatrician decided to give him intravenous liquids. We were unable to go into the operation theater with Jimmy, but he was very cooperative with the staff. He was always trusting and openly accepted other people. He separated from us easily and went with the nurse without a fuss.

When we could finally see him, he was lying in a baby crib, and he was being held down by sandbags on his arms and legs. He couldn't move. His eyes were full of fear. He looked at me as if to plead with me to free him, but his life depended on his being attached to the IV, and the hospital staff wouldn't let me. I saw the fear of abandonment and the plea in his eyes, and my heart was breaking. In addition, our visit was limited to a half hour. Moke Chee went to kiss him and hold his little fingers, but the charge nurse intervened and pushed her away.

Moke Chee screamed, "He's my baby! You have to let me hold my baby!" Another nurse came in and grabbed Moke Chee from behind. I said, "That's not necessary," and I hugged Moke Chee.

During that commotion, Moke Chee noticed the drip from the IV stopped and called it to the attention of the nurse. The nurse said it hadn't stopped, and we said, "Please at least look at it. It's not dripping. Don't tell us it hasn't stopped when we can see with our own eyes that it has. There's no point in having the IV in him if it's not dripping."

The nurse checked the IV and said, "It only stopped momentarily. It's fixed now. You have to leave."

We asked that Moke Chee be allowed to stay with Jimmy overnight to comfort him and to have an extra set of eyes on the IV. Our request was refused. We went home worried about leaving Jimmy and worried Sheana might get the same rotavirus illness; thankfully, Sheana was fine.

The house seemed so empty without all the energy Jimmy created. Moke Chee's mother had many, many questions. We shared only reassuring information with her and told her Jimmy would be fine and be able to come home in the morning.

My father-in-law was unusually stoic, but he didn't eat dinner that night. Moke Chee said, "Pa, eat. Jimmy is where he needs to be and will be home as good as new in the morning."

Moke Chee didn't sleep at all that night. I could feel her toss and turn and hear her whispered prayers until daylight. We bathed and paced until eight o'clock and called a trishaw to take us to the hospital. Jimmy was better and sleeping when we arrived. The nurses took his IV out, and Moke Chee was able to hold him, but before he could be discharged, he had to be able to take rice porridge without vomiting or having diarrhea.

Jimmy didn't eat much. Usually, he had a hearty appetite. Thank God he could hold down what he was able to eat. When Jimmy was ready to be released from the hospital, Grandmother had the driver waiting in the hospital lobby for us. The driver told us Grandmother didn't want Jimmy returning home in a trishaw. That pleased me.

The day before we were to leave, we visited Auntie Gan one more time. She had been so supportive and generous to us by purchasing imported toys and clothing for the children beyond anything we could afford. Her house was an easy walk from Moke Chee's house, and when we walked back to Moke Chee's house, I noticed a Jaguar Mark II parked in front of my in-laws' house. The gaggle of Irving Road street urchins surrounded the car. It was far too luxurious and looked out of place on Irving Road.

As we drew nearer, I could see that the front door of the house was wide open. I was worried that something bad had happened to the old folks while we were away because the doors were always locked. I could hear voices coming from the house. I didn't recognize the man's voice, but my mother-in-law was shouting something to the effect of: "Go away, you devil. I can see your horns."

We entered, and I saw a man I had not met but recognized. He was the teenager, now a man, that I had seen in Moke Chee's photo albums. He was standing in the sitting room next to the family altar. He was talking to my father-in-law, who was also standing, not sitting, next to his favorite lounge chair.

My mother-in-law was standing in the doorway leading back to the kitchen shouting insults with a pained expression on her face. My father-in-law ignored her protestations while listening to the man with an expression of hopefulness on his face.

The man also ignored my mother-in-law. He was almost as tall as my father-in-law and had very refined features like him and like Teh Eng, except—unlike them—he was wearing what looked like a very expensive white long-sleeved silk shirt with French cuffs and an expensive-looking tie. The man was Tou Shi, the teenage boy Moke Chee had a crush on as a school-girl. He stopped talking to my father-in-law in mid-sentence and shifted his gaze to Moke Chee as we entered the house. He looked Moke Chee up and down as if eyeing an item at auction and trying to determine its selling price and said, "Ah Chee, long time, no see. You are even more beautiful than I remember."

Moke Chee seemed stunned to see him and offended by his comment. She turned to me and said, "Jim, this is Tou Shi," and then said to him, "This is my husband, Jim."

He didn't acknowledge my presence and spoke to Moke Chee in Hokkien. "I just got into town and learned you're leaving for the States. I stopped by to see you and to tell you that you don't have to go. You can stay here with me."

I was outraged. Moke Chee snapped back in English, "What do you take me for? You're asking me to give up my husband and children to be your concubine. Get out." She was holding Sheana in her right arm and pointed to the door with her left.

He shifted his feet, and his face reddened as if uncomfortable that she had replied in English. He answered in Hokkien, "No, it's not like that. My divorce has finally gone through, and I'm free to marry."

Moke Chee snapped back in English, "That's your business

and has nothing to do with me."

He continued speaking in Hokkien, not suspecting or not caring that I understood what he was saying. "Your father tells me you're leaving for the States tomorrow, and I'm here to tell you that you don't have to go."

Moke Chee scolded him in English, "Who do you think you are to tell me what I have or don't have to do."

He said, "You can stay here and marry me."

Moke Chee said, "That's ridiculous. You're making a fool of yourself. I love my husband."

He said, "You and I had feelings for each other once. Then I had to spoil it by having a fling in college and making a mistake and then having to do the honorable thing."

Moke Chee said, "That was a long time ago. I was an impressionable schoolgirl back then. Now, I'm a happily married woman with two children."

He said, "That doesn't matter. I still have feelings for you, and it can be like it was, and I will accept you along with your children and raise them as my own."

I heard enough. I clenched my fist. I was watching his Adam's apple move as he spoke. His neck was thin and looked fragile. His trachea could easily be crushed with one punch. He tried to act as if I were a nobody, not even acknowledging my presence, trying to steal my wife and children. He was arrogant and stupid.

My mother-in-law moved into the sitting room between him and me and made a spitting gesture toward him, calling him a double-headed snake. She told Moke Chee not to listen to his lies and pleaded with my father-in-law to throw him out.

Moke Chee said, "Get out. I'm not interested." She took the children—Sheana still in her right arm and Jimmy by the hand—and walked past my mother-in-law to the back of the house.

Finally, my father-in-law said, "You've had your say. It's best if you leave."

Tou Shi persisted. He obviously was a man used to getting

what he wanted and was determined to get it. He shouted after Moke Chee, "I'll give you two years. If things don't work out for you in the States during that period, just say the word, and I'll send the first-class airfare for you and the children to come back."

Moke Chee ignored him and kept on without breaking her stride. My father-in-law reclined in his recliner and picked up the afternoon newspaper as if nothing had happened. My mother-in-law locked and bolted the front door and went to the back of the house.

An odd but comforting thought flashed through my mind as Tou Shi stood on the stoop outside the front door slipping his feet into his shoes: If I were sent to Vietnam and killed there—it could certainly happen within the next two years—there was a man with the financial resources and social position to ensure that Moke Chee had a comfortable life and that our children would receive the best education money could buy. I didn't share that thought with Moke Chee. I didn't want to upset her by talking about me being killed in Vietnam, but the thought of what would happen to Moke Chee, our children, and the old folks if I were killed in Vietnam was always with me. Everything was viewed through the lens of being sent to Vietnam.

Departure

May 28 arrived, and six cars full of family and friends pulled up outside 70c Irving Road. Moke Chee's mother elected to say goodbye to her daughter, grandson, granddaughter, and son-in-law at home. She made chocolate custard for her son-in-law one last time. I coaxed Shaggy into her cage and put the sarong that I wore for pajamas that night in the cage with her. I hoped my familiar scent would keep her calm.

My father-in-law got into the front seat of the car we rode in. After all our transactions in Malaysia, I had three thousand ringgit cash, about a thousand U.S. dollars left over, and an extra forty U.S. dollars. I no longer needed Malaysian currency, so I gave all the Malaysian currency to my father-in-law to tide him over until Moke Chee and I were settled.

Flight Back to Chicago

We checked in at the Penang airport. We were scheduled to fly to Singapore and then change flights and fly to Hawaii, where we would change flights and fly to Los Angeles, and then change planes once more to Chicago. It was about thirty-four hours of traveling. With the time difference, we would arrive in Chicago on May 29.

We boarded a propeller aircraft, and when we were at cruising altitude, it was possible to hear a dog barking. I could see the curious looks on other passengers' faces. Then there was a rumbling, tumbling noise coming from underneath the cabin. It sounded like the aircraft was falling apart. Suddenly, the barking and the rumbling sounds from under the cabin stopped. Shortly after, a male crew member entered the cabin from the curtain up forward carrying Shaggy. The stunned passengers all said in unison: "It's a dog."

When the crew member passed me, I said, "That's my dog. If you let her, she'll stay right here under my feet."

He replied, "I'm sorry, Sir, we can't do that."

He took her to the back and opened a door. I was worried it was an exit door but found out it was one of two toilets on the plane, and he locked Shaggy in there. Shaggy remained quiet.

When we landed in Singapore, we learned that Shaggy had destroyed her cage, but fortunately, the airline had another cage for her. I had to pay sixty Singapore dollars for the cage.

The airline wouldn't take American dollars, and there was no time to go to a money changer. Fortunately, Moke Chee's cousin, Sui Lay, had come to the airport to see us and paid for the new cage. He also negotiated with the customs officer, one of his former students, to suspend the forty-eight-hour animal quarantine period, allowing us to pass through with Shaggy.

Aside from the episode with Shaggy, our trip went smoothly. We boarded the jet to Hawaii. The plane made a stop in Da Nang, where it picked up a few homeward-bound teenage soldiers, and then to Guam. Armed soldiers got on the plane in Guam and checked everyone's passports. They paid particular interest in the soldiers and other draft-age men, including me. We weren't allowed to get out of our seats while they checked each passport. That took the better part of an hour. Sheana fell asleep sucking on her bottle, but Jimmy was having a more difficult time and wanted to be walked, but I wasn't allowed to walk him.

Finally, we were released and on our way. Sheana slept most of the time, but Jimmy was unable to sleep. Moke Chee held Sheana while I held Jimmy. Other passengers and even the flight crew occasionally held the children to give us a rest.

When we arrived in Hawaii, I was called by a customs officer to report to the baggage area of the airport because Shaggy refused to eat or drink water. The customs official was worried about her. Once I arrived, Shaggy drank some water and ate. They allowed me to take her for a walk, and she did her business. The customs agent asked if I was staying in Hawaii, and I told him I had to report to my draft board in Chicago. He said he had never seen a dog like Shaggy and asked if "Pariah" was a rare breed of dog. I didn't want to lie, but I also didn't want to tell him "Pariah" is what all mixed breeds are called, so I said, "There are only a handful like her."

He said, "In that case, we won't quarantine her here if you promise to keep her away from other animals and to call a vet at the first sign of any illness."

I said, "I promise I will." I played with Shaggy a little more and then coaxed her back into her cage.

I went to the passengers' lounge and found Moke Chee and the children. We boarded our next plane to Los Angeles. The plane ride was bumpy. Jimmy still had not slept. He wasn't able to take the bottle and spit it up. All he was able to keep down was water. We changed flights in Los Angeles and finally were on the last leg to Chicago. It was dark out, and the cabin lights were dimmed, and Jimmy finally fell asleep. Then the plane landed in Las Vegas. Jimmy and Sheana both slept through the landing, and Moke Chee and I were relieved because we were also able to sleep. But that was short-lived.

A party of revelers boarded at Las Vegas. They were loud and smelled of alcohol and cigarette smoke. Both babies woke before we took off, and neither fell asleep again. A thoughtful flight attendant offered to carry Jimmy for a while, and he rewarded her kindness by vomiting on her. Moke Chee and I apologized profusely and worried that Jimmy was getting sick again. The journey was wearing on all of us, and while I didn't want to go back to Chicago, it was a relief to arrive there. My mother and father were waiting for us.

I wondered what my parents thought as the four of us arrived. I was single when they saw me off alone on January 2, 1962, and now I'd come back on May 29, 1966, with a wife, two children, and a dog.

My mother and father were waiting for us at the arrival gate. I worried about how they, particularly my mother, would receive Moke Chee. My mother and my sister treated my brothers' wives shabbily. Moke Chee had experienced white bigotry while studying in England and traveling in Europe. I prayed my family would hold their bigotry in check. I was glad my mother wanted to hold the children. It was a sign, I thought, that she accepted and loved them. We had sent her clippings of the children's hair and had selected my mother and father as Jimmy's godparents when we had him baptized.

Also, we selected my sister, she being my mother's favorite child, as Sheana's godmother when she was baptized. I thought that would endear my mother and possibly even my sister to Moke Chee and the children. I was sure my brothers would treat Moke Chee with respect.

I was so exhausted by the time our plane reached Chicago that it was a relief to have my father and mother carry the children to the luggage receiving room. We gathered our belongings along with Shaggy, who, like all dogs, instantly went to my father wagging her tail, wanting to be petted. There was something about my father that made dogs, little children, and—too often—other women attracted to him. We piled our things in my father's Chevrolet and were at my parents' house in less than a half hour.

My mother sat in the front seat next to my father. She pulled the silver foil off of a Hershey's Kiss and turned toward the back seat, holding the chocolate nugget in the palm of her hand. Before I could tell my mother she shouldn't give Jimmy chocolate because he was ill on the plane, he grabbed the nugget with his tiny fingers and, as with everything he encountered at that age, plucked it in his mouth to explore its attributes. Fortunately, Jimmy was able to hold the chocolate down. My mother gave him another despite my protests, and by the time we got home, his face and hands were covered in milk chocolate.

We settled in my old room, a breezeway off the side of the main house. My parents had prepared the room for our arrival with two used baby beds that they had picked up at house sales. The breezeway was the part of the house where I had lived since I was a teenager. At first, the baby beds looked out of place in my old room. Back in my high school days, I could only dream of having a wife and children and a home and a good steady job. Now, I had the most important part of that dream. I thought being in my old room with Moke Chee, Jimmy, Sheana, and Shaggy should have felt strange. But it didn't.

The next day was the Memorial Day holiday, so my sister

and brothers and their spouses and children came over to visit. Moke Chee had packed a bag full of gifts from Malaysia to give to my parents and siblings and various family members and friends. They looked at Moke Chee as if she were from another world, which she was compared to our sheltered whites-only world. They didn't know what to make of her gifts. They appreciated the gifts, but they could not disguise the suspicion that showed in their eyes.

Gift-giving, which was an innate aspect of Moke Chee's Malaysian culture, was foreign to my family and friends, for whom gift-giving was only obligatory on special occasions. To them, a friendly visit was not a special occasion. They were unfamiliar with the concept and pleasure of a gift-giving culture.

I had hoped for a quiet return home, and finally, everybody left and the four of us and Shaggy retired to my room for the night. The fold-up sofa bed that I had slept in alone for nearly ten years I now shared with Moke Chee. The bed spring sagged in the middle, as I remembered, which caused, as if we needed a cause, Moke Chee and I to roll into each other's arms.

The four of us and Shaggy slept soundly until dawn when Jimmy climbed out of his crib and crawled into bed with Moke Chee and me. Shaggy jumped into our bed after him. I felt Jimmy's diaper, which was heavy and saggy, so I got up to change him. Moke Chee got up and changed Sheana's diaper. It was the early morning of Tuesday, May 31.

We could hear my parents in the kitchen and joined them and saw them off to work. My mother kissed the children goodbye while my father urged her to hurry so as not to be late for work. Seeing the joy on my mother's face when she kissed the children strangely made me feel sad. I couldn't remember ever being kissed by my mother or even hugged by her or receiving a loving comment. Her overindulgence of Jimmy and Sheana seemed to be an attempt to fill what she had missed in raising her own children.

I was also gripped by a sense of fear and doom as Moke

Chee and I waited, pacing the kitchen floor until eight o'clock. I couldn't tell you how often I stopped at the kitchen sink and turned on the faucet for a drink of water to quench my parched throat. No matter how often, my throat remained parched while the perspiration oozed from the palms of my hands. But now it was eight o'clock. It was time to call my draft board.

I lifted the yellow Bakelite telephone receiver from its cradle on the wall-mounted rotary-dial telephone above the kitchen table. Dialing a telephone was a strange feeling. I hadn't used a dial telephone in years. I had no telephone in Malaysia, and when I had to make a call, I picked up the receiver and an operator was at the other end to make the connection for me. Now, after I dried my palms on my pants leg, Moke Chee called out the seven numbers written on the telegram sent to me by the draft board. The last number was a zero. I listened to the clicks the rotor made going back to its natural position. It seemed to take forever.

Finally, the dial was back to its neutral position, and the connection was made, but what I heard was that irritating buzzing noise from the other end, indicating the line was busy. I didn't get through. Their telephone was already busy. I redialed immediately. The same result. I was too slow and clumsy to get through right away. I called again at ten-minute intervals and again got a busy signal. I started calling every five minutes. I had the number memorized by the time I finally reached a man with a chipper and youthful-sounding voice on the other end.

He said: "You have reached the Chicago Selective Service Board. This is Charles Smyth speaking; how may I help you?"

I said, "My name is James Wolter, and I've been ordered to call to make an appointment for a physical."

He asked for the spelling of my name, my birthdate, and my Selective Service number. After I gave him that information, he said, "It says here that you're married and in Malaysia. Is that so?"

"Yes. But I'm in Chicago now and reporting for my physical."

"And do you have a marriage certificate?"

"Yes. Two."

"Only one will do. And it says you have two children?"

"Yes."

"Both were born in 1965, but not twins. Is that correct?"

"Yes."

"And do you have birth certificates for them?"

"Yes. Both are issued by the State Department and signed by Secretary Rogers."

"Good. Have photocopies of your marriage certificate and your children's birth certificates made and send the photocopies in, and you will be reclassified."

"I have them right in front of me. It would be no trouble for me to bring them in."

"That won't be necessary. Just drop the photocopies in the mail. You do have our mailing address, don't you?"

"Then, I don't have to report for a physical today?" I asked in trepidation.

"That won't be necessary. You're being reclassified. Is there anything else I can do for you today?"

"Are you sure?"

"Absolutely. Just get the photocopies to us within a week."

"It says in the telegram that I'll be arrested by U.S. Marshals if I don't report for a physical. Marshals won't come looking for me?"

"Right. I've marked your folder 'Reported, reclassification pending.' Just make sure the photocopies are in this week. Mark the envelope 'Attention: Charles Smyth.' "

"That's it?" I was confused and then worried. What if he didn't have the authority for this?

"That's it. Anything else I can do for you?"

"Thank you. No. I'll have the photocopies in the mail today." I let out a big sigh of relief. More of disbelief. I felt disoriented, with the need to clear my head.

I hugged Moke Chee and said, "I'm free. I don't have to go

in. I won't be drafted. I won't be sent to Vietnam. Let's get the children. I want to go outside and breathe the fresh, clean air. I'm free. I'm going to live. I won't have to kill kids."

Moke Chee hugged me, and we kissed. A real kiss. The kind of deep and passionate kiss that said: I'm going to live, and we will be together and raise a family.

We gathered the children, who were still in their pajamas, and went outside and stood under my favorite maple tree—the same tree I climbed as a young boy. I took a deep breath of fresh air. The air was fresh and spring-flavored. The sky was high and baby blue. I was free, and my family was safe.

I wrapped one arm around Moke Chee, who was holding Sheana, and held Jimmy in my other arm. Our hug under that mighty maple tree became, at that moment, our signature "family hug" of gratitude, which we practice to this day. I took in another deep breath of air and stood holding Moke Chee with our children. For the first time in four months, I felt free— free from worry about going to Vietnam, free from worry about hunting and killing teenagers or being killed, and free from worry that another man would raise my children. I was alive and free and with my family—and I would remain with them in America. I was overjoyed, yet still filled with guilt. I wondered who would be sent in my place and said a silent prayer of thanksgiving. I then prayed that the man who would be sent in my place would return home safely unscarred and get to have a wife and raise a family. Oh, how I prayed.

EPILOGUE

Moke Chee and I celebrated our sixtieth wedding anniversary on September 10, 2023. We are both retired and still live in the Chicago area.

Moke Chee became a freelance commercial artist, a preschool teacher, and the owner of a secretarial business.

I became a special education teacher, a public school administrator, a university professor, and an administrative law judge.

Baby Jimmy grew up to become a neurosurgeon, as Moke Chee predicted. He is the father of two grown children and the grandfather of one.

Baby Sheana grew up to become an attorney. She is married to an attorney and is the mother of three grown children: two sons and a daughter.

As a family, we visited Moke Chee's family every other year. Sheana and Jimmy spent many years creating their own memories with Moke Chee's father, mother, and Nanny.

Moke Chee's father died in 1976, followed by her mother in 1977. Nanny passed away in 1984.

Shaggy lived until 1972.

Note: Today, Kuala Trengganu is called Kuala Terengganu, and Alor Star is called Alor Setar.

ACKNOWLEDGMENTS

First and foremost, I must thank my wife, Moke Chee, who inspired, encouraged, read, and offered corrections to this book. I must also thank Dr. Yap Lay Leng and Dr. Chong Tian Hoo for reading early drafts of the book, providing helpful suggestions, and offering encouragement.

Editor Katherine Sopranos deserves much credit and appreciation for making my rambling recollections readable for you, the reader.

This book is dedicated to Robert (Bob) Hoyle, Returned Peace Corps Volunteer Philippines II, who provided me with decades of support, encouragement, and unconditional friendship and whose passing motivated me to write this story of love, failure, adventure, and triumph.

ABOUT ATMOSPHERE PRESS

Founded in 2015, Atmosphere Press was built on the principles of Honesty, Transparency, Professionalism, Kindness, and Making Your Book Awesome. As an ethical and author-friendly hybrid press, we stay true to that founding mission today.

If you're a reader, enter our giveaway for a free book here:

SCAN TO ENTER
BOOK GIVEAWAY

If you're a writer, submit your manuscript for consideration here:

SCAN TO SUBMIT
MANUSCRIPT

And always feel free to visit Atmosphere Press and our authors online at atmospherepress.com. See you there soon!

ABOUT THE AUTHOR

From left: Fong Moke Chee, her father Fong
Fung Chiew, and Jim Wolter in 1963

A lifelong Chicagoan, **JIM WOLTER** has been dedicated to education, serving as a special education teacher, a public school administrator, a university professor, and an administrative law judge. Now retired, his hobbies and creative endeavors include writing and sculpting. Jim is an experienced public speaker and has short stories published in *Worldview Magazine* and an essay published in *Peace Corps Worldwide* and in *U.S. News and World Report*. Northern Illinois University has serialized online his discussions about the innovations he created while teaching in Malaysia. As a sculptor, his works are installed at several locations in Illinois, including a metal sculpture called *Summer Reader* at Northern Illinois University's Reading Center, a sculpture at the Winnetka Public Library in Winnetka, Illinois, and a desktop ceramic St. Patrick at the Irish American Heritage Center in Chicago.